BECAUSE OF CHRIST

Because of Christ

Memoirs of a
Lutheran Theologian

Carl E. Braaten

William B. Eerdmans Publishing Company

Grand Rapids, Michigan / Cambridge, U.K.

Published 2010 by
Wm. B. Eerdmans Publishing Co.
2140 Oak Industrial Drive N.E., Grand Rapids, Michigan 49505 /
P.O. Box 163, Cambridge CB3 9PU U.K.

Printed in the United States of America

16 15 14 13 12 11 10   7 6 5 4 3 2 1

Library of Congress Cataloging-in-Publication Data

Braaten, Carl E., 1929-
Because of Christ: memoirs of a Lutheran theologian / Carl E. Braaten.
p.   cm.
Includes bibliographical references.
ISBN 978-0-8028-6471-0 (pbk.: alk. paper)
1. Braaten, Carl E., 1929- 2. Theologians — United States — Biography.
3. Lutheran Church — United States — Clergy — Biography.
4. Theological seminaries — United States — Faculty — Biography. I. Title.

BX8080.B672A3 2010
230′.41092 — dc22
[B]

2009045881

www.eerdmans.com

Contents

CONTENTS

Preface

This book is a *theological* autobiography. It tells the story of my life as a theologian, starting where it all began — on the mission field in Madagascar. There the seeds of my faith and understanding were sown by American Lutheran missionaries — my parents, teachers, and matrons at the Missionary Children's Home in Fort Dauphin. In these memoirs I intend to give a personal account of the ins and outs of the theological schools, movements, and personalities I encountered in my vocation as a Lutheran theologian. The story I am telling unavoidably unfolds as a chronicle that includes many conflicts and controversies. The very struggle for the truth of the gospel entails the negation and at times even the condemnation of rival doctrines. Some of these are blatant heresies that flourish within the church; others are alternative religions or ideologies whose most virulent forms threaten the survival of the Christian faith.

The theologian's task is to turn the spotlight of the gospel on the intellectual challenges of our time and to keep the church from crossing the line from orthodoxy into heresy. Heretics are not tarred and feathered or burned at the stake nowadays. No one pays a high price for propagating heretical propositions. A heretic in the Catholic Church may have no difficulty finding a good job in a Protestant seminary. Some of today's best sellers major in heresy, for example, Dan Brown's *The Da Vinci Code,* to cite one example of the resurgence of gnosticism in American religion. Nevertheless, heresy is debilitating; it causes spiritual anemia; it substitutes ideology for real theology. This is a condition that has stricken large segments of Christianity in Europe, no doubt a major reason why their beautiful churches are open for tourists on weekdays but the pews inside them are mostly empty on Sundays.

But I am not interested in pinning the label "heretic" or "apostate" on any theologian. Oh, well, there may be a few such, especially those in outright denial of the divinity of Christ or the resurrection of Jesus. For without the divinity of Christ there can be no confession of the Tri-unity of God, and without the reality of Jesus' resurrection the gospel becomes an empty promise. Hence, a controversial narrative of theology in our time will not hesitate to render a negative judgment on any theological idea that empties the gospel of its substance. How is one to tell the difference between ideas that are incompatible with the gospel and the ones that are gospel-friendly? Paul Tillich once suggested that the best symbol for the function of theology is that of John the Baptist, depicted in the Isenheim Altarpiece, painted by Mathias Grünewald (ca. 1513-15). John the Baptist is standing to one side pointing to the dying Savior on the cross. In a more abstract idiom the criterion of the gospel truth is, in Luther's German phrase, *was Christum treibt* (what conveys Christ). Everything we do in the church — preaching, teaching, evangelizing, serving the world, and caring for the poor — is on account of Christ, *propter Christum!* I have chosen this phrase — in its English translation, "Because of Christ" — as the title of my memoirs because it identifies the center of my existence as a Christian theologian. *Propter Christum* is used in conjunction with *sola gratia* and *per fidem* to affirm that sinners are saved by grace alone through faith on account of Christ. Divine grace and human faith are operative in the Bible and in Christianity solely because of Christ. Some contemporary theologians have written copiously to argue that Christ-centeredness is a liability in theology. I confess that I remain stubbornly and unashamedly guilty in their eyes.[1]

---

1. The modern attack on the principle of Christocentricity was launched by H. Richard Niebuhr, who ridiculed it as "unitarianism of the second article." Whatever Niebuhr meant by that, some of Niebuhr's pupils have taken up the attack and carried it

Preface

A theologian does not construct a system of Christian doctrine from scratch. Even a pigmy in theology can see a lot when standing on the shoulders of a giant. We are in the same situation as those to whom Jude wrote his letter, appealing to them "to contend for the faith which was once for all delivered to the saints" (Jude 3). A theologian of the church "will judge doctrine and reject doctrine that is contrary to the gospel."[2] The ancient creeds and confessions of the church instruct us on how to read and interpret the Scriptures. It is not the task of a church theologian to invent a new Christianity out of his or her religious experience and imagination, such as the Re-Imagining Conferences of radical theological feminists attempted to do.

Since I am a Lutheran theologian, these memoirs will inevitably reflect the distinctive principles and emphases of the Lutheran tradition. Whereas some of my Lutheran friends and colleagues have joined other churches, especially Roman Catholic and Orthodox, I remain a Lutheran by religious experience and theological conviction. Though I have witnessed and lament the near collapse of confessional theology in Lutheran seminary education, the eclipse of catechesis in Christian education, massive ignorance of doctrine on the part of the laity, and wanton disregard of church discipline among bishops and pastors, such enfeebling problems neither make me less Lutheran nor tempt me to become something else. I have never been able to imagine myself as other than Lutheran under the existing conditions of church division. A chief reason, I suppose, is that I taught Lutheran symbolics enough

---

further. This is particularly true of Gene TeSelle in his book *Christ in Context* where he states flat out that Christocentricity is incompatible with radical monotheism of biblical faith. It is also emphatically the case with the theocentric ethics of James Gustafson, who, like John Hick, does not believe that the doctrine of the incarnation makes sense in a post-Copernican view of the universe. They are not alone. The writings of Tom Driver, Rosemary R. Ruether, and Paul Knitter also go far to deconstruct the classical belief that Christ is key to the Christian understanding of the triune God and the gospel of salvation.

2. Article XXVIII of the Augsburg Confession states: "according to divine right it is the office of the bishop to preach the gospel, to forgive sin, to judge doctrine and reject doctrine that is contrary to the gospel." But this is no less true of the office of pastors and theologians of the church in their own jurisdictions, for pastors in the congregations they serve and for theologians in the institutions in which they teach.

years to make me keenly aware of the chief doctrinal differences between the Lutheran understanding of the Christian faith and all others. Even after fifty years of ecumenical dialogues there still remains something distinctive about the Lutheran faith-experience, its interpretation of the Bible and understanding of the gospel. Some who belong to other churches may surely share that type of experience, and many who belong to Lutheran churches seem not to have a clue as to the content and meaning of the Lutheran Confessions.

Many of the great leaders of the ecumenical movement have been Lutheran — Anders Nygren, Hans Lilje, Franklin Clark Fry, to name a few. Many of my favorite twentieth-century Lutheran theologians wrote their systematic theologies, not only for Lutherans, but for the worldwide church, such as Gustaf Aulén, Edmund Schlink, Wolfhart Pannenberg, and Robert W. Jenson. Thanks to their efforts, the sharp edges of many church-dividing differences have been significantly abraded through bilateral dialogues. Some of the mutual condemnations of another era have been successfully removed, and in some cases new agreements have led to full communion between church bodies once separated. Such ecumenical progress is a gift of the Holy Spirit, and that is reason enough to believe that churches will continue to find paths to greater Christian unity. However, it is not the function of ecumenism to melt down the various types of Christian experience. A Jesuit is a Jesuit and not a Dominican or Franciscan or Benedictine. Though members of these orders are all Roman Catholic, they do not cease to retain their historic distinguishing characteristics. Similarly, Lutherans and Calvinists and Wesleyans and Pentecostals — however many bridges they may build to reconcile the differences that heretofore have precluded altar and pulpit fellowship — will assuredly always retain the distinctive marks of their founding DNA. If I were to join the Roman Catholic Church, as a Lutheran I would have no difficulty with the "Catholic" part, since I share the belief of the Apostles' Creed in "the holy catholic church," but I would be at a loss about what to do with the "Roman" part. I was not brought up Roman and I have never been motivated to become one. However, I do hope and pray for the day when Lutherans will be reconciled with their Roman Catholic brothers and sisters, united by faith in the gospel of Jesus Christ as baptized members of his One Body. I have no doubt — and I have repeatedly so argued for decades — that such a reconciliation between world Lutheranism and the Roman Catholic Church will include a papal ministry that serves the unity of the church. However, such a ministry will need to exercise its care for the whole church in a new way for the sake of the gospel and its universal mission. What that means should now be at the forefront of new rounds of multilateral ecumenical dialogues that Pope John Paul II called for in his encyclical *Ut Unum Sint*.

These memoirs relate my struggle to reclaim the original intent of the Lutheran Reformation. Luther did not set out to create a new Christianity, let alone a Protestant denomination, but rather to summon the church to become truly evangelical, catholic, and orthodox. These three words also convey my own self-understanding as a Lutheran theologian — *evangelical* without being Protestant, *catholic* without being Roman, and *orthodox* without being Eastern. It is true that those who are not Lutheran lay claim to the same marks of theological identity. Such marks aim to circumvent the reductionistic label of "Protestantism." What is the meaning of being Protestant? If it means not being Roman Catholic, that does not adequately describe the fullness of Luther's reforming work and legacy.

My quest for truth is the red thread that runs through the story I am about to tell. In college I became a philosophy major on the urging of friends who convinced me that this field of study offers the greatest opportunity to engage in the pursuit of truth. After college I was awarded a Fulbright Scholarship to study philosophy at the Sorbonne, University of Paris. My research project was to compare the philosophies of Søren Kierkegaard and Jean-Paul Sartre, with particular reference to the concept of freedom. I took a course on phenomenology taught by Maurice Merleau-Ponty, on existentialism by Jean Wahl, on Kant and Hegel by Jean Hypollite, and others. After a dizzying year of immersion in philosophical questions, I concluded that the ultimate truth I was seeking in an existential way could not be found in the study of philosophy. At that time I was also reading two books by Jacques Maritain, *True Humanism* and *Introduction to Philosophy*. Maritain was a French Thomist philosopher I had met once when he gave a lecture at St. Thomas College in St. Paul, Minnesota. I mulled over the proposition from the Thomist tradition, that theology is the science of God and divine things and philosophy is its handmaid *(ancilla theologiae)*. Why loiter in the outer court of the temple if one can enter into the holy of holies? So I turned in earnest to the study of theology.

The quest for the *gospel* truth has been at the forefront of my teaching of Christian dogmatics. Its existential poignancy stemmed from the circumstances of my missionary origins. My parents were sent as missionaries to Madagascar, and it was there that I grew up. What sense does it make to export western Christianity to people who never asked for it? Were the missionaries justified in what they were doing by the noncoercive means of teaching and preaching? The missionaries believed that the gospel conveyed truth and was not propaganda. They were communicating to the Malagasy people a message that they would not otherwise have a chance to hear. But if that gospel is not absolutely true — the promise of God unto salvation and eternal life — the missionaries were wasting their time and sacrificing their lives for nothing. The very idea that what they were doing was all in vain is deeply troubling. Were the missionaries doing what Christ commissioned his followers to do? If yes, that settles it; there is no higher commander in chief. This is the essential nugget of truth that proves the folly of the fashionable pluralistic theologies of religion that have invaded the mainline Protestant churches and virtually put an end to their commitment to world evangelization.

Paul Tillich was my most important mentor on my way to becoming a theologian. Yet, I knew I could never become a Tillichian. I could never fit the categories of German idealism — à la Hegel and Schelling — into my head. Moreover, the idea of becoming the disciple of a great theologian seemed at odds with being a disciple of the Great Master. At one time I tried to be Kierkegaardian, the year I went to Paris on a Fulbright Scholarship. Howard Hong, my philosophy professor at St. Olaf College and the translator, with his wife Edna, of the *Collected Works of Søren Kierkegaard,* inspired me in that direction. The effort did not last a semester. I thought I saw too much truth in thinkers Kierkegaard criticized. When I read Karl Barth's Romans commentary, it was like a religious experience, but partly on account of Tillich's influence and the fact that on some important doctrines Barth was anti-Lutheran, I could never become a Barthian. I admit this with some regret, because I believe that Karl Barth was the greatest theologian of the twentieth century, and perhaps the greatest Protestant theologian since John Calvin.

I confess to being somewhat eclectic in my thinking. My love for Luther was chastened by what I learned from reading Calvin. As a Lutheran I always had a profound affinity for the epistles of Paul, but then I have loved to preach even more from the Gospel of John. As I studied the church fathers under Georges Florovsky and Harry Austryn Wolfson at Harvard, Augustine was my natural favorite, but there was so much to learn from Origen. So it went, I could not come down hard on one side and ignore the other. In modern Protestant theology there was Kähler against Ritschl, and I learned from both, there was Bultmann but also Schlink, Pannenberg but also Moltmann. My thought has moved dialectically between *Sic et Non*, often leaving me with the feeling that were I to belong strictly to one school of thought, it would naturally be easier to be more rigorously consistent.[3] But I do not believe that would have brought me closer to the truth.

My decision to write a theological autobiography means that many important aspects of my life — some even more important than theology — will not be included. I will not tell much about my family life — nearly sixty years of marriage to LaVonne; we are together parents of four children, grandparents of eleven, and great-grandparents of four, and there is no end in sight. A more complete autobiography would tell about my parents and siblings, my hobbies and travels, friends and colleagues, sports and trophies, health foods and health clubs, politics and business, and much more. My theological odyssey will read something like an intellectual travelogue, in that I have been something of a peripatetic student and teacher. I have studied in many schools, taught in many cities, lived in many countries, traveled on many continents, bought and sold many homes.

Next I will tell about growing up in Madagascar, where my faith was nurtured, giving rise to my first theological questions.

---

3. Ralph Waldo Emerson is often quoted as having said "Consistency is the hobgoblin of little minds." In fact, he said, "A foolish consistency is the hobgoblin of little minds." But he did not explain the difference between a foolish and a wise consistency.

CHAPTER ONE

Growing Up in Madagascar

1930–1946

My three siblings, Agnes, Arlene, and Folkvard, were born on the mission field in Madagascar. I was born in St. Paul while my parents were on furlough after a seven-year term of service as missionaries in the southern part of the island. My father, Torstein Folkvard Braaten, and my mother, Clara Agnes (Titterud), were commissioned to serve as missionaries by the Norwegian Lutheran Church in America, one of the predecessor bodies of the Evangelical Lutheran Church in America. The standing joke was that I was the only one in the family legally qualified to become president of the United States. My father was born in Norway and came to America at the age of nineteen. After graduating from Concordia College in Morehead, Minnesota, and Luther Seminary in St. Paul, Minnesota, he married Clara Titterud, and then volunteered for missionary service. Together they served as missionaries in Madagascar from 1922 to 1956. They spent many beautiful retirement years in Northfield, Minnesota. My mother loved to attend musical concerts at St. Olaf College, and my father was equally avid in attending theological lectures. Every morning during their coffee break they listened to the chapel services broadcast by the college's radio station, WCAL. It was a much deserved change from their hard years on the mission field.

Madagascar is the fourth-largest island in the world, 1,000 miles in length, with a population of sixteen million, predominantly mixed Asian and African. The Malagasy language is of Malayo-Polynesian origin, spoken in many dialects throughout the island. Many of the natives still practice the traditional animistic religion that has a strong emphasis on maintaining contact with the dead. Diviners, otherwise known as witch doctors, are believed to possess the ability to initiate contact with the ancestors of the living. Christianity was brought to Madagascar by the Protestant London Missionary Society, which gained many converts, opened schools, and translated the Bible into the Malagasy language. Today about 45 percent of the people are Christian, half Roman Catholic and the other half Lutheran, Reformed, and Anglican. Madagascar became a French colony in 1895, and after a bitterly fought national uprising it gained full independence in 1960.

Through an agreement with the Anglican and Reformed mission societies, the American Lutheran missionaries were awarded the mission territory in the far south of Madagascar. At the very southeastern tip of Madagascar lies a beautiful harbor town called Fort Dauphin. That was the headquarters of the Lutheran mission, the place where I grew up from year one until I left the island after my junior year of high school. Each missionary was assigned an outlying district in which to work, to preach the gospel, teach the Bible, build churches, open schools, train evangelists and catechists, dispense health care, plant gardens, and exemplify a Christian lifestyle.

We missionary children lived together in a boarding school while our parents were at their mission stations. Twice each year we lived with our parents during a short and a long vacation period. At the home for missionary children we related to each other as brothers and sisters under the supervision of a matron. Even as teens, no dating was permitted. nor was any overt exchange of thoughts or feelings about sex. We attended a schoolhouse with two rooms, one for the little kids (first through sixth grades) and one for the bigger kids (seventh through twelfth grades). We learned the four R's. The fourth was religion, which meant Christianity. We studied the Bible and memorized lengthy passages, especially the psalms, the nativity story, the Sermon on the Mount, the fourteenth and seventeenth chapters of John's Gospel, the eighth chapter of Romans, as well as various other Bible verses. The Lutheran principle of *sola Scriptura* was observed without question. Yet, as I reflect on the practice of Bible reading and interpretation, it was never done solo, but always in conjunction with Luther's *Small Catechism* and the study of church history, learning about the inspiring lives of the saints, martyrs, and missionaries.

The Lutheran missionaries came from the tradition of late-nineteenth-century Norwegian pietism. This meant that the Bible was treated not so much as a source book of orthodox doctrines but more as the living word of God that speaks to the heart. Yet, I can recall none of our teachers speaking disparagingly of "dead orthodoxy" as some pietists did, as though pure doctrine should be held in low regard. The theology of these evangelical Lutheran missionaries was what I would call "neo-orthodox pietism." One of their heroes was Ole Hallesby, professor of systematic theology at the Free Faculty of Theology in Oslo (1909-1952). Some of his many writings were the most treasured in my father's library, especially Hallesby's books *Prayer* and *Why I Became a Christian*.

Our teachers were not biblical scholars, nor did they buttress the Bible with theories of plenary inspiration and verbal inerrancy. We were spared what Philip Melanchthon called "the wrath of theologians" *(rabies theologorum)*, who turn the Bible into a battleground to prove its infallibility. I recall learning about Ussher's chronology and a literal six-day creation, but never thought either was that important to believe. Of course, the missionaries taught that the Bible is the infallible Word of God, not merely a record of human thoughts about God. Therefore, the authority of the Bible was the bedrock of the entire missionary enterprise. Years later, upon entering the seminary, I learned that Lutheran theologians in America were engaged in a fierce "battle over the Bible." Some accepted and some rejected the modern methods of higher criticism. Nothing in my religious upbringing prevented me from being open to all the modern methods of interpretation, provided they rendered the scriptural texts more intelligible. Just as we were taught to confess the full humanity of the *incarnate* Word of God, it seemed to follow that we should also accept the full humanity of the *written* Word of God. Accordingly, the Bible is subject to our human ways of knowing, like every other ancient document written in Hebrew or Greek.

3

Missionary children grew up in a multicultural context. Growing up amidst Malagasy, French, Métis, Chinese, Indians, Arabs, Norwegians, and Americans, we were exposed to many religions, languages, colors, cultures, and cuisines. Recent decades have witnessed strained and noisy clamors and special pleading for multiculturalism in American neighborhoods, churches, and schools, as though that would create a panacea of greater justice and equality in society. Then I realized, rather belatedly, what a gift it was for children of foreign missionaries to have acquired a global multicultural perspective in a perfectly natural way.

The missionaries established a school for their children in which all the subjects were taught in English. The only unusual thing about it was that every school day opened with morning devotions — Bible reading, prayers, and hymn singing. After devotions we studied the Bible, the history of Christianity, and Lutheran doctrine. I was not an exceptional student by any means. I was not an avid reader, though I was quick in arithmetic. I can remember counting the minutes for the bell to ring to mark the end of the school day — and the signal that it was time for sports. Our team sports were soccer and volleyball. Tennis was my first love; I got my first racquet at the age of nine. Since we were in Madagascar during the years of World War II, our tennis came to an end when there were no replacements for worn-out gut strings and tennis balls. Other sports included bike riding, mountain climbing, swimming, body surfing, sailing, hunting, and fishing — we loved the outdoors and were very active.

The missionaries took the third commandment very seriously. The weekly routine of work and chores was interrupted by long hours of Sunday worship. The church services were in the Malagasy language, often lasting two hours or more. The sermons seemed endless because we did not understand much of the church talk. We could speak and understand quite a bit of the ordinary language of daily life, salted with the usual four-letter words. The Malagasy are a very musical people and love to sing hymns — never skipping any stanzas like we do in the States. They dressed up for church in their finest clothes, and would be shocked to see the casual and sloppy way many of their fellow Christians in America dress when they go to church. After a lengthy church service with the Malagasy Christians, we attended Sunday school for missionary children in English. In our early teens we had to take two years of confirmation class. The day I was confirmed was the first time I wore a pair of long pants that my mother sewed. Confirmation was a very solemn occasion. We learned our lessons, but beyond that we were made aware that the promises we would be asked to make were decisions for life. The Lutheran missionaries did not advocate the kind of "born-again theology" that denies baptism to infants. Confirmation was a time when teenagers confirmed the vows their parents made on their behalf when they were baptized as babies. My mother took me aside and asked if I realized the seriousness of the vows I was about to make. I said I did, but did I really? I have often felt that growing up in this missionary colony was like being in a pressure cooker. Yet, I am thankful that my parents and teachers never used any coercive measures to transmit the Christian faith to their children.

When I became a pastor of the Lutheran Church of the Messiah in North Minneapolis, I tried to teach confirmation class exactly as it had been taught to me — Rambo style. It was not easy, because the confirmands did not take naturally to the idea that Christianity was something to be learned by heart. I did not back off. It came as a shock to me to discover that many of my fellow pastors gave up expecting students to learn by rote Luther's *Small Catechism* and important passages of Scripture. They thought it was possible to learn the meanings without memorizing the words. They seemed to think that if children are required to learn Christian teachings by rote, they will later rebel and leave the church. I was convinced that those for whom confirmation comes too easily are the first ones to use it as a graduation ceremony. Polls indicate that many are confirmed but few remain with the church. Why? Taking the kids bowling and on hayrides is a poor substitute for serious Christian education.

Once in my confirmation class in Madagascar we discussed the Bible passage "And there is salvation in no one else, for there is no other name under heaven given among men by which we must be saved" (Acts 4:12). I asked the confirmation teacher, who happened to be my uncle, K. F. Braaten, the superintendent of the mission, whether that means that all the heathen in Madagascar who die without having heard the gospel of salvation would go to hell. He answered wisely, as I think back on it: "Our task is to preach the gospel so that all may believe and be saved. But it may well be that those who die without having any chance to hear the gospel may in the end be given a second chance." The second chance he had in mind was probably based on the belief that when Christ descended into hell he "preached to the spirits in prison" (1 Pet. 3:19). Who were these spirits? They were people who had never heard the story of salvation in their lifetime. In reality, it was not a second chance; it was in effect their first chance. This was not, of course, an idea my uncle invented on the spot, but one taught by some seventeenth-century Lutheran dogmaticians. Such an idea was more than I could comprehend at the time, but the answer stayed with me, so much so that later I adopted a version of it as my own.

Where we grew up in south Madagascar there were only two kinds of Christians, Lutherans and Catholics. Our friends were children of French colonialists, people in government and business. They were almost all Catholics. I knew nothing about ecumenism, but I learned later that the personal experience of coming to know persons of other churches lies at the root of ecumenism. The word got back to our parents that my brother and I were fraternizing with French girls, and they were Catholics. Uffda! My father called my brother Martin and me into his office to ask about this. Is it true? He told us about the differences between Lutherans and Catholics — we believe this and they believe that. I do not remember his exact words. Nothing bad came of it. I believe that our father was more curious than worried. The fraternization continued without the missionaries' blessings. Since the missionary children lived in the same dormitory, it was considered taboo for them to fraternize. The only alternative was for the guys to venture outside the missionary compound to meet the French girls; truth be told, what transpired was all very innocent stuff.

The Lutheran mission in Madagascar proved to be a huge success. The missionaries finally worked themselves out of a job. The time came when the Malagasy Lutheran Church could govern itself, support itself, and propagate the faith without the supervising presence of missionaries. In China this same sort of thing was called the "Three-

Self Movement." That was severely criticized by both Protestants and Catholics, because it was organized under the aegis of the Communist regime. The Communists wanted to rid Christianity of all foreign influence. Whatever their malevolent intent, it has turned out to be providential, because the spread of Christianity in China is exploding beyond anyone's wildest imagination. This is exactly what the world missionary movement has been trying to accomplish from the beginning, to transform foreign missions into indigenous churches.

The Malagasy Lutheran Church that the missionaries left behind now reflects the kind of theology and church practices they taught. This means that the Malagasy Christians live conspicuously in a countercultural manner. In a polygamous society the Christian men are permitted to have only one wife. On the occasion of baptism adults are expected to get rid of their idols and amulets that supposedly ensure health and happiness. No longer do they consult witch doctors as mediums to communicate with their ancestors. Christians who lapse back into heathen practices are subject to strict codes of church discipline. The missionaries were very leery of every form of syncretism. Not even drums were allowed in church worship; the sounds and rhythms seemed too reminiscent of the pagan ritual dances.

When I left Madagascar in 1946, World War II had just come to an end. Not a tear did I shed when the time came to leave the island. I could not wait to get back to America and the benefits of civilization I had been deprived of during my teen years. When I landed on American soil, I felt that I had come home at last — the land of my birth. I have always been a sports nut, and am so even today. As a child I longed for things Madagascar could not provide — basketball and tennis. As soon as I came to the United States, the first thing I did was to buy a tennis racquet. When I went to Augustana Academy for my senior year of high school, I spent all my spare hours in the gym trying to catch up on basketball. It was too late; I soon discovered I would never excel at either sport. Yet, as I approach my eightieth year, I still play a competitive game of tennis, both singles and doubles.

In spite of the limited educational resources at the school (no science lab, for example) for missionary children in Fort Dauphin, almost all went on to graduate from college, many went to the seminary to become pastors, and some returned to Madagascar as missionaries. For some reason I happened to be the only one of the missionary children to earn a doctorate in theology and to become an academic theologian. This I cannot explain because there were no role models among the missionaries; not one had an advanced degree in theology, and none of my teachers encouraged the study of theology. I do remember, however, that my father read whatever theological books he could lay his hands on, and when I gave him copies of books I wrote, he read every word of them, underlining and making copious marginal comments. When later I scanned the pages for his comments, I discovered that they were always thoughtful.

Chapter Two

Augustana Academy and St. Olaf College

1946–1951

When I returned from Madagascar in the spring of 1946, I lived with my uncle and aunt, Kittel and Anna Braaten, on Elliott Avenue in South Minneapolis. They were retired missionaries from Madagascar. Immediately I got a job at Bridgeman's Ice Cream Parlor as a busboy earning fifty cents an hour. We never had ice cream in Madagascar; for two weeks I indulged myself to the limit. The first day on the job I went with the other busboys to a hamburger shop down the street. I had never seen the kind of food they were serving and did not know how to order. The guy on the stool next to me ordered a hamburger and a malt. I did not know what that was, so when it came my turn to order I simply said, "Same thing." When I bused the dishes, customers would comment, "Where have you been? Where did you get that tan?" It was after all March in Minnesota, and I was sporting a dark midsummer tan. Not wanting to get into a conversation about just having come from Madagascar, anticipating what the next question would be, "Where's that?" I lied and said I had been in Florida. Was that a white lie or what?

When I made enough money to buy a bike, I quit Bridgeman's, got a job with Western Union, and spent the rest of the summer biking in and out of traffic in downtown Minneapolis delivering telegrams. Once in a while some fat cat would tip me a quarter, and I thought, "Gee, thanks, how generous!" It was my first taste of how people at the low end of the pay scale felt about working, a subject that Studs

Terkel, my favorite columnist writing for the *Chicago Tribune,* made into a best seller, *Working: People Talk about What They Do All Day and How They Feel about It.* When subsequently I worked at various menial jobs to pay for my education, I felt I could have made a contribution to Terkel's book. It wasn't work that I minded so much as the poor wages and working conditions.

In the fall of 1946 I attended Augustana Academy for my senior year of high school, in Canton, South Dakota. The Academy was a boarding school, serving as a home away from home for many missionary children. It was also a Lutheran high school, fostering a kind of piety unlike anything I had experienced. Most of the students came because their parents wanted them to live in a Christian atmosphere, supposedly free of the temptations thought to be typical of public high schools — cigarettes, booze, and sex. The Academy served as a kind of reform school for a few students who had run into trouble with the law. The student body was consequently a mixed bag, some ultrapious students and a few downright hell-raisers. I had three roommates. One was a senior from a rough neighborhood in Chicago whose parents were going through a divorce; another was a junior farm boy from Wahoo, Nebraska, who told about his weird fondness for sheep. Another boy was a sophomore from Denver, a tough kid who loved to box. One night he said he had had enough of the Academy. He sold me his boxing gloves for ten dollars, and with money in his pocket, he climbed down the fire escape with a duffle bag containing all his belongings, caught a freight train, and headed out of town. That's the last we saw of the kid from Denver.

Revival meetings were standard fare at the Academy. The visiting evangelists used high-powered emotional appeals for personal confessions and testimonials. They wanted students to be "born again." Were these really Lutherans? These preachers came from a wing of Midwest Lutheranism much influenced by low-church Swedish and Norwegian revival movements, associated with the Lutheran Bible Institute in Minneapolis. One evening, after a revival meeting in chapel, one of these evangelists went from room to room, getting students to kneel down and coaxing confessions out of them. He came to our room, insisting that there must be some things we needed to confess.

We all remained silent. My roommates were as uncomfortable with these methods as I was. The missionaries I grew up with in Madagascar never did anything like that. They baptized us as infants, taught us Luther's *Small Catechism,* and raised us on a rather steady regimen of Christian practices. There was never a time we were led to believe that we needed to be "born again." Luther's counsel was a good one: when in doubt or despair, console yourself, saying, *"baptizatus sum"* (I have been baptized).[1]

In the spring of 1947 I visited St. Olaf College to explore whether that was the school I should attend in the fall. It happened to coincide with the time that Norwegians celebrate *Syttende Mai* (May 17), the day that marks Norway's declaration of independence, similar in significance to our Fourth of July. The weekend I was there the college on the hill was abuzz with patriotic music, national costumes, folk dances, and ethnic pastries that Norwegians enjoy at their festivals. I thought to myself, if this is college life, I can't wait to get there.

Thus I enrolled as a college freshman in the fall of 1947, with my older brother, Martin,[2] who had just completed his tour of duty with the U.S. Army. Perhaps mostly by default — I had no clear career objective — I embarked on a preseminary education, following to the letter the recommended program of prerequisites for the study of theology. Tuition at that time was almost free for children of missionary parents, thanks to a generous policy on the part of this Lutheran church college that took into account that missionaries were generally among the lowest-paid clergy, and besides, the president of the college, Clemens S. Granskou, had himself been a missionary to China. At the time of my graduation four years later, my total indebtedness to the college was $400. My brother, who graduated at the same time, owed nothing because his army service entitled him to the G.I. Bill of Rights.

In my senior year at the Academy I met LaVonne Gardner. That would turn out to be the most important thing that happened that

---

1. Luther's full saying is: *"Ecce, ego baptizatus sum, et credo in Christum crucifixum."*

2. My brother entered the army with the name of Folkvard; he left it using his second name, Martin. A lot of people had a hard time pronouncing Folkvard, which was a common name in the Braaten tribe. Growing up in Madagascar, his nickname was "Tack" or "Tak."

year, though at the time I did not know it. The next year she went to Waldorf College in Forest City, Iowa, and I went to St. Olaf College. We did not meet again until my senior year of college. Since Waldorf was only a junior college, LaVonne came to St. Olaf as a junior. By chance we happened to cross paths on campus in the fall of 1950, greeted each other, and before long started dating. By Thanksgiving we were going steady.

The study of Christian theology rests on the foundations of the classical humanistic disciplines. These include the history of Western philosophy, from the Greek pre-Socratics to modern European existentialism and phenomenology, as well as American pragmatism and process metaphysics. My major in philosophy included a special concentration on Kierkegaard. We read *Either/Or, Philosophical Fragments,* and *Concluding Unscientific Postscripts.* Copies of the translations by Howard and Edna Hong were made by using the old A. B. Dick mimeograph machines that bled ink and left blue stains to the touch. A course in logic — the science of learning how to reason and argue — was a requirement for a major in philosophy.

The classical languages were also prerequisites, the two biblical languages, Hebrew and Greek, as well as Latin. French and German were not considered prerequisites for the first theological degree, but were required by most postgraduate programs leading to a doctor's degree in theology. Equally important, of course, was the study of the English language and literature. That was my second major. The freshman course in English required one theme a week and a major research paper for the semester. More than any other, this course prepared me for a career of writing books and articles[3] and as an editor of theological journals and textbooks. In addition, courses in world history and modern European history were required, not my favorite subjects, mostly because of the boring way they were often taught. With tongue in cheek the famous historian Arnold Toynbee referred to history as "one damn thing after another." Since then I have learned to love to read history — especially the biblical history of salvation, the history of Christianity, and the history of theology.

---

3. See the bibliography of my publications in the appendix of this book.

In my senior year I was given the opportunity to write an honors paper in philosophy. I chose to write on the topic "The Concept of Freedom in the Philosophy of Jean-Paul Sartre." It proved to be a useful exercise. In applying for a Fulbright Scholarship to study at the Sorbonne, University of Paris in 1951-1952, I had to submit a research project. I proposed to write on the concept of freedom in the writings of Søren Kierkegaard and Jean-Paul Sartre. It would be a comparative study of two very different philosophers, one holding a Christian viewpoint and the other an atheistic one. It proved to be a winning strategy. I was awarded a Fulbright in the spring of 1951.

I was graduated from St. Olaf College in June 1951, *magna cum laude,* with a grade point average of 3.77, and with departmental honors in three majors, philosophy, English, and French. I had four B's on my transcript, in freshman Norwegian, European history, biology, and unified physical science. It did not take long to figure out that I was not going to be a scientist. In my junior year I was one of six elected to the Phi Beta Kappa Society, an organization founded in 1776 at the College of William and Mary, the preeminent academic honors society for the liberal arts. My brother Martin also graduated with departmental honors in history and French. Our parents could not attend the graduation ceremony; they were still on the mission field.

CHAPTER THREE

The University of Paris–Sorbonne

1951–1952

When I was awarded a Fulbright Scholarship to study philosophy at the Sorbonne in Paris, the first thing I did was to tell LaVonne. We were engaged but our plan was to postpone marriage until LaVonne finished her senior year of college. When I applied for the Fulbright, we were not engaged. But now, what should we do? I could decline the award, but neither of us wanted that. I could accept and go by myself. But that seemed selfish and risky — who knows what a year apart would do to our relationship? We could get married and go together. That had two negatives: first, LaVonne would have to skip her senior year of college, and second, the amount of the stipend was meant for a single person. Could the two of us survive on $150 a month in Paris? We could count on no other source of income. The money we planned to earn during the summer would go to pay for travel expenses. My mother had a saying, "You can't live on love and the north wind." We decided to try anyway. Our parents must have thought it inadvisable, but they did not openly oppose our plan. We were married on September 16, 1951, at Estherville Lutheran Church, Estherville, Iowa. This was the town where LaVonne's parents, Lloyd and Olivia Gardner, lived and worked. My brother Martin was not able to be my best man because he had joined the Marines and was in training.

Several days after we were married, we took a train to New York City and caught the SS *DeGrasse*, a passenger boat of the French Line. On board we met other Fulbright students bound for Paris. I recall especially the Ortons and the Suderows, two couples with whom we socialized in Paris. LaVonne and I got "seasick" while the boat was still in harbor, during lunchtime. We asked ourselves in total bewilderment, "How is it possible to get seasick while the boat is still tied to the pier?" We got our answer. We had been told to take Dramamine before we set sail. We each had taken two pills, to make sure we would not get seasick. The pills made us sick, causing a different reaction in each of us. LaVonne became very drowsy and slept for hours in the cabin. I became a motor-racing wreck unable to relax; I walked the decks and occasionally stopped in to see how LaVonne was. The next day we were okay.

One week later we docked in Le Havre, and after going through customs we boarded a train to Paris, not knowing where we would eat or sleep that first night. Paris was still suffering from the deprivations of World War II. For supper we had a bowl of chicken soup, which turned out to be spoiled. Fortunately I remembered enough French to voice our complaint and told the cashier we would not pay for inedible food. We found a room for the night, and the next day we went to a bureau that listed apartments for rent to foreigners. The owners could charge Americans many times more than the local French were able to pay. Americans were thought to be rich — and by comparison we were — so we were easy targets for price gouging. We rented an apartment that we had to share with its owner, Madame Chevaux. Her name means "horses" in French. A nasty nag she was. We had to share her kitchen. She would snoop around to see what LaVonne was cooking. When we told her we were having French toast, she snorted, "There's nothing French about it." One time a friend from St. Olaf College, Arthur Olsen, visited us for several days and slept on a sofa in our living room. A few weeks later another friend from St. Olaf, Wally Sue, stayed with us and also occupied the living room. Madame Chevaux objected and said something to the effect that what we were doing was immoral. It violated her French sensibility; imagine, a young married couple hosting a single man! So we found a small apartment on the north side of Paris, solely ours. We packed our bags and left this miserable woman.

Paris in the winter is depressingly gray and gloomy, fostering moods of despair, angst, ennui, and nausea. I became convinced that it is no accident that the world's leading existentialists and nihilists are Parisian philosophers sipping wine on the Left Bank of the Seine. When we were in Paris, Jean-Paul Sartre (1905-1980) and Albert Camus (1913-1960) were enjoying their heyday. I am not sure "enjoying" is the right word, because it is hard to imagine Sartre or Camus enjoying anything. Sartre's magnum opus was *Being and Nothingness*. The plays of Sartre and the novels of Camus were the steady fare of the youth who had lost faith and hope during the war years under the German Nazi occupation. At that time I had never read a word of Paul Tillich. Years later when I read Tillich's bon mot: "Existentialism is the good luck of Christian theology," it struck me that he was exactly right. Why? Because existentialism poses the questions of life and death, to be or not to be, questions about the meaning and destiny of life, with piercing and excruciating acuity. These are the sorts of questions to which the gospel of Jesus Christ does provide answers. In that year I descended into the slough of despondency and dread, and at times felt the "nausea" that Sartre wrote about in his novel by that name. I endured this condition in the quiet interiority of my own soul. I did not talk about it. I tried not to let LaVonne know the depths of my misery. Years later LaVonne confessed that she was undergoing similar feelings that year. We kept each other unaware of what each of us was experiencing.

We attended weekly services at the American Church in Paris, at 65 Quai d'Orsay. It is a large Gothic church founded to serve not only the expatriate American community, but also a wide variety of English-speaking people from many countries and denominations. The senior pastor was a Presbyterian, Dr. Clayton Edgar Williams, whose sermons were carefully crafted to address a multinational congregation. The United Nations Organization had its headquarters in Paris and held its assemblies there at that time. Dr. Williams invited LaVonne and me to a monthly dinner at the church, followed by a colloquium featuring a guest speaker. The group was an outstanding mix of visiting professors, scientists, writers, artists, Fulbright students, most of them Americans on some kind of mission in Paris. We met and listened to many famous people — authors, politicians, economists, etc. — many of them attached to the United Nations. It was the most high-powered concentration of intellectual dialogue I had ever experienced. These encounters made us aware of how much we had to learn and how fortunate we were to be in Paris at that time.

Besides attending lectures in philosophy at the Sorbonne, LaVonne and I frequently went to the National Opera House of Paris. LaVonne was studying French at the Alliance Française. There she met Lutheran missionaries studying the French language in preparation for going to Madagascar. She also sang with the Paris Philharmonic Chorus and Symphony. We were kept busy doing many new and exciting things. Our participation in the educational and cultural opportunities that Paris offered was slowed considerably when in February the doctor informed us of what we already suspected — LaVonne was pregnant. What a shockeroo! I do not recall but LaVonne remembers that it threw me for a loop. LaVonne started losing weight. We worried about what becoming parents would mean for our future. Would this throw a monkey wrench into our plan for me to enter Luther Seminary in the fall of 1952? We knew that we needed to return to the States sooner rather than later. Our funds were drying up and I needed to get an early start on a summer job in Minneapolis. We felt we had to get settled into an apartment, save some money, and await the birth of our first child.

CHAPTER FOUR

Luther Seminary

1952–1955

Becoming a student at Luther Seminary in the 1950s was a simple matter. The seminary belonged to the Evangelical Lutheran Church (ELC), formerly known as the Norwegian Lutheran Church in America; it was its only seminary. This church was like an extended ethnic family — all the pastors seemed to know each other. My father personally knew the president of the church, Johan A. Aasgaard, as well as the president of the seminary, Thaddeus F. Gullickson. It was assumed without question that his son would be accepted as a student. There were no forms to fill out, no psychological tests, and no committee interviews. I recall writing a letter to President Gullickson, informing him of my plan to attend the seminary in the fall of 1952. The ELC operated with a high level of trust and transparency. Even more special, there was no tuition. Everything was free. This was a seminary of the church in every sense; the cost to educate its future clergy was covered. Such a policy had much to do with the high degree of loyalty the church could expect from its clergy. How utterly different from current procedures, rules, and regulations that apply in Lutheran theological education. Now there prevails a lack of trust and loyalty. Everything functions by bloated committees determined by the quota system, combined with a kind of "don't ask, don't tell" moral discipline — or lack thereof — in seminary life.

The seminary education that was offered students at Luther Seminary in the 1950s was a moderate form of Midwest Lutheran pietism.

The professors were all Lutherans of Norwegian descent, except for two Latvian refugees from the Russian Communist occupation of their country. There were no female teachers or students. The only woman in sight was the office secretary of the president. There were no deans — no dean of faculty or dean of students — and no committees. President Gullickson ran everything, with the assistance of one janitor. That was all the bureaucracy there was to deal with a student body of around three hundred. Gullickson was from a generation of hard-working pastors who had survived the Great Depression. Matriculation was a requirement for acceptance into the middler year. One needed a passing academic record and no reports of immorality, bearing on matters of sex or alcohol. Students received a slip of paper in their mailbox, which called for a yes or no answer. The question was, "Do you believe in Jesus Christ as your personal Lord and Savior?"

I recall one student in particular, let us call him John Johnson. In the coffee shop he talked like a true believer who knew it all. He knew the pious lingo and had been a lay preacher. But he flunked out the first year and was not allowed back. It was hard to figure. Then we heard a story that allegedly came from the president. It may have been apocryphal. In any case, as the story goes, a young man came to the seminary, and like John Johnson he flunked out his first year. He protested to the president, "This can't be because I had a direct call from Christ." "What do you mean?" the president asked. The student answered, "I was driving a tractor one day, and I looked up and saw the letters *PC* written across the sky. That was a sign that I should get down from my tractor and 'preach Christ.'" The president said to him, "Young man, those letters don't mean 'preach Christ' but 'plow corn.'"

One of my first days at the seminary I noticed a bunch of students outside the library intensely engaged in argument. As I stuck my head into the huddle someone turned to me and asked, "Whose side are you on?" I had no clue what they were arguing about. One of the upperclassmen told me that the campus was aflame with heated controversy pitting two professors against each other, one a pietist, George Aus, and the other orthodox, Herman Preus. George Aus taught that persons are free to accept or reject the offer of salvation. He liked the picture of Jesus knocking at the door. The person on the inside has his hand on the doorknob. He is free to choose to open the door or to keep it shut. George Aus often told the story of how he became a Christian. One day he made a decision to accept Jesus and let him into his heart.

George Aus's theology of decision was typical of American evangelicalism; most of the students were pietists who believed the same way. Herman Preus took the other side of the debate. To support his view he cited Luther's *Bondage of the Will*, which Luther wrote to refute Erasmus, the humanist of Rotterdam, who had written *A Diatribe concerning Free Choice*. Luther argued that on account of the fall human beings are not able to accept the gift of salvation until their enslaved will has been liberated by the Holy Spirit. God not only foresees who will believe, but he sees to it that they will believe. Luther's explanation of the third article of the Apostles' Creed expresses the matter clearly: "I believe that by my own reason or strength I cannot believe in Jesus Christ, my Lord, or come to him. But the Holy Spirit has called me through the Gospel, enlightened me with his gifts, and sanctified and preserved me in true faith."

At first I took Aus's side of the debate. It seemed to make perfect sense. After all, I had just spent a year in Paris filling my head with the existentialist ideas of Kierkegaard and Sartre, precisely on the concept of freedom. The key idea of existentialism is that humans are not free not to choose. Sartre said, *"Il faut choisir!"* We must choose; we cannot escape the terrifying burden of freedom to construct our own reality and destiny. What we choose to be is what we are. That sounds like Erasmus, not Luther. At that time I had not yet read *Bondage of the Will* or any of Luther's writings, except, of course, his *Small Catechism*. So I gave Aus a pass and disliked Preus very much, both his style and the substance of his teaching. However, *mirabile dictu*, by my senior year I had changed my mind. Three things accounted for this 180-degree turnabout. First, I had started reading Luther, in particular his three treatises written in 1520, *The Freedom of a Christian, The Babylonian Captivity of the Church*, and *To the Christian Nobility of the German Nation*, as well as his *Commentary on Paul's Epistle to the Galatians*. Second, Luther's radical understanding of justification — by grace alone, through faith alone, on account of Christ alone — was tonic for my soul. The gospel of grace that led Luther through the darkest hours of his *Anfechtungen* met my need for the assurance of unconditional forgiveness "without any merit or worthiness on my part."[1] Third, I came to know Professor Edmund Smits, a Latvian refugee, who quietly and persistently lured me into a study of the Lutheran scholastics. From there he had me read parts of the *Summa Theologica* of Thomas Aquinas. From that point forward I could no longer accept the decisional theology of evangelical pietism.

Edmund Smits ("Smitty," the students affectionately called him) was my favorite teacher, even though he did not teach any core courses in church history or dogmatics. He was allowed to teach a few noncredit electives; I was one of the few students who signed up for them. He was more qualified to teach classical Lutheran theology than any of the tenured professors. They seemed to resent his superior qualifications. In my middler year students learned that his teaching position was in jeopardy. The faculty failed to support his reappointment, so the seminary board of directors was considering letting him go. The students got wind of this and rallied to his support with a letter-writing campaign and personal testimonies. Why, we wondered, was the faculty opposed to him? One reason was that he championed the spirit of classical Lutheran orthodoxy (seventeenth century), and another was that he was a friend and ally of Herman Preus. I recall one conversation with Dr. Smits in which I doubted the claim of confessional Lutheranism to possess the pure truth of Scripture. Smits said to me, "Carl, orthodoxy is a vision, not an achievement." That was sweet music to my ears, a bit of wisdom I tucked away in my mind and heart and have cherished ever since.

Luther Seminary's curriculum was modeled after the traditional European division of theology into four parts: Bible, church history, dogmatics, and practical theology. Almost all the courses were required, six in Bible, five in church history, six in dogmatics, six in practical theology, leaving almost no room for electives. The other Lutheran seminaries followed this same pattern. Then they all embarked on what came to be a favorite faculty adventure — curricular revision. With every revi-

1. From Luther's explanation of the first article of the Apostles' Creed.

sion the number of required courses was reduced, allowing students to elect subjects of greater appeal to them. This was not a salutary development. Too often students would shop around for slough-off courses and some teachers would jazz up their electives to attract students. The result was the dumbing down of the curriculum, thus minimizing the scholarly study of theology for pastoral formation. Traditionally the Lutheran pastor could be counted on to know the Bible, church history, doctrinal theology, and the essentials of Word-and-sacrament ministry. That is no longer true, as any well-versed layperson can testify. Because the tail (electives) is allowed to wag the dog (core courses), the Lutheran pastor is no longer esteemed as a theologian. Today's seminary has acquired all the characteristics of a community college.

What lies behind the watering down of the theological curriculum in today's seminaries is the fact that many students, perhaps most, are ill prepared for the academic rigors of theological study. The curricular prerequisites have been dropped, or at least are not enforced. The decline of real theology at the seminaries is part of the larger story of American Christianity, both Protestant and Catholic, of accommodating the culture of American religion. Its hallmark is experiential religiosity divorced from dogma. I agree with Harold Bloom: "Gnosticism . . . is now, and always has been, the hidden religion of the United States, the American religion proper."[2] Instead of bucking the tide, the seminaries have more or less capitulated to the trend of lowering entrance requirements to meet the competition for students. Language requirements were the first to go.

As one who went on to do graduate studies in theology, I have always been grateful that our generation had to slog through an old-fashioned curriculum that in principle covered all the basics from A to Z. The problem was not the curriculum as such; it was that most of the professors were unqualified to teach their subject matter. Very few held an earned doctorate in their field. Warren Quanbeck, considered the most brilliant member of the faculty, had a doctor's degree in New Testament theology from Princeton Seminary. After a few years of teaching the New Testament he became a professor of dogmatics, a

2. Harold Bloom, *The American Religion* (Simon and Schuster, 1992), p. 50.

discipline for which he had no special training. Nevertheless, Warren Quanbeck gained the reputation of being the most gifted theologian of the Evangelical Lutheran Church. He was appointed as one of the few Lutheran observers at the Second Vatican Council. He was a frequent delegate at the assemblies of the Lutheran World Federation. To my knowledge Quanbeck did not leave behind an impressive theological legacy of books or articles that advanced the cause of Christian theology in America.

The professor of Old Testament, John Milton, used class time to disprove the JEDP documentary hypothesis. His favorite phrase was "the essential Mosaicity of the Pentateuch." I was no biblical scholar, but even then I thought the idea that Moses wrote the first five books of the Old Testament was laughable. Some of the most creative work in theology was being done by Old Testament professors at that time. Milton never mentioned the name of Gerhard von Rad. We learned none of the best Old Testament theology being written in the 1950s. We met the same fate in New Testament theology. We heard not a word about Bultmann, demythologizing, hermeneutics, the quest of the historical Jesus, new interpretations of Pauline theology, or any of the hotly debated issues in New Testament studies. We were left to read about these things on our own. What we learned was that there were many interesting things that our professors were either ignorant of or chose to shield us from. When I went on to graduate school, I soon realized that I would need to learn Old and New Testament theology almost from scratch. What I learned about the Bible at Luther Seminary was scarcely superior to what I learned from my missionary teachers in Madagascar.

The professors at Luther Seminary were sincere, hardworking, pious, and pastoral, but they were not good teachers and most were not theologically well educated. We wrote lots of exams, but they were seldom returned with comments or corrections. The same thing happened with term papers. All the jokes applied — like, the professors threw them down the stairs; the ones that got to the bottom got A's. I must have been lucky; a lot of mine made it to the bottom.

As I reflect back on my seminary experience, I am grateful about one thing — the psychologizing craze had not yet hit seminary education. That came later, with the onslaught of CPE (clinical pastoral education) that softened the brains of students so they could not take theology seriously. Students would begin their sentences with "I feel" rather than "I think."

During the middler year the faculty gave students their internship assignments. The internship requirement had been dropped during the Second World War, so that graduating seniors would more quickly be available to enlist as military chaplains. The requirement had not yet been reinstated in the catalogue the year I entered the seminary. Nevertheless, the faculty went ahead and assigned me to a parish in Williston, North Dakota, under an ultraconservative Lutheran pastor, Casper B. Nervig. They were thinking, most likely, that on account of my alleged liberal tendencies, I needed some straightening out under a hard-nosed conservative Lutheran.

Nervig was a well-known author of a book entitled *Christian Truth and Religious Delusion.* Its table of contents carried some interesting chapter titles. For example, the title of chapter 2 was "The Evangelical Lutheran Church — the Church of Truth." Chapter 3 was "Catholic Churches: Much Truth — Much Error." Chapter 4 was "The Reformed Churches: Much Truth — Some Error." For Pentecostalism the title was "Some Truth — Much Error." The book contained a stunning diagram of a large tree. The roots of the tree were embedded in the Bible. The tree trunk grew straight upward representing five hundred years of creeds and church fathers who taught the pure Christian truth. Farther up, the tree branched out, deviating from the center; one branch represented Roman Catholicism and the other Eastern Orthodoxy. The sixteenth-century Lutheran Reformation was straight in line with the roots of the tree, the Bible, and the first five centuries. A whole slew of branches here and there represented the many familiar denominations and sects. The place at the very top of the tree, straight in line with the Bible, the first five centuries, and the Lutheran Reformation, was held by the Evangelical Lutheran Church. I was a member of this church; I should have felt so proud. Instead, I laughed. Imagine, we were the blessed possessors of the full Christian truth, without error. How fortunate to be assigned to an internship under this pastor's tutelage. But I would have none of it.

I went to see the president, T. F. Gullickson, and told him that since I planned to go on to graduate school, I could not accept the internship assignment. He said, "But the faculty has voted unanimously in favor of it." I explained that the catalogue did not stipulate internship as a requirement when I entered the seminary. That meant that I was not obligated, no matter how the faculty voted. He could not disagree.

The faculty's unanimous vote would not be its last. Students at Luther Seminary had to preach a senior sermon as a requirement in homiletics. I chose to preach on two texts, the story of Thomas doubting the resurrection of Jesus and the story of John the Baptist asking, "Are you he who is to come, or should we look for another?" The title of my sermon was "The Vertical and Horizontal Dimensions of Doubt." The faculty always sat together in one of the front rows, looking stern and serious. I was scared and pumped up for the occasion. What I said somehow struck a nerve; faculty members were visibly displeased. I distinguished between two kinds of doubt. There is doubt as the intellectual form of sin. A good example was Satan's question to Eve in the Garden of Eden, "Did God say?" Then there is doubt as a necessary condition of intellectual inquiry, for example, the Cartesian *dubito ergo sum*. The latter should be encouraged in a theological school, but, I said, that was not the case here at Luther Seminary. The spirit of questioning was suppressed in the classrooms; it was assumed that students were there to get cooked answers to questions they were not even asking. The professors did not take kindly to what seemed like my sowing the seeds of freethinking.

I have called this my "thousand dollars sermon." The seminary tradition was to award the highest-ranking senior a $1,000 grant from the Lutheran Brotherhood Insurance Company. That year the faculty voted to give it to the president of the student body, who was not at the top of the class. Some students protested the injustice in writing to the newly elected president of the seminary, Alvin Rogness. I viewed the whole affair as the faculty's revenge for my refusal of internship and my sermon's implicit criticism of the tendency to confuse the vertical *(coram deo)* and horizontal *(coram mundo)* dimensions of doubt.

During my senior year I did supply preaching in two rural congregations in southwestern Minnesota. I would hold service in one congregation at 9:00 A.M. and in the other at 10:30 A.M. The two services were identical — the liturgy, hymns, and sermon. There were fewer than a hundred at each service. I asked the president of one of the church councils, "Why don't we combine the two congregations and have only one worship service, since the two services are exactly the same? We could hold it at one church one Sunday and at the other the next, and so forth." He answered, "That would be impossible!" I asked, "How come?" He said, "We just don't agree." I asked, "What is the disagreement all about?" He explained that earlier in the century the two congregations had split over a dispute on Lutheran doctrine. "What doctrine?" I asked. He said it had to do with the controversy on election and free will. I asked him, "On what side of the dispute was your congregation?" He paused and then said, "I can't remember. It's so long ago." Now the two congregations have merged. The controversy resolved itself when the old warriors were laid to rest in their respective graveyards. But I would bet dollars to donuts that the old controversy between Aus and Preus on election and free will is still alive at my alma mater, and will continue as long as there are pietists and confessional Lutherans around to debate the issue. Or it may be the case that many younger faculty members — many coming from non-Lutheran denominations — may not know enough of the tradition to engage in argument.

The only other controversy gripping Luther Seminary and the ELC had to do with the Bible. The question was hotly debated: "Is the Bible the Word of God or does it contain the Word of God?" President Gullickson and other ELC theologians and pastors firmly held that the Bible *is* the Word of God. The ELC accused the United Lutheran Church (ULC) of holding the liberal view, namely, the idea that the Bible only *contains* the Word of God. For ammunition they cited what Joseph Sittler wrote in his first book, *The Doctrine of the Word*. Sittler attempted to lead Lutheranism away from a fundamentalist approach, with its insistence on the verbal inerrancy of the Bible. In its place Sittler developed a dynamic concept of the Word of God, drawing on new ideas from neo-orthodox theologians, notably Karl Barth, Emil Brunner, Gustaf Aulén, and Anders Nygren. Sittler's ideas were rejected by Gullickson as too liberal. The controversy could not be resolved by appealing to the *Book of Concord,* because it contains no explicit doctrine on the Bible as the Word of God, let alone its literal inerrancy and verbal inspiration. American Lutheranism was scarred by the controversy between modernists and fundamentalists in the 1920s. Another generation of Lutheran theology was needed to work its way beyond the controversy in a way that both acknowledges the authority of the Bible in matters of faith and morals and accepts the modern methods of historical criticism.

In the spring of 1955 I was thrilled to receive letters of acceptance from the divinity schools of Chicago, Yale, and Harvard to do doctoral studies in theology. I chose Harvard for two reasons: (1) Paul Tillich was leaving Union Seminary in New York to become a university professor at Harvard, and (2) Harvard offered a more attractive financial package. When word got to the seminary faculty that I was going to Harvard, some lamented that the "liberal" was heading to the hotbed of Protestant liberalism, with its strong background in New England Unitarianism. A professor of Old Testament, John V. Halvorson, took me aside and counseled for my benefit — he was genuinely concerned — that I should go to Concordia Theological Seminary in St. Louis rather than Harvard Divinity School. There my liberal tendencies would be counterbalanced by the conservative orientation of the Missouri Synod. I said, no thanks; such a proposal ran completely against my grain of thinking. That would have been like jumping from the frying pan of pietistic biblicism into the fire of biblical fundamentalism. Even today, as I write these memoirs fifty years later, the Missouri Lutherans are still stuck in the same rut of a fundamentalist interpretation of the Bible. For example, they still officially adhere to a literal belief in the creation of the world in six days, to heck with modern scientific cosmology. Every historical account must be accepted as factually inerrant.

I left Luther Seminary clearly committed to the tradition of Lutheran confessional theology. In going to Harvard I had no intention of becoming a liberal Protestant theologian; I wanted to embark on a plan of studies that would eventually qualify me to become a Lutheran professor of dogmatics. There was no professor at Luther Seminary that modeled what that meant, nor did I know of anyone in American

Lutheranism. At Harvard I planned to learn what it takes to do dog-matic and systematic theology in the mainstream of the Christian tra-dition, of course, from a Lutheran perspective. I was full of optimism and hope. At last I would meet Paul Tillich.

CHAPTER FIVE

Harvard Divinity School

1955–1957

We — LaVonne, Craig (three years old), and I — pulled a U-Haul trailer filled with all our earthly belongings from St. Paul, Minnesota, to Cambridge, Massachusetts. LaVonne had worked at Campbell Mithune Advertising Agency for two years, buying a $25 savings bond with every paycheck. We rented an apartment on Wendell Street, within easy walking distance of the divinity school. With a lot of work we were able to make this modest apartment into a comfortable home for the next two years at Harvard. It became a cozy place where with meager means we did a lot of entertaining — pizza, and a little beer and wine. We drove a nifty 1951 Chevrolet coupe. To make ends meet LaVonne worked as a part-time secretary for Pastor Henry Horn at University Lutheran Church. To help out on the grocery bill LaVonne cooked dinner five nights a week for three Lutheran divinity students — Paul Lee, Bill Norby, and Roger Johnson. Every mealtime was given to theological table talk, which usually meant Tillich talk. LaVonne also typed term papers for students at thirty-five cents a page. I did supply preaching in nearby Lutheran congregations and tutored a few university students in French. That's how we made it through two years of graduate school without incurring any debts.

At Luther I had read a few of Tillich's writings, starting with one of his earliest books translated into English, *The Interpretation of History* (1936). I wrote a book review of it for a class in church history, taught by E. Clifford Nelson; it was one of five books recommended for extra reading. Tillich was fast becoming famous; articles and photos appeared in *Time, Newsweek,* and *Life* magazines. He was being hailed as the "apostle to the intellectuals," and though not really an existentialist, he somehow became popularly associated with the wave of existentialism among the avant-garde literati. Tillich was often invited to preach in college chapels and lectured to large gatherings on university campuses throughout the United States. He came to St. Olaf College in 1954; a few seminarians who went to hear him returned buzzing about the fantastic things they had heard. Paul Lee suggested that I read *The Protestant Era* (1948). I read the chapters dealing with the Reformation doctrine of justification through faith: "The Protestant Principle and the Proletarian Situation," "The Formative Power of Protestantism," and "The Protestant Message and the Man of Today." Tillich's interpretations were new to me and provided grist to my quest for a kind of Lutheran identity with theological integrity and relevance for the modern world. For the next years "identity" and "relevance" became the two poles around which my thoughts were to revolve.

Naturally I signed up for every class taught by Tillich. The first one was a departmental seminar called "Four Types of Love." The four types were *agapē* (New Testament), *eros* (Plato), *philia* (Aristotle), and *libido* (Freud). It was not a successful seminar. Other members of the department of theology — John Dillenberger, John Wild, and Walter Leibrecht — were too intimidated by Tillich's presence to contribute anything significant. Students gave Tillich their exclusive attention and ignored what anyone else had to say. Tillich's word was received as authoritative; every utterance was parsed. A saying attributed to George Buttrick, the preacher at Harvard Memorial Chapel, was quoted around campus: "There are two great minds in the world, God's and Tillich's."

Nathan Pusey, president of Harvard University, was a devout Episcopalian layman; frequently he read the lessons at Sunday morning worship in Memorial Chapel. Upon his inauguration Pusey pledged to return the divinity school to its glory days. He succeeded in assembling a remarkably talented faculty: Frank Cross in Old Testament; G. Ernest Wright and Krister Stendahl in New Testament; John Dillenberger, Paul Lehmann, and Richard R. Niebuhr in theology; Georges

Florovsky and Milton Anastos in the history of Christianity; George Buttrick in homiletics; and John Wild in philosophy of religion. In addition, a few famous scholars were already on the faculty, such as Robert Pfeiffer in Old Testament, Amos Wilder in New Testament, George Hunston Williams in church history, and Harry Austryn Wolfson in patristics. With Paul Tillich's arrival Nathan Pusey achieved almost overnight the renaissance of Harvard Divinity School, making it arguably the premier school of theology in America, or at least equal to Yale and Chicago, and superior to Union, Princeton, and Vanderbilt.

My program of study was shaped by what I thought would best prepare me to become a systematic theologian. Tillich taught me by his example and guidance that one does not become a systematic theologian by reading what present-day theologians are saying. Tillich did not spend much time lecturing on contemporary problems in philosophy and theology. He drew students into the study of the classics, starting with the ancient Greeks. He was not a master seeking to make disciples — little Tillichian toadies. Those who sucked up to him he tended to keep at arm's length. Tillich's advice was: Don't read me but read the texts of the great tradition. Go to the sources of the classical Christian thinkers — *ad fontes.* That is exactly what I tried to do. I read the church fathers — Irenaeus, Origen, Athanasius, Cyril, Tertullian, Cyprian, Augustine, the Cappadocians, etc. — with Florovsky and Wolfson. I read the medieval scholastics and mystics in Tillich's seminars, as well as Luther and Calvin with Dillenberger.

In my second year at Harvard Tillich asked me to be his teaching assistant, a position for which I was paid quite handsomely. My job was to read the term papers that students wrote for Tillich's lecture courses and seminars. Students made it known that they did not appreciate receiving my critical comments in the margins of their papers. I could hardly blame them. I was a mere fellow student; what did I know? Some were Unitarians whom I found to be rather shallow and pitifully ignorant of the robust teachings of the Christian tradition, particularly on the doctrine of the Trinity and Christology taught by the ancient fathers and doctors of the church. On one embarrassing occasion some Unitarian students complained to the dean of the faculty, Douglas Horton, about the way their papers were being graded. I was not inclined to give an A for what I thought was a Unitarian misinterpretation of Tillich's thought. The dean called me into his office and heard my side of the story. He put his arm around me and said, "Don't worry about it. You're doing just fine."

One day a famous photojournalist, Alfred Eisenstaedt, from *Life* magazine, came to Harvard to take pictures for a cover story on Paul Tillich. He asked for one student to sit for pictures with Tillich, and I was chosen. Wow! I was told by the photographer that Tillich and I were about to appear on the cover of *Time* magazine. We posed this way and that way, frontwards and sideways. The week the story was to appear, the Suez Canal crisis erupted, an international conflict that pitted Egypt against Israel, the United Kingdom, and France. As bad luck would have it, the notorious mug of Gamal Abdel Nasser appeared on the cover instead. Nasser had blocked passage in the canal by sinking forty ships, and that became the major story of the week.

Paul Tillich meant a lot to me. Years later I published a number of pieces evaluating Tillich's theology, indicating agreements and disagreements.[1] Here I will recount only what Tillich meant to me as my doctor-father on my way to a Th.D. (doctor of theology). Harvard offered two graduate degrees, a Ph.D. and a Th.D. A Ph.D. was designed mostly for future teachers of religion; it focused on the history and philosophy of religion and contemporary religious thought. That degree required only a reading knowledge of two modern languages, German and French. A Th.D. required a reading knowledge of the biblical languages, Hebrew and Greek, as well as Latin, German, and French. The theological doctorate (Th.D.) focused on the history of Christianity and the classics of Christian theology. The Th.D. route

---

1. My writings on the thought of Paul Tillich spanned many years. Here are some of them. "Paul Tillich as a Lutheran Theologian," *Record* (Chicago Lutheran Theological Seminary) 67, no. 3 (August 1962): 34-42; "Paul Tillich and the Classical Christian Tradition," in *A History of Christian Thought*, ed. Carl E. Braaten (Simon and Schuster, 1967), xiii-xxv; "Eschatology and Ontology in Conflict: A Study of Paul Tillich's Theology," in *Christ and Counter-Christ* (Fortress, 1972), pp. 54-66; "The Contemporary Significance of Justification in the Theology of Paul Tillich," in Braaten, *Justification: The Article by Which the Church Stands or Falls* (Augsburg Fortress, 1990), pp. 41-62; "Paul Tillich on the 'Protestant Principle and Catholic Substance,'" in Braaten, *That All May Believe* (Eerdmans, 2008).

was the appropriate choice for me. I wrote major papers on Augustine, Origen, Nestorius, Boehme, Luther, Schleiermacher, Barth, Nygren, and Tillich. My main focus was on Trinity and Christology in the history of Christian thought. By the end of my second year it was time to face the rigors of the doctoral examinations, five days of writing, morning and afternoon. Even though I did not feel ready for the ordeal, I had to go through with it, since we were running out of money. The professors were very busy people working on their own projects. As it turned out, I passed with flying colors. Perhaps they were too busy to read them with care.

Tillich was very helpful to me. He wrote a letter of recommendation in support of my application to become a Kent Fellow of the Society for Religion in Higher Education. It was an honor to be accepted into this prestigious society of scholars. Tillich also wrote a letter recommending me for the Sinclair Kennedy Traveling Fellowship, a generous grant of Harvard University that would make it possible to study for a year in Germany. From among the many great German universities I chose Heidelberg, because it was reputed to have the strongest theological faculty in the world.

After passing the comprehensive exams I made an appointment to see Tillich to discuss a possible topic for my dissertation. Five minutes into the conversation Tillich said, "This is what you must do, write on Martin Kähler's concept of the historical Jesus. Translate his book, *Der sogenannte historische Jesus und der geschichtliche biblische Christus,* write a lengthy introduction for it and that will be your dissertation." Who is Martin Kähler? Tillich said Kähler had been his professor of dogmatics at the University of Halle. I did not know enough to ask any questions or make any comments. I had seen Kähler's name once or twice in connection with something Tillich had written on the doctrine of justification. I thanked Tillich for the suggestion and went directly to the library. There I found the book in question and a half-dozen others by Martin Kähler. None of them had been translated into English and all were printed in the old German script, where the *s* looks like an *f*. I read fast and furiously and by nightfall I knew I had my dissertation topic in the bag. What a relief. I have known students who have struggled for years to find a suitable subject on which to write, chasing down one blind alley after another.

All that remained to do was to pack our suitcases and trunks, and book our passage to Le Havre, France, on the SS *United States,* America's greatest ocean liner. We took a train to Paris, where we were met at Gare Saint Lazare by my brother Martin and his wife Betty. They were in Paris for a year of language study in preparation for missionary service in French Cameroon. We bought their car, a sporty convertible, a Hillman Minx made in Britain. We were on our way to Heidelberg, not knowing what resources the university library might have for my research on Martin Kähler. For once we had plenty of money in the bank. I had been awarded a Lutheran World Federation scholarship for overseas study. That, together with the Harvard fellowship, meant we could look forward to living in relative ease and doing a lot of traveling.

CHAPTER SIX

The University of Heidelberg

1957–1958

The University of Heidelberg indeed had a great faculty of theology. The most notable professors were Gerhard von Rad (Old Testament), Günther Bornkamm (New Testament), Hans Freiherr von Campenhausen (church history), Heinrich Bornkamm (church history), Edmund Schlink (systematic theology), Peter Brunner (systematic theology), and Wolfhart Pannenberg (systematic theology). Students were free to attend any of the lectures or seminars of these great scholars. Since my interest was contemporary systematic theology, I listened mostly to the lectures of Schlink, Brunner, and Pannenberg. But taking courses was not the real purpose of my study in Heidelberg.

I had come to Heidelberg on a singular mission: to translate Martin Kähler's book *Der sogenannte historische Jesus und der geschichtliche biblische Christus,* and to write the dissertation Paul Tillich had assigned — on Kähler's approach to the problem of the historical Jesus. I knew this would be a tough assignment. My knowledge of the German language was limited. I had taken a course in German at the University of Minnesota; I managed to pass the language exam for a Harvard Th.D., but that did not mean I was proficient in German. When I arrived at the university, I discovered that a pro-seminar (led by Johannes Wirsching, who later became a professor of systematic theology at the University of Berlin) was being offered that very fall on Kähler's book on the historical Jesus. What luck! A Kähler renaissance was taking place in German theology at that time. Neither Tillich nor I could foresee how timely the assignment of this topic would be. Kähler's thought was being drawn into the controversy surrounding Rudolf Bultmann's programmatic call to demythologize the New Testament. Both Bultmann's disciples and his critics appealed to Kähler in dealing with the question of the relation between history and the kerygma, between the historical Jesus and the kerygmatic Christ. Could it be that my research project on Kähler would turn out to be theologically relevant after all? Instead of having to delve into some musty old volumes to unearth some dry-as-dust ideas of no relevance for today, I was facing the happy prospect of spending a year in Heidelberg coming to terms with the most consequential issues in contemporary theology. I wrote my seminar paper comparing Kähler and Tillich on the place of the historical Jesus in Christology. Although Tillich did not believe that Kähler's answer to the question of the historical Jesus was adequate in our post-Bultmannian situation, he did accept one of Kähler's ideas, namely, to keep faith free and independent of the always-oscillating results of historical research. Believers need not look to historians for a green light to believe in Jesus as the Christ. The certainty of faith must not be based on the sinking sands of historical probability.

The year in Heidelberg was very special for LaVonne and me — it was the beginning of a lasting friendship and collaborative relationship with Robert (Jens) and Blanche Jenson. We did not always believe it would turn out that way. In the summer of 1957 LaVonne and I learned that the Jensons were also going to Heidelberg. Jens was planning to study for a doctorate in theology at the university. Jens and I had had little to do with each other at Luther Seminary. He was from Luther College and I, from St. Olaf College. Both of us were saddled with the prevailing stereotypes: Luther College stood for Lutheran orthodoxy and St. Olaf College for Christian humanism. I was the guy who had studied philosophy (existentialism and phenomenology) at the Sorbonne; that was enough to make me some sort of liberal. Jens was the brain trust of the seminarians who supported Herman Preus in his conflict with George Aus.

I did not anticipate that Jens and I would have a lot to do with each other in Heidelberg. Then one Sunday afternoon as LaVonne and I were strolling down Hauptstrasse in Heidelberg, we saw Robert and Blanche Jenson coming our way. By the time we recognized each other, it was too late to turn around or cross the street. We met, we exchanged greetings, talked about our living accommodations, and before we went our separate ways, Blanche suggested that we get together. This we did, again and again, back and forth, we to their humble place in the suburb of Neckargemünde and they to our small city apartment on Mittlerer Gaisbergweg. There was so much to talk about. All the frontline theological issues were being treated in the lectures and seminars. Jens and I would mull over everything we were hearing and learning.

One day a well-known Lutheran pastor, Carroll Hinderlie, arrived in Heidelberg with his large family. He was on a study leave to catch up on what was going on in theology. It was rumored that he was being groomed to teach New Testament at Luther Seminary. Its president, Alvin Rogness, was known to be one of his best friends. After attending a few lectures he told Jens and me that it was a waste of time; the professors were not teaching anything he didn't already know. Wow! Here was the citadel of the rebirth of confessional Lutheran theology after the Nazi period; here a Lutheran systematic theology was being shaped as an alternative to Barthianism and a Lutheran theological critique of Bultmann's demythologizing program was being mounted; it was the launching pad of the theology of hope that Pannenberg was pioneering through his essays on hermeneutics, eschatology, and history. And there was nothing here that a pastor from Midwestern Lutheran pietism did not already know? Unbelievable.

The year in Heidelberg was very special in another respect. LaVonne and I met Wolfhart and Hilke Pannenberg. That was the start of a lifelong collaborative friendship. We did not know then that Pannenberg would soon become the most famous Lutheran systematic theologian in the world. Once I asked Johannes Wirsching, the leader of the Kähler seminar, whether there was anything new developing in German theology beyond the standoff between Barth and Bultmann. He said, yes, that Pannenberg was the leader of a study group made up of some of his fellow graduate students constructing a new theological concept of history. This was an interdisciplinary group working to create a way beyond the opposition between Bultmann's critical interpretation of the New Testament and Barth's theological exposition of church dogmatics. Pannenberg realized that theology cannot have much of a future when dogmatics is divorced from exegesis. The group came to be known in subsequent debate as "the Pannenberg circle," comprising biblical exegetes, church historians, and theologians. Pannenberg, being the systematician, drafted the comprehensive synthesis informed by the various exegetical and historical insights. The circle published a volume of essays appropriately entitled *Revelation as History* (1961). Its fundamental unifying theme is that God reveals himself indirectly through historical events. This meant that theology as the "study of God" cannot be separated from the study of history.

The next time we met the Pannenbergs was in 1965. Wolfhart became a visiting professor at the University of Chicago Divinity School. Knowing that I had recently returned from studying in Germany, Jerald Brauer, dean of the divinity school, asked if I knew of any bright new star on the horizon of German theology. I was quick to answer, "Of course, Wolfhart Pannenberg, professor of systematic theology at the University of Mainz." So Brauer invited him to teach for a semester. It was not a happy experience for Pannenberg. In Germany Pannenberg was treated as a VIP; he was used to lecturing to hundreds of students and leading large seminars. At Chicago there was no welcoming host, no planned reception to meet other members of the faculty. Six students signed up for his seminar on Christology. Who is Wolfhart Pannenberg anyway? No one had heard of him, and he was not accorded the respect due to a *Herr Professor*. Of the six students, three were auditors, and to Pannenberg's dismay students thought nothing of missing a session. One student reported to Pannenberg that he would need to miss class to take his wife to the doctor. That sort of thing would never happen in Germany.

That year in Germany LaVonne and I met Roy and Norma Harrisville, which was the start of a lasting friendship. Roy had received a Lutheran World Federation (LWF) grant to study at the University of Tübingen. Jens and I had also received an LWF grant. We met Roy at a youth hostel in Bonn, at an LWF conference to orient all LWF scholars to the social, political, and cultural situation in Germany. Roy had received his doctorate in New Testament from Princeton Seminary under the supervision of Otto Piper. The three of us argued theology late into the night, each one holding his ground in relation to the others. Roy, as I recall, was defending the anti-Bultmannian stance of his doctor-father, Otto Piper; Jens was in support of certain aspects of Bultmann's theology; and I was speaking out of a Tillichian frame of reference, which was both for and against Bultmann. Whereas Tillich and Bultmann were two Lutheran theologians worlds apart in their thought structures, Tillich welcomed the debate on demythologizing that Bultmann started. However, for Tillich the prefix "de-" did not mean the "elimination" of but rather the "interpretation" of myth. During Roy's year of study in Tübingen he met Ernst Käsemann, one of Bultmann's greatest students. Roy's mind made a 180-degree turnabout that year. Since then Roy has become one of the most creative mediators of the Bultmann-Käsemann legacy and a productive interpreter of the New Testament in his own right.

In the spring of 1958 LaVonne and I bought a 1956 Mercedes, a beautiful black sedan in perfect condition. Jens, Roy, and I made an unforgettable trip to Basel, Switzerland, to hear Karl Barth, the most famous theologian in the world. When we approached the Swiss border, Roy discovered that he had forgotten his passport. What to do? The borders were not open at that time. So we devised a plan. We had Roy crouch down on the floor in the back seat and threw some jackets over him, and Jens and I handed our passports to the border guard. He looked into the car but did not poke around. So he waved us through. On the return trip we tried the same ruse, but it did not work. The guard told everyone to get out of the car and then found Roy hiding. It was past midnight. We pleaded that we were mere theological students who had come for a day to hear a famous Swiss professor lecture at the University of Basel. But we had no way to certify Roy's identity. So the officer in charge called some bureau in Tübingen that kept the registration of foreigners. Roy was legally registered, so the guards let us pass. With a huge sigh of relief we went on our way, saying, "If this had happened in the States, who knows how long we would have been detained?"

One day I received a letter from Tillich informing me that he was to be in Hamburg on a day in May. If I wished to discuss my dissertation, I could meet him for breakfast at his hotel. I answered that it would work out fine because I needed to drive to Hamburg anyway to ship our Mercedes to the States. So we met again. As we entered the restaurant, I noticed that Tillich was being profusely congratulated by the maître d' and others. I asked Tillich what that was all about. He answered, "Haven't you heard? It's in all the papers. I was awarded the Goethe Medallion." This was a German national prize awarded annually by the Goethe Institut, the German cultural institution that honors persons who have achieved excellence in promoting cultural exchange. That was a big deal for Tillich, because after the war Tillich had been designated persona non grata in Germany on account of his criticism of some of the policies of the United States.

In the late 1950s Tillich was being rediscovered in Germany as a major systematic theologian. Tillich had fled from Germany in 1933 on account of his conflict with the Nazi government. During the intervening years Tillich was unknown in Germany. If anyone remembered Tillich, it was because his name appeared, always in a negative light, in a few footnotes in the early volumes of Barth's *Church Dogmatics*. In the late 1950s Tillich reentered German theology as a fresh new voice beyond the stalemate between the Barthians and Bultmannians. In the winter of 1958 I attended a seminar taught by Edmund Schlink dealing with Tillich's systematic theology along with the thought of Karl Barth (Reformed), Paul Althaus (Lutheran), and Michael Schmaus (Roman Catholic). Schlink expressed surprise to discover the churchly orientation of Tillich's *Systematic Theology*. Barth had tagged Tillich with the label "theologian of culture." However, the first volume of Tillich's systematics opens with the words: "Theology, as a function of the Christian church, must serve the needs of the church." Barth couldn't say it any better. Tillich was reclaimed by German theologians as one of them, especially among younger theologians. Wolfhart Pannenberg, in particular, welcomed the third volume of Tillich's systematics, especially part IV on "Life and the Spirit." He referred to this section as an outstanding example of an attempt to develop a theology of the Spirit within the broad horizon of an overall interpretation of life.

The year I encountered the renaissance of Lutheran theology in Heidelberg convinced me that my future in theology would necessarily move beyond the categories I had learned from Paul Tillich's systematic theology. I owed a great debt of gratitude to Tillich for what he meant to me as a teacher of the classical Christian tradition. However, the crucial issue in theology after World War II was how best to deal with Christianity as a historical religion. In the last analysis Tillich's thought tended to place the categories of history and eschatology into the procrustean bed of a philosophical essentialist ontology that owes more to Plato than to the Bible. When I published my first theological book, *History and Hermeneutics,* it became clear that my theological thinking had switched onto quite a different track. I did not find in Tillich's theology a solution to the hermeneutical problem posed by the linkage of the Christian faith to historical events.

I read a lot of Bultmann and his many critics that year in Heidelberg. Upon returning to the States, Roy Harrisville and I translated and edited selected essays published in two symposia on the theology of Rudolf Bultmann, with responses from his critics. The two volumes are: *Kerygma and History* (1962) and *The Historical Jesus and the Kerygmatic Christ* (1964), published by Abingdon Press. My dissertation on Kähler dovetailed with all the themes and problems that we covered in these books. In 1964 Fortress Press published my translation and introduction to Martin Kähler's work, under the English title *The So-Called Historical Jesus and the Historic Biblical Christ.* Again it was the category of history that dominated all these publications. Although many insights and accents in Bultmann's theology fascinated me, I was convinced that Bultmann's demythologizing of the New Testament dissolved the objective reality of history into the existential moment of decision. This became incontrovertibly clear in the way Bultmann sidestepped the historicity of the resurrection of Jesus. The apostolic kerygma was emptied of its historical contents. My Heidelberg experience urged me to discover a different way forward in theology than along the lines of either Tillich or Bultmann. Little did I know at that time that meanwhile Wolfhart Pannenberg and a few of his fellow graduate students were steeped in research and conversations on how best to deal with the theological problems with which I was simultaneously grappling. When the Pannenberg circle published their manifesto, *Revelation as History*, the effect on me was as though I had won the lottery. For me this book of essays signaled the way forward beyond Barth, Bultmann, Tillich, and the entire older generation of dialectical and existentialist theologians.

Editing and publishing the two books on Bultmann's theology catapulted me almost overnight to the forefront of the movement to transmit German theology to the English-speaking world. I was eager to do this work of mediation for two reasons: first, there was nothing going on in American Lutheran theology that I could constructively move forward, and second, there was likewise nothing in American Protestant theology with which I could identify. Although I had been a student of Tillich, I was in no way a Tillichian, and furthermore I never regarded Tillich's theology as American. It was thoroughly Germanic. If not Tillich, then what? The process theology being taught at the Chicago Divinity School, based on the metaphysics of Alfred N. Whitehead and Charles Hartshorne, could not gain my interest because its fundamental thought structure blurred the distinction between the Creator and the creation, God and the world. Boston personalism was impossible to take seriously because it was Unitarianism with no Christology. Then there were the two Niebuhrs, H. Richard and Reinhold, but neither one was a theologian in a strict sense. As was generally typical of liberal Protestant theology, neither of the Niebuhrs wrote theology within the framework of the doctrine of the Trinity with a high Christology to match. The two Niebuhrs made significant contributions to religious thought in America in different respects, but the theological legacy they left behind was extremely thin, leaving no firm theological foundations on which to build.

Close to the time of our departure from Heidelberg I received a letter from Alvin Rogness, president of Luther Seminary, inviting me to serve as a part-time instructor starting in the fall of 1958. He also offered to work with the district president, Elmer Reinertsen, to find me an appropriate call to the parish ministry somewhere in the Twin Cities. Luther Seminary had a five-year rule. One had to serve five years as a parish pastor before being eligible for a full-time position on the seminary faculty. I thought the rule was an unnecessary obstacle, but I was willing to abide by it, somewhat grudgingly. Later I changed my mind and supported the intent of the rule. Those who teach future pastors had better ground their teaching of theology in the skills and practices of the ordained ministry. The fruitful years of parish experience in North Minneapolis prepared me to teach the required post-internship course to seniors in pastoral theology for many years.

We returned to the United States in May 1958. Our son Craig was six years old, our dog Heidi was a purebred German shepherd, LaVonne was pregnant with our second child, and I was filled with the latest news from the front lines of the German theological battlefield.

CHAPTER SEVEN

Lutheran Church of the Messiah and Luther Seminary

1958–1961

I received a call to serve as the pastor of a Lutheran congregation in North Minneapolis, Russell Avenue Lutheran Church. District President Elmer Reinertsen ordained me on August 30, 1958, with my father Torstein F. Braaten and my uncle Kittel F. Braaten assisting. The same day LaVonne gave birth to Martha, our second child, so she missed the occasion. We moved into the parsonage across the street from the church on the corner of Russell Avenue and Sixteenth Street. There we planned to live for at least the next five years. At the same time, I was invited by Alvin Rogness, the president of Luther Seminary, to teach part time in the areas of church history and contemporary theology. The Evangelical Lutheran Church required that any professor teaching at its seminary needed to serve at least five years as a parish pastor. At the time I did not think that the rule should apply to me, but later I became convinced that it was a wise rule. Should not anyone teaching future pastors have hands-on experience of what the church's ministry is all about?

The church was located in a predominantly Jewish neighborhood. At least three synagogues were within walking distance. At the first congregational meeting I suggested that our church would make a more effective witness if we changed its name to Lutheran Church of the Messiah. The reference to the Messiah would remind our Jewish neighbors and ourselves that at a very deep level Christianity and Judaism share common ground — both are messianic faiths. Christians believe that the Jewish Messiah has already come, Jews that he is still to come. Christianity began as an offshoot of Judaism. The apostle Paul, speaking to the Gentiles in Rome, tells them they are "a wild olive shoot" grafted on to the olive tree, and that the branch does not support the root but the root supports the branch (Rom. 11:17-18). The congregation approved the change unanimously; the new name of the church was meant to be a theological statement and a witness to our Jewish neighbors.

To my surprise I took to the parish ministry like a fish to water. I enjoyed everything about it, except the poor salary. We had learned frugality during the lean years in graduate school, so we managed to survive from week to week. My first challenge as the new pastor was to call on all members of the congregation, to get to know who they were, where they lived, and what expectations they had. Next I called on all lapsed members and occasional visitors whose names the previous pastor had kept in a rolodex. That stratagem worked marvels. I remembered the sage advice of a veteran pastor whose name I cannot remember: "It takes a lot of shoe leather to grow a congregation." New people started coming to church, bringing their children to Sunday school, attending adult forums, and joining one of the women's circles or the men's group. I am normally a shy person and an introvert. However, I did not find ringing doorbells and calling on strangers difficult. As a Fuller Brush man in the summer of 1952, that's exactly what I learned to do day after day eight hours a day.

At our first communion service I noticed something strange. After the sermon and the offering, the service bulletin called for a final hymn and closing prayer, followed by an organ interlude. Then I saw half of the congregation get up and walk out. When the communion liturgy began, only those who felt worthy enough came forward to the altar rail for the bread and wine. I was dismayed and found this practice unacceptable. The next Sunday I preached a sermon — I still have it — entitled "The Communion of the Unworthy." The text was 1 Corinthians 11:23-32. Members of the congregation had been intimidated by a misinterpretation of the verse that warns that those who eat the bread and drink the cup *unworthily* will bring judgment upon themselves. No one wished to do that, so the safest thing was to skip the Lord's

Supper. I told the congregation that I understood where they were coming from, but the words in 1 Corinthians were not meant to scare us away. They were not meant to separate the sheep from the goats, the worthy from the unworthy. We are all unworthy. The reason we come to the Lord's Table is precisely so that we, unworthy sinners that we are, may receive the new worth that Christ bestows on us. When we eat the bread and drink the wine, we receive the benefits of Jesus' death and resurrection. I also said that if there is another mass exodus of those who feel unworthy, I would join them out the door. It is not the case that some are worthy and others are unworthy. Then I told them that the real point of the Corinthian passage was to protest the unholy practice of the Christians in Corinth of dividing the body of Christ between the wealthier ones who served themselves first and the poor who were served last. The sermon worked like magic. We got rid of the organ interlude and made the Lord's Supper an integral part of the whole service. The immediate result was that communion attendance more than doubled.

The district president sent annual forms for pastors to fill out. Our numbers were good in every respect. But I refused to waste my time keeping records — how many attended church each week, how many communed, how many were confirmed, how many baptisms, weddings, funerals during the year, and so forth. Who cares? I was too busy getting the numbers to grow to be bothered by record keeping. I never heard a word from the district president, so I assumed he was also too busy to read the reports. My guess is that he would look at the bottom line, to see the amount of our annual pledge and whether the monthly checks were coming in on time.

With so much new activity at the church, it seemed we were bulging at the seams. Some members began to talk about the need for a new building. All we had was the sanctuary and the basement. We needed a Sunday school building and a parish hall. The church council brought the proposal to the annual meeting, and there we heard the usual pros and cons. The most unforgettable comment was made by a so-called pillar of the congregation to oppose the building. "At the rate we are growing, pretty soon the building will be too small anyway. It's better for us to wait and see what happens." In other words, let us do nothing.

Money was a real problem for most of the families. The majority of the members were lower middle class, and many were single mothers receiving ADC (Aid to Dependent Children). Only one person was a college graduate, an attorney. One man operated a Phillips 66 gas station. I was told that the previous pastor always filled up his gas tank there. So I also patronized this man's station. I noticed from the church directory that he lived next door to a sister congregation several miles away. I asked him why he drove all the way to our church since he lived next door to Christ Lutheran Church. He said, "It's cheaper." Ha! Ha! Maybe we'll change that. So we did. The congregation hired an outside expert to lead an ambitious building fund drive, and when it was over this man had quadrupled his pledge.

During the years at Lutheran Church of the Messiah I encountered the entire gamut of pastoral challenges and crises.

- Eleven-year-old Lynette Gustafson, caught on fire while playing with matches, burned herself to death. Preaching at her funeral without sobbing was one of the hardest things I've ever had to do.
- A faithful parishioner whose husband was an alcoholic handed me his gun to dispose of; she was afraid he would use it on the family in a fit of rage.
- I called on a woman to ask her to consider teaching Sunday school. I noticed a bad scar on her wrist. She confessed that she had slashed her wrist in a suicide attempt. I pondered, am I making a mistake in asking her to teach a class?
- The phone rang in the middle of the night and a woman with five kids told me her husband had just been killed in a car accident. What does one say in the face of such tragedy? Why does God let bad things happen to good people and good things happen to bad people? I have never found a satisfactory answer to the problem of theodicy.
- I invited a Palestinian seminary student to speak at our Sunday evening potluck forum. He told about the plight of Christians in Palestine. The next morning I received phone calls from members of the Zion Society for Israel asking for equal time. I denied the request because the purpose of the event was to hear the story of a fellow

Christian from another part of the world and not to take sides in a political controversy.

- I had been alerted by other pastors that sooner or later I would have to deal with the Masons. At a funeral service of one of their Masonic members, they told me what they would like to do. I told them whatever they wanted to do after the service was up to the family and them, but they would play no part during the funeral liturgy. And they didn't.

- A former seminary student from Luther Seminary moved into our neighborhood with his family. He had left the seminary because it was too liberal. He was carrying on the old fight for biblical inerrancy in the ELC, namely, that every word of the Bible is literally and factually true. Like so many conservative evangelicals, he believed also that biblical prophecy was being played out in the Holy Land today. To support the rebirth of Israel was to side with God in realizing his plan for the "last days" — the return of Christ, the battle of Armageddon, the rapture, and so forth. This young man seemed to believe that Hal Lindsey's *Late Great Planet Earth* was the true interpretation of Holy Scripture. Knowing that I was teaching at Luther Seminary, he wrote a letter to the church council accusing me of the same heresies he had leveled against the seminary and the ELC. I must be a modernist in his definition or the seminary would not have asked me to teach there. As president of the church council, I invited this man to appear at its next meeting to explain the accusations, and then I would respond. When both of us finished what we had to say, there was a pause for discussion. Then I asked the church council for a vote of confidence and for a word of censure against the person undermining my ministry by spreading false charges. Either I was or I was not preaching and teaching in accordance with the doctrinal standards spelled out in the constitution of the ELC. The church council gave me a vote of confidence; this man never set foot inside our church again.

- Two of the deacons in charge of counting the Sunday offerings would leave with the collection plates before the final prayer of the church and the benediction. I asked them to wait until the end of the service before they start counting. One of them said they did it to save time,

48

and besides, "That long prayer don't mean nothing anyways." That was just another sign that we had some teaching to do.

- One week LaVonne and I wanted to buy a piece of furniture for which we did not have the money. This was before the day of credit cards. So on a Saturday afternoon I called on the treasurer to ask to be paid in advance. He came to the door obviously inebriated but not so bad that he could not heed my request. This was the man who had earlier commented on my preaching: "You don't preach sin and guilt hard enough." I thought I was preaching both law and gospel, according to good Lutheran homiletics. But this guy apparently was looking to the sermon for punishment to assuage his guilt. I was not sure that hammering hard on the sin of drunkenness would do him any good.

- Much of the poverty among our members was caused by the problem of alcoholism. Many of the males would go on weekend binges and waste their wages, leaving their wives and children bereft. One man, the father of one of my seminary students, made a very generous pledge to the building fund. When he was in default of meeting his pledge, I was given the assignment of making a house call. He came to the door in a drunken stupor. I had my answer. It was either the bottle or the pledge, and I knew which was more likely to win out.

- I tried to take sermon preparation seriously. Sunday afternoon I would read the pericopes for the next Sunday and let the words bounce around in my mind for several days. Then I would read a few of the great sermons preached on the Gospel text, some ancient and some contemporary. I would read a few reliable commentaries to make sure I was informed by the best exegetical scholarship available today. On Thursday I would construct a sermon outline, then write it out word for word. I never trusted myself to ad-lib my thoughts from the pulpit. Strange things come out of the mouths of preachers who improvise their lines on the spot. On Friday and Saturday I would practice the sermon out loud so my tongue would not trip over the words. After church one Sunday a young man who attended regularly — I knew he was a philosophy major at the University of Minnesota — greeted me at door and said, "I enjoy your preaching but you say pretty much the same thing every Sunday."

Ouch, that hurt. That kind of candor keeps a preacher humble and honest, or at least free of any delusion of grandeur.

One day the phone rang. It was Warren Quanbeck calling to inquire whether I would consider teaching at the Lutheran Theological Seminary in Maywood, Illinois. He had received a call from Donald Heiges, the dean of the Maywood seminary, with the information that George Forell had suddenly resigned to return to his former teaching position at the University of Iowa. The job would be for only one year, but if I took it they would consider me for the permanent appointment. This was by all odds the premier place for a systematician in Lutheran theological education. Joseph Sittler was the previous occupant of the chair in systematic theology. It was an honor to be asked. It would, however, mean to sidestep the five-year rule and most likely disqualify me from ever teaching at my alma mater Luther Seminary. It would mean leaving the parish sooner than expected, and just when things were going well. It would also mean switching synods, from the Evangelical Lutheran Church to the United Lutheran Church. I had a lot of relatives and friends in the former and knew almost nobody in the latter, so I might feel like a fish out of water. After discussing the proposition with LaVonne, we decided to accept the offer. Thus, once again we packed up kit and caboodle and moved to Maywood in the fall of 1961, our seventh move in ten years.

During my three years of parish ministry I led three lives — full-time pastor, part-time teacher, and part-time author and editor of theological publications. I still had to finish writing my dissertation on Martin Kähler and then defend it before the faculty at Harvard Divinity School. I felt confident that I knew more about Kähler than anyone on the faculty except Paul Tillich. On the day of the defense Tillich arrived with his memory of his former dogmatics professor refreshed from reading my dissertation. I assumed he would be supportive. At one point the New Testament professor, Amos Wilder, challenged Kähler's idea that the believer's faith is not dependent on the results of historical research into the life and teachings of Jesus. Wilder persisted in pressing me with his questions. Tillich then looked at him and said, "Amos, you can't be serious!" Wilder sank back into his chair, and that was the end of his interrogation. I left Harvard with a Th.D. in 1960.

Fortress Press published my translation and introduction of Kähler's book on the historical Jesus — a classic still in print after more than forty years.[1] Roy Harrisville and I coedited two volumes on Bultmann's theology.[2] The first article I wrote was on the Lutheran doctrine of justification,[3] a lifelong focal point of my theology. The article argued that if faith is a work we must do for salvation, then faith does not justify. Justification by faith has been misconstrued in the tradition of Lutheran Pietism in a semi-Pelagian sense. If we believe in Christ, then God will justify us. Well, how much faith do we need and how earnest must it be? How is that much different from asking, how many good works must we do to merit God's love? The logic of "if/then" makes salvation conditional on something we must do to gain God's favor. Luther taught that our wills are in bondage; faith is not an act humans can perform by their own free will. Faith is purely a gift of grace; it is not a prerequisite but a consequence of God's justifying activity. This article was my kiss good-bye to what George Aus was teaching at Luther Seminary. This kind of semi-Pelagianism works like a fifth column against the whole point of Luther's reformatory message. That first thing I wrote may turn out to be the truest, in terms of my deepest "here I stand" convictions.

The most enjoyable thing I did during my parish years was to take the lead in founding *dialog: A Journal of Theology.* After returning from Heidelberg the Harrisvilles invited the Jensons and the Braatens for lunch in their new home in St. Anthony Park. Roy was the new professor of New Testament at Luther Seminary. We were reminiscing about the good times we had in Germany when one of us blurted out,

1. Martin Kaehler, *The So-Called Historical Jesus and the Historic Biblical Christ,* trans. and ed. Carl E. Braaten (Fortress, 1964).

2. *Kerygma and History: A Symposium on the Theology of Rudolf Bultmann,* trans. and ed. Carl E. Braaten and Roy A. Harrisville (Abingdon, 1962); *The Historical Jesus and the Kerygmatic Christ,* trans. and ed. Carl E. Braaten and Roy A. Harrisville (Abingdon, 1964).

3. "The Correlation of Justification and Faith in Evangelical Dogmatics," in *The New Community in Christ,* ed. James H. Burtness and John P. Kildahl (Augsburg, 1963).

"Why don't we start our own journal of theology?" I volunteered to be the coordinator of the project. We drew up a list of theologians and pastors in the Twin Cities who might be willing to associate themselves with our dream — Lavern Grosc, Thomas Basich, Loren Halvorson, Philip Quanbeck, James Burtness, Kent Knutson, and the three of us.

Loren Halvorson told us that Martin Marty was coming to the Twin Cities on a speaking engagement; perhaps he might be willing to meet with us to discuss our plan to start a new Lutheran journal. We picked him up at the airport and brought him to Luther Seminary, where we discussed the nature and purpose of the journal. Marty seemed supportive. He was a recent graduate of Concordia Seminary in St. Louis and had just received his doctorate from the University of Chicago Divinity School; he was already becoming known as a bright new name in American religion. The discussion came around to a name for the journal. As the leader of the project, my mind was made up; it was going to be *dialog: A Journal of Theology.* Marty was asked what he thought about that. He said it was too *au courant,* overused and fashionable. It wouldn't wear well. I countered that the concept of dialogue is grounded in classical philosophy; it has stood the test of time; we are still reading Plato's dialogues. Of course, one may object that if dialogue becomes merely a ping-pong game between opposing ideas, that would not necessarily advance the cause of truth. However, the Socratic dialogues were always conducted in search of truth. That was also our intention for the journal we were about to launch.

Subsequently, the group met at a restaurant to decide on the editorial structure — the editor in chief, the managing editor, associate editors, book review editor, circulation manager, and business manager. We assembled a roster of distinguished Lutheran theologians from around the world — Peter Brunner, Helmut Thielicke, Nils Dahl, Anders Nygren, Edmund Schlink, Wolfhart Pannenberg, Regin Prenter, Per Lønning, Aarne Siirala, Martin Heinecken, Krister Stendahl, George Lindbeck, and many others. We entered into an agreement with Sacred Design Associates to print the periodical, advertise it, and maintain the subscription list. I was elected editor in chief. James Burtness was the managing editor; the associate editors were Roy Harrisville, Kent Knutson, Robert Scharlemann, and Franklin Sherman; Robert W.

Jenson was the book review editor. The first issue came out in January 1962; its theme was "Crisis in the Church." Can it be that even forty-five years ago we were talking about "crisis" in the church? *Plus ça change, plus c'est la même chose.* Or to quote the Preacher, "There's nothing new under the sun" (Eccles. 1:9). I do not really believe that, but sometimes it seems that way.

We who launched *dialog* felt that we were somewhat out of step with our church, the Evangelical Lutheran Church. Unlike any previous generation of pastors and theologians, we were all fresh out of graduate school with doctorates from Harvard, Yale, Princeton, Union, Chicago, Heidelberg, and Edinburgh. Our mentors were the greatest theological minds of the twentieth century. What was the crisis? Looking back on those times, I do not now think there was much of a crisis, certainly not as compared with Lutheranism in America today. No accusations were being made against any part of the church — its officials, theologians, or pastors — of heresy, heterodoxy, antinomianism, political correctness, ideology-mongering, and the like. In my introductory essay I set forth the assumptions and aims of the new journal. What appeared to be a crisis was merely the need for what Vatican II called *aggiornamento,* bringing the church and its theology up to date. To do that is always dangerous without the corresponding movement that Vatican II called *ressourcement,* going deeply into the sources *(ad fontes)* for renewal. We felt that the ELC was lagging behind in both respects. The church was becoming rapidly urban with a rural mind-set. Its theology was emerging from nineteenth-century Midwest pietism and was in danger of lapsing into Protestant evangelicalism, or worse, fundamentalism.

The journal *dialog* was calling for dialogue — between the Word of God and the world of today, between the divided churches, between theological schools, between European and American theology, between current questions and obsolete answers. The saying was going around, "The Lutheran church is the Republican Party at prayer." When John F. Kennedy was running for president against Richard Nixon, a number of prominent Lutherans came out in support of the Catholic Democrat. That sent shock waves through American Lutheranism, from the perspective of which there were two things wrong with Jack Kennedy: he was a Catholic and he was a Democrat. We realized that we were politically, socially, and culturally more liberal than the older generation. We were tired of having our seniors warn in church periodicals against the dangers of the world church, socialism, the welfare state, liberalism, federalism, the Supreme Court, big government, and so forth. As a pastor I was inundated with free copies of *Christianity Today, Christian Economics, Word Alone* (yes, that existed back then too), and *Through to Victory* — all rightist, reactionary, romanticist, and old-guard conservative. Their editorial perspectives fairly reflected the mind-set of many pastors and lay folks in the ELC, but certainly not ours.

Even in those preecumenical days we observed that the word "alone" was doing a lot of mischief in American Lutheranism. The Lutheran *sola*s had become tools of anti-Catholic propaganda, thus leading Lutheranism down the path of Protestant reductionism. When we say *"sola Scriptura,"* some take that to mean "without tradition." But that is impossible, because the slogan itself is a piece of tradition. It is nowhere to be found in Scripture. If *sola Scriptura* means the Word alone, then what about the sacraments? The Word never stands alone in the theology of the Lutheran Confessions. When we say "faith alone," that has been taken to mean "without works," and that has led to antinomianism, a heresy in itself. Does not Scripture say that "faith without works is dead"? We were not rejecting the Lutheran *sola*s as such, but only rampant misinterpretations of them.

dialog made a big splash when it came out. By the end of its first year of publication it had almost five thousand subscribers. But that is also when Sacred Design Associates of Minneapolis, an independent producer of art materials for churches, went bankrupt. *dialog* became completely independent and organized itself as a nonprofit corporation under the laws of Minnesota. Kent Knutson was elected chairman of the board of directors of Dialog, Inc. Lawrence Brings became the treasurer. He was the CEO of T. S. Denison and Company, Inc., the publishing house chosen to take over the responsibilities of printing, advertising, and handling subscriptions. Eventually *dialog* severed its relationship with Lawrence Brings and Denison, and relocated its office to Luther Seminary in St. Paul. There Sylvia Ruud as treasurer almost single-handedly kept the journal a solvent enterprise for many years, until it moved to Pacific Lutheran Theological Seminary under the editorship of Ted Peters.

Having received the letter of invitation from Dean Donald Heiges to join the faculty of the Lutheran seminary in Maywood, Illinois, we said our good-byes to the members of the Lutheran Church of the Messiah and to our colleagues at Luther Seminary. I looked forward to a new venture as visiting professor of systematic theology, honored to be following in the footsteps of two well-known Lutheran theologians, Joseph Sittler and George Forell.

CHAPTER EIGHT

Lutheran School of Theology, Maywood Campus

1961–1967

The Diversity of the Maywood Faculty of Theology

Coming to Maywood, a western suburb of Chicago, and joining the faculty of the Lutheran School of Theology changed the course of our lives, the family's and mine. We were entering into a different part of American Lutheranism. It seemed relatively free of pietism, legalism, biblicism, ethnocentrism, and low-church liturgical and sacramental practices. At Luther Seminary all the faculty members, except for the two Latvian refugees, were of Norwegian descent and belonged to the Norwegian Lutheran Church in America — monocultural to the core. Both LaVonne and I found Maywood to be a refreshing change. I was the only one of Norwegian heritage on the diverse Maywood faculty. The others reflected the ethnic pluralism of American Lutheranism — two of Danish background (Johannes Knudsen and Axel Kildegaard), two of Finnish (Walter Kukkonen and Eino Vehanen), six of German (Armin Weng, Stephen Bremer, Robert Fischer, Robert Marshall, Morris Niedenthal, and James Scherer), one of Latvian (Paul Kirsons), one of Estonian (Arthur Vööbus), one of Swedish (Gerald Johnson), and one of British (Donald Flatt). What unified the faculty was not ethnicity or piety but rather commitment to the basic principles of Lutheran theology and to high academic standards. From the day I set foot on campus I sensed that this was the right place for me. But would the feeling be mutual? Would the faculty accept me with the same degree of enthusiasm that I felt for this challenging place to do theology?

I had only a few months to make a mark before the faculty would begin its search for a permanent appointment to the chair of systematic theology. However, the dark cloud of job insecurity did not weigh heavily on my mind. All the courses I was given to teach were up my alley — Christian dogmatics and ethics, the history of Christian thought, contemporary theology, etc. I wrote out my lectures word for word and delivered them with passion and conviction. Naturally, as could be expected, the dean of the faculty, Donald Heiges, queried the students on what they thought about the new professor. In general they seemed to give me high marks. As a sports lover I spent most of my spare hours playing games with the students — softball, touch football, tennis, billiards, and ping-pong. They invited me to join them off-campus to talk theology over beer and pretzels. Being only a few years older than most of the students, it was easy to be both their teacher and a friend. I was the students' choice for the permanent appointment, and they made it known to the administration and the faculty.

The day came when the faculty met to deliberate and vote to fill the chair in systematic theology. Understandably they were looking for an established name to occupy the position, someone of the stature of Joseph Sittler or George Forell. I was just out of graduate school and the parish, with no books or articles to list on my résumé. Some writings were in the pipeline, but none had yet appeared in print, with one exception. The first issue of *dialog* appeared in January 1962, in time for the faculty to weigh the significance of the fact that I was its editor in chief and the author of the introductory essay and one of the articles entitled "The Crisis of Confessionalism." The publication of this independent theological journal was the most exciting thing that had happened in American Lutheran theology for a long time. The other Lutheran journals, *Lutheran Quarterly* and *Concordia Theological Monthly,* did not engage in contemporary theological debate. The latter was preoccupied with the intramural interests of the Lutheran Church–Missouri Synod. *Lutheran Quarterly* was chiefly a repository of noncontroversial articles in church history, edited by the prominent Lutheran historian Theodore Tappert. When Tappert got wind of our plan to start a new Lutheran journal, he pleaded with us to throw our energies into the *Quarterly*. We explained that *dialog* would be completely different; it would be a journal of theology — contemporary and controversial. The *Lutheran Quarterly* had to stay clear of theological disputes in American Lutheranism. Its editors and financial support came from the various seminaries, representing church bodies not yet in fellowship with each other. In contrast, for us the idea of a *noncontroversial theology* was an oxymoron. How could students schooled in the controversies of present-day theology play possum for the sake of the politics of Lutheran unity?

The faculty did not manage to find an established Lutheran theologian for the position. On the day of the vote there were only two candidates, Philip Hefner and myself. Hefner was a recent graduate of the seminary, still studying for a Ph.D. at the University of Chicago Divinity School. He was well known to every member of the faculty. I was told that the vote would be nip and tuck, since Hefner was the favorite son. But he had no parish or teaching experience and had not published anything. In my favor was the fact that I was already functioning in the position, with a bit of a track record in teaching, three years part time at Luther Seminary and one semester at Maywood. In addition, I was an ordained pastor with three years of parish experience and an editor in chief of a new Lutheran theological journal. My academic résumé included a Fulbright Fellowship at the University of Paris, a Lutheran World Federation Scholarship for study at the University of Heidelberg, and a Harvard doctorate. The faculty meeting took place, and after dealing with regular business I was asked to leave the room while the faculty discussed the merits of the two candidates. I sat in the faculty lounge for about an hour, sipping coffee. After the votes were cast and counted, I was invited back into the room and greeted with applause at the announcement that I had been elected. One of the distinguished senior members, Johannes Knudsen, confided to me that the vote was eight to four in my favor, and that although he had voted for the other candidate for reasons of personal loyalty, he was happy to welcome me as a colleague and was looking forward to a fruitful collegial relationship. That is exactly what happened; Knudsen became a great colleague, a close friend of the family, and a lively conversation partner for many years. He was a patristics scholar, an authority on the life and thought of N. F. S. Grundtvig, and a leading architect of the merger that produced the Lutheran Church in America (LCA), bringing together the AELC (American Evangelical Lutheran Church) Danes, the Suomi Finns, the Augustana Swedes, and the ULCA (United Lutheran Church of America) Germans.

I was very happy to receive the vote of confidence from my colleagues. Some of them were recognized as leaders in their fields of specialization. Arthur Vööbus was an internationally famous Syriac scholar and historian, teaching the New Testament. Robert Marshall was an outstanding teacher of the Old Testament; he was elected bishop of the Illinois Synod and later became the presiding bishop of the Lutheran Church in America. Robert Fischer was a leading scholar of Luther and the Reformation and of Lutheranism in America. James Scherer was an internationally known missiologist and author of many books and articles. Grady Davis was the author of a standard textbook on sermon design used widely in teaching homiletics. It felt good to be surrounded by colleagues who respected intellectual work and theological productivity. I resolved not to disappoint the trust these colleagues placed in me.

New Frontiers in Theology

I wasted no time in getting down to the business of writing and publishing. During the six years at Maywood I published articles in a wide variety of journals besides *dialog,* including *Koinonia, Church History, Lutheran World, Theology Today, Journal of Religion, Una Sancta, Lutheran Quarterly,* and *Journal of Ecumenical Studies.* I wrote and published my first book, *History and Hermeneutics,* volume 2 in a new series entitled New Directions in Theology, edited by William Hordern. I dedicated this book in memory of my teacher, Paul J. Tillich, who had just died in 1965 at the age of seventy-nine. But the book was not about Paul Tillich. It was essentially an introduction to the theology of Wolfhart Pannenberg, presented in the context of modern theological options. Pannenberg was the founder of a new approach, sometimes referred to as eschatological theology or theology of hope. Pannenberg took up the most disputed questions in theology, and as far as I was concerned, his answers were more adequate than those of any other leading theologian. His genius lay in his ability to overcome a series of glaring dichotomies in the theologies of both Barth and Bultmann, say, between revelation and history, faith and reason, the historical Jesus and the kerygmatic Christ, the historicity of the resurrection and the interpretation of faith, Israel (old covenant) and the church (new covenant), Scripture and tradition, Word and sacrament, *Heilsgeschichte* and world history, etc. My book was the first extensive elaboration of Pannenberg's theology in the English-speaking world, and, what is more, I touted it as a solution to the problems inherent in modern theology. Pannenberg was appreciative. In the foreword of his book *Basic Questions in Theology,* volume 1, he writes: "I must not fail to mention the excellent presentation of my thought by Carl E. Braaten in his *History and Hermeneutics.*"[1] If he was pleased, I was even more so.

Pannenberg's theology was becoming one of the major options in modern theology. E. Frank Tupper wrote a book on the theology of Pannenberg, in which he wrote: "Pannenberg's impact upon American theologians began to materialize in the latter half of the 1960's, perhaps most conspicuously in the writings of Carl E. Braaten."[2] I did not mind at all being referred to as an American representation of the new school of eschatological theology or, as it was better known, the theology of hope.[3] James Robinson and John B. Cobb launched a series of volumes, entitled New Frontiers in Theology, in which German and American theologians engaged in dialogue on three different themes. The first dealt with "The Later Heidegger and Theology," featuring the thought of Heinrich Ott, the young Swiss theologian who suc-

---

1. Wolfhart Pannenberg, *Basic Questions in Theology,* vol. 1, trans. George H. Kehm (Fortress, 1970), p. xviii.

2. E. Frank Tupper, *The Theology of Wolfhart Pannenberg* (Westminster, 1973), p. 27.

3. I wrote several articles dealing with the futuristic eschatology of hope: "The Theme of the Future in Current Eschatologies," *Record* (Lutheran School of Theology, Maywood Campus) 71, no. 3 (August 1966): 5-10; "Toward a Theology of Hope," *Theology Today* 24, no. 2 (July 1967): 208-26.

ceeded Karl Barth as professor of theology at the University of Basel. Ott was claiming a close affinity between the philosophy of the later Heidegger and important aspects of Barth's theology, and at the same time was critical of Bultmann's use of the early Heidegger. The world of theology responded to Ott's discovery with a huge yawn. Heidegger's thought, whether of the earlier or later period, never gained much traction in British and American theology. The case of Ott demonstrated once again how short-lived a theology is that depends too closely on the conceptuality of a particular philosophy.

The second volume in the New Frontiers in Theology trilogy focused on the new hermeneutical theories of Gerhard Ebeling and Ernst Fuchs. Hermeneutics is the science of interpretation. The so-called new hermeneutic of Ebeling and Fuchs was a synthesis of recent historical-critical studies of the Bible, the theology of Rudolf Bultmann, and the history of modern hermeneutical reflections, from Schleiermacher to Wilhelm Dilthey, and Martin Heidegger. This new trend was being heralded as a lively new option that overcame the hiatus between the Barthian and Bultmannian schools of theology. I saw it as an inferior alternative to that of Wolfhart Pannenberg, so I gave an address at the American Theological Society in Chicago entitled "How New Is the New Hermeneutic?"[4] I started out by saying that more important than whether the approach of Ebeling and Fuchs is *new* is whether it is *true*. Publishers are looking for a profit so they need to market their goods to people with "itching ears," for whom relevance to the new is more preferable than faithfulness to the old. In fact, in my view the theologies that turn out to be the most relevant are those that intentionally eschew novelty in favor of renewing the faith "once for all delivered to the saints" (Jude 3b).

I did not believe that the Fuchs-Ebeling line offered much promise in furthering the interpretation of Scripture, which is what hermeneutics is supposed to do. My own reading of Fuchs and Ebeling convinced me that theirs is a failed approach for two reasons: (1) they do not illuminate how the faith of contemporary believers gains access to

---

4. Carl E. Braaten, "How New Is the New Hermeneutic?" *Theology Today* 22, no. 2 (July 1965): 218-35.

the biblical message, and (2) their reliance on contemporary existentialism obstructs a full hearing of the total biblical message. The hermeneutical problem is how to bridge the gap between our life today and what the biblical text has to say. Every preacher knows something about this problem. Schleiermacher tried to bridge the historical gap between the author's past and our present situation by an act of psychological imagination. Dilthey followed in the same line and so did Bultmann. The defect of this psychological-existentialist approach to hermeneutics is that it limits the biblical text to an understanding of the possibilities of human existence, and is unable to interpret the text as the history of the acts of God. The Bible does indeed reveal a lot about human experience and behavior, but more importantly it conveys a message about the acts of God in history, culminating in his self-revelation in the person of Jesus. Barth was right — the Bible is not humanity's word about God but God's word about humanity.

Fuchs and Ebeling wished to go beyond Bultmann's restriction of the text to its understanding of existence. They moved from talk about existential understanding to language event (Fuchs's *Sprachereignis*) or word event (Ebeling's *Wortgeschehen*). The later Heidegger called language the house of being or the voice of being. (When Heidegger spoke of "being," theologians translated it as "God.") We can agree with Fuchs and Ebeling that for Christian theology the hermeneutical problem can be stated as a question: How can the Word of God that took the form of human language in the Bible be understood and translated into contemporary language without losing any of its power and meaning? Good question! Fuchs and Ebeling reduced everything in the New Testament, including Jesus, to language events. Jesus is a word event. What then happens to real history, to real historical events, like the crucifixion of Jesus and his resurrection? They were surely historic events creative of language; they are revelatory only when the historical facts are kept indissolubly connected with the interpretive words. In Fuchs and Ebeling all theology shrinks to the linguistic exchange between the Word and faith. The concept of language event cannot by itself span the wide chasm of the centuries between the history of salvation recorded in the Bible and the times in which we live. The actual bridge is history itself, the history of the people of God, in the church in which the Bible is preached as the Word of God to the world under the active guidance of the Holy Spirit. It is finally the Spirit who bridges the gap between the ancient Scriptures and the contemporary church. Apart from the living voice of the Spirit in the church, the Bible is a dead letter.

The third volume in the trilogy of Robinson and Cobb, *Theology as History,* engaged in dialogue with the theology of Wolfhart Pannenberg. Neither of the two previous approaches, those of Ott and of Fuchs/Ebeling, that leaned on the philosophy of Martin Heidegger took history seriously. For Pannenberg the reality of history is decisive in solving theological problems, whether we are dealing with the idea of revelation, the resurrection of Jesus, or the significance of the Old Testament. So also history is the key to hermeneutical theory, a concern lacking in the theologies of both Barth and Bultmann. Hermeneutics should assist theology and preaching to express the full content of the Bible in the context of the contemporary world. I became convinced that Pannenberg offered the most fruitful way forward for churchly theology today. Pannenberg adopted an image from Hans-Georg Gadamer of "merging horizons." The horizon of the present-day interpreter and the horizon of the biblical text must somehow be merged. Pannenberg developed the concept of universal history in light of the biblical revelation of the one God who is creator and redeemer of the world. The hermeneutical gap is bridged by the continuing history of God's unfolding plan for the world. Every new article or book that came from Pannenberg's pen persuaded me that he had the most adequate answers to the basic questions of theology today.

Reuniting with Paul Tillich in Chicago

While I was at Maywood Paul Tillich popped into my life again. After five years at Harvard University Tillich was invited to continue his teaching career at the University of Chicago, beginning in 1962. When I learned that Tillich was to give a lecture course entitled "Protestant Theology in the Nineteenth and Twentieth Centuries" during the spring quarter of the 1962-1963 school year, I asked Jerald Brauer, dean of the divinity school, for permission to have the lectures tape-recorded. Tillich lectured from an outline and longhand notes; thus, when it came time for me to edit them, I had no manuscript against which to check the spoken word. I transferred Tillich's voice to a typed manuscript, doing as much editing as necessary to produce a readable text. Tillich granted permission to have the manuscript published as a book, with the proviso that we entitle it *Perspectives on Nineteenth and Twentieth Century Protestant Theology.*[5]

When Paul Tillich was at Union Theological Seminary, he lectured on the history of Christian thought. The lectures were stenographically transcribed by Peter N. John, once a student of Tillich. Harper and Row Publishers asked me to edit Peter John's text for publication under the title *A History of Christian Thought.*[6] Later the two previously published volumes were combined into one, covering the mainstream of the Christian tradition from its primitive origins to modern existentialism.[7] Amazingly, the book is still in print over forty years later and is widely used both as an introduction to the great ideas in the history of Christianity and to the way in which Tillich drew from the sources for his own constructive thinking.

I invited Tillich to give three lectures at Maywood, which he graciously agreed to do. LaVonne prepared a lunch for us, and after lunch he took a nap in our bed. Thereafter we named the pillow he used the "Tillich-pillow."

Service on Three Church Commissions

Whoever succeeded Joseph Sittler and George Forell as a systematic theologian in Chicago would most likely be expected to serve the national church body in various capacities. I was asked to serve on three church-wide commissions, which always met in New York City. The

5. Paul Tillich, *Perspectives on Nineteenth and Twentieth Century Protestant Theology,* edited and with an introduction by Carl E. Braaten (SCM, 1967).

6. Paul J. Tillich, *A History of Christian Thought* (Harper and Row, 1968).

7. Paul J. Tillich, *A History of Christian Thought,* ed Carl E. Braaten (Simon and Schuster, 1972).

first one was organized by the Board of Social Ministry of the Lutheran Church in America (LCA), on the theme "Studies in Man, Medicine, and Theology." The study group of consultants was formed with an equal number of theologians and physicians. Their purpose was to contribute a Lutheran voice to the discussion of medical ethics in a Christian context. We were asked to take into consideration the historic Christian witness, the needs of persons, the welfare of society, and the new dimensions of medical science and technology. Papers were produced on the relation between medicine and theology, abortion, the dying patient, and birth control. The paper I wrote was published as a booklet entitled *The Ethics of Conception and Contraception*. Our effort was but a small first step on the part of the LCA to tackle the issues bearing on medical ethics. Since then the issues in bioethics have become infinitely more complex and controversial. This study was important for me; for the first time it forced me to delve deeply into the foundations of Lutheran ethics, particularly with reference to the nature of marriage as an order of creation, responsible decisions in family planning, and the morality of contraceptive means.

The second LCA commission on which I served dealt with the doctrine of the ministry. The purpose of this study was to prepare for the mergers that created the Lutheran Church in America. Certain tensions needed to be resolved between the low-church and the high-church tendencies in American Lutheranism. The commission reached a dead end and was dissolved and replaced by another, and that in turn ended in failure. None of the mergers among Lutherans in the late twentieth century succeeded in resolving the historic disagreements on the ordained ministry that can be traced to Luther himself, though millions of dollars were spent in trying to do so.

The third LCA commission was organized by the Board of Social Ministry. It was mandated to produce a social statement on "sex, marriage, and the family." I had already broached aspects of this topic in my paper on the ethics of conception and contraception. This commission called for three papers, one from a psychological perspective, one from a sociological perspective, and one from a theological perspective. I was assigned the theological paper. Early in our discussions it became clear that the psychological and sociological perspectives reflected the new "situation ethics" popularized by Joseph Fletcher. Floyd Martinson was the sociologist from Gustavus Adolphus College. He made the sociological observation that "many church people have discovered that 'breaking the rules' is not as bad as the church had said it would be and that 'keeping' them is not as satisfying."[8] I knew we were headed for trouble. Christa Klein has written about the encounter between my paper from the perspective of Lutheran theological ethics and the amoral relativism espoused by nominal Lutherans drinking from the poisoned wells of liberal Protestantism. This is what Christa Klein wrote in her report: "Carl E. Braaten of the Lutheran School of Theology at Chicago divided the group between those who favored what was labeled his 'ontological-normative' method and those who preferred a more 'situationalist' approach. . . . His draft places human sexuality within the scheme of God's creation and redemption. Sexual differentiation of male and female is creation in the image of God who is love."[9]

What I went on to say about marriage and divorce, sexual intercourse within and outside of the marriage vows, and the perversions of sexuality such as prostitution and homosexuality was well within the framework of traditional Lutheran ethics, magisterially set forth by Helmut Thielicke in his three volumes of *Theological Ethics*. Some members of the consultation responded that my approach was authoritarian; it presumed to know in advance what is right and wrong, without taking into account all the variables in each situation. Don't tell your teenager how to behave with her boyfriend in the back seat of a car. Don't be legalistic; that is the worst thing possible. Let them figure it out when they get into the situation. That is "situation ethics," popularly construed.

We were lectured that the church needs to listen to what works in pastoral counseling and what fits the changing times in which we live. In situation ethics it is morally more meaningful to ask how I feel about myself in the context of interpersonal relationships than to pre-

8. Christa R. Klein with Christian D. von Dehsen, *Politics and Policy: The Genesis and Theology of the Social Statements in the Lutheran Church in America* (Fortress, 1989), p. 106.

9. Klein and von Dehsen, *Politics and Policy*, p. 107.

sume to know the will of God in advance and to obey his command-ments. We heard from these antinomian Lutherans — that's not the evangelical ethic of love. In the end the commission could not agree on anything authoritative from a biblical-theological point of view. I saw the handwriting on the wall: Lutherans were joining the liberal Protes-tants calling for a new morality — love without law. Franklin Sherman, my colleague and professor of Christian ethics at the Lu-theran School of Theology at Chicago, resigned as a member of the commission, indicating his frustration by saying: "The LCA was about to position itself right smack in the middle of the *Zeitgeist*."[10]

The "Return to Rome" Controversy

The bishop of the Illinois Synod asked me to deliver an address to an assembly of pastors on the ecumenical significance for Lutherans of the Second Vatican Council. This turned out to be a watershed experi-ence for me; it drew me into a nationwide controversy that made head-lines in the *New York Times*, the *Minneapolis Star*, and virtually every daily newspaper in the country. The headlines read: "Lutheran Theo-logian Urges 'Return to Rome.'" My address was entitled "The Trag-edy of the Reformation and the Return to Catholicity."[11] Notice, it does not say return to Rome or to the Catholic Church. The full-length version of my speech was printed in an abridged form in the Lutheran journal *Una Sancta*,[12] edited by Richard John Neuhaus. This was the text used by the Religious News Service to report that I was advocat-ing a Protestant return to the Roman Catholic Church. Of course, that was far from my mind. The unabridged version printed in the *Record* explicitly disavowed that notion. It says,

---

10. Klein and von Dehsen, *Politics and Policy*, p. 110.

11. Printed in the *Record* (Lutheran School of Theology, Maywood Campus) 70, no. 3 (August 1965): 5-15.

12. The editor of *Una Sancta* gave the address a different title, "Rome, Reformation, and Reunion," *Una Sancta* (June 1966): 3-8. For reasons of space the editor asked me to cut the article by two thousand words; that resulted in the removal of numerous nu-ances and qualifications in the longer version.

If evangelical catholics harbor the hope of reunion with Roman Catholics, they certainly do not and cannot mean return to the Roman Catholic Church as Roman. The concept of "return" is inadequate simply because it suggests that the Protestant party is the prodigal wanderer who has to come home, while the Roman Church is like the waiting Father. . . . Furthermore, the concept of "return" which grates upon Protestant nerves does not reflect Pope John's admission that responsibility is divided, and there is equal blame on both sides. The idea of a mutual advance converging upon the future fulfillment of what is valid on both sides is a better working hypothesis. It does not require either side to deny its own history, but through further historical development, it allows for a future reconciliation.[13]

The editor of the *Christian Century,* Kyle Haselden, wrote an editorial attacking my proposal as "odious" and "dangerous." He dubbed it "Protestant Hara-Kiri."[14] To illustrate the relationship between Lutheranism and the Roman Catholic Church, I used a parable that likened Protestants to exiles. Lutherans, I said, are Catholics in exile. The parable harked back to World War II when Hitler's army invaded and conquered France. Many French patriots left France and rallied around General Charles de Gaulle, to fight to liberate their beloved fatherland. Now, what if the free French forgot the reason for their exile, and as ex-patriots made a permanent home for themselves in another country under another government with no plan ever to reunite with their fellow countrymen?

The editor of the *Christian Century* rejected the very idea of Protestants as exiles. Rather, he said, they are emigrants. When emigrants leave the old country, they generally do it for good. I wrote a response in which I said that Luther never intended to emigrate out of the Catholic Church, to found a new church named after him. Perhaps Protestants understand themselves as emigrants who have founded their own

13. Carl E. Braaten, "The Tragedy of the Reformation and the Return of Catholicity," *Record* 70, no. 3 (August 1965): 13-14.

14. "Protestant Hara-Kiri," *Christian Century* (June 22, 1966).

permanent denominations. Of course, Lutherans too are protestants, but only in the sense that they continue to *protest* the conditions in the Roman Catholic Church that brought about their separation. As Catholics in exile, Lutherans must continue their struggle until the conditions are right for reconciliation and reunion with those from whom they are separated. That is the purpose of Lutheran involvement in the ecumenical movement, to restore the unity of the church that was fractured by schisms and heresies.

My ecumenical address caused a hullabaloo among pastors and laypeople who read the headlines calling for a return to Rome; it unleashed a torrent of angry letters and hate mail, not only against me but also against Catholics. Here are a few choice excerpts.

A Lutheran pastor: "The stand you are taking borders on treason to the faith you confessed at your ordination."

A Lutheran pastor from Brazil: "Your theological perspective is being formed and informed by a childish rebellion. Your total motivation seems to be to get attention at any cost, like a child that beats his head on the floor."

A Lutheran laywoman: "The Catholic Church has certainly not made any worthy reforms. Catholics still believe the Pope is God. Roman Catholics strive to convert people to their faith, not to bring Christ to people."

An anonymous writer from California: "You and your ilk are trying to establish a 'Hell Hole' comprised of religious queers and communist conspirators under atheistic control to eliminate the Christian Church and Christ's teachings. Hurrah for the devil's little helper and the communist Big Shot — spelled with an 'i.'"

I did receive some affirmative letters that equally misunderstood my proposal, saying, in effect, "It's about time someone makes a long-overdue proposal for Protestants to return home to Rome." These could not be taken seriously because they were only reiterating Rome's standard appeal to Protestants.

The *Christian Century* referred to the whole squabble as the "Braaten Brouhaha" in a final comment in which the editor tried to smooth things over, without admitting any fault or anti-Catholic bias on his part. Fortunately for me, the controversy ended with the publication of a symposium in a follow-up issue of *Una Sancta*.[15] Four leading ecumenists participated — Albert Outler, a Methodist theologian at Perkins School of Theology; Warren Quanbeck, a professor at Luther Seminary and an official observer at the Second Vatican Council; Robert McAfee Brown, a Presbyterian theologian at Stanford University; and George Lindbeck, a Lutheran theologian at Yale Divinity School, also an official observer at Vatican II.

Robert McAfee Brown summed up the affair quite well: "Having read what Professor Braaten actually wrote, I am forced to the conclusion that he has been the victim of an unusually bad press. . . . It would seem that Professor Braaten's article is a significant next step in the ecumenical dialogue." Albert Outler wrote, "Even on my first reading of *The Christian Century*'s stern reprimand of Carl E. Braaten, it struck me as intemperate and implausible. . . . 'Reunion by return,' the *Century*'s pet peeve, is expressly ruled out. . . . Nowhere is there a whiff of reunion by repudiation. . . . To mislabel his proposal 'reunion by return' is a phobic reaction that will edify none but the immobilists on both sides."

George Lindbeck wrote: "Why the furor? Why object as strongly as some have done to Carl Braaten's 'Rome, Reformation and Reunion'? Why misrepresent him? Substantially the same points have been made by others besides Braaten without arousing such excitement. . . . I myself have said (or intended to say) everything Braaten has, and practically no one took exception." Warren Quanbeck, who was my teacher at Luther Seminary, wrote, "A careful reading of Professor Braaten's article in *Una Sancta* leaves a different impression than was created by the news reports. Examination of the article makes it plain that the author does not regard a 'return to Rome' as an appropriate or desirable way of achieving the unity of the church. . . . The reports that Professor Braaten advocates a 'return to Rome' therefore misrepresent his concern and understanding of the problem."

While the four symposiasts were mostly supportive of my proposal, they questioned whether the exile image fully expressed the complex re-

---

15. "Rome, Reformation, and Reunion: A Symposium," *Una Sancta* 23, no. 3 (1966): 12-33.

lations between Catholics and Protestants that have evolved over 450 years. I have to concede the point. After all, exiles do seek to "return" to their homeland. When Castro dies or is overthrown and a new government is installed, many Cuban exiles plan to return. But I still think the exile image retains its bite. Exiles cannot return to their homeland until a radical change in government takes place. Did not the Reformers protest what they decried as a tyrannical regime in control of the western Catholic Church? Is it not the case that the institutions they improvised were provisional and born out of necessity? They would become obsolete as soon as the reforms they called for took effect.

What did I learn from this controversy and my exposure to the public media? Several things: first, don't trust anything you read in a newspaper, especially the headlines; second, don't underestimate the intensity of anti-Catholic feeling among Protestants, including Lutherans; and third, be aware that ecumenism is hard work leading to a future no one can predict. Meanwhile, we must never give up the work for church unity; it conforms to the prayer of our Lord that "all may be one."

My ecumenical experience while at Maywood was enhanced by joining a dialogue group sponsored by Calvert House, a Roman Catholic ministry at the University of Chicago. There I met a new breed of Roman Catholic theologians who interpreted the Second Vatican Council as an invitation to enter the world of modernity *(aggiornamento)* without worrying much about ecclesiastical authority. Two became famous: Andrew Greeley and John Dominic Crossan. These two Irish Catholics were even at that time (in the 1960s) nonconformist and fearless mavericks who said what they thought. The Vatican Congregation on the Doctrine of the Faith has since come down hard on theologians who deviate from traditional Catholic teachings, for example, Charles Curran, Hans Küng, Leonardo Boff, Edward Schillebeeckx, Roger Haight, and many lesser-knowns. Even though I am profoundly opposed to ancient and modern versions of heresy and apostasy, I could not function well in an authoritarian system of thought control. In my opinion the dogma of papal infallibility continues to be the biggest ecumenical problem facing the churches.

In the spring of 1966 I was granted a Simon Guggenheim Fellowship offering a generous stipend. We were now six in our family; LaVonne and I were parents of two sons (Craig and Kristofer) and two daughters (Martha and Maria). It would be costly to transport a family of our size overseas for a year of postdoctoral studies. We chose to go to Oxford, England, to register at Mansfield College, a part of the University of Oxford. Robert and Blanche Jenson were there. Jens was the dean and tutor of Lutheran students at Mansfield College. I planned to write a book on theology from a futurist eschatological perspective.

CHAPTER NINE

Mansfield College — Oxford University

1967–1968

A Tumultuous Year

Our family of six[1] took the *Queen Elizabeth* to Southampton, England, and then we boarded a train to Oxford. Robert and Blanche Jenson met us at the station and escorted us to the lovely house they had rented for us on Woodstock Road. The two-story house was quite large with a magnificent, well-kept garden, full of rosebushes and many other plants. Our daughters, Martha and Maria, were placed in a poor grade school attended mostly by children of the lower class, where teachers had low expectations of their students and taught accordingly. Craig, our older son, attended Magdalen College School for Boys. The one thing that bothered him the most was witnessing the principal regularly flogging teenage boys who broke school rules. The best part of his experience was playing on the school's tennis team, earning the privilege of playing an end-of-the-year tournament at Wimbledon, the All-England Lawn Tennis Club.

LaVonne soon learned the art of brass rubbing. Brass rubbings are created by laying a sheet of black or white paper on a flat brass plate and rubbing with a wax stick. The metal plate is embedded in the con-

---

1. LaVonne and I now had two boys and two girls: Craig Martin, fifteen years old, Martha LaVonne, nine years, Maria Christel, seven years, and Kristofer André, three years.

crete floor of a church, designed to be a lasting memorial to a prominent person — such as a knight, abbot, or merchant. It was necessary to get the rector's permission before entering the church to make a brass rubbing. LaVonne visited churches as far away as Cambridge, to make rubbings of the most famous personages.

My sabbatical year in Oxford was one of the most turbulent years in America's history. Our nation was involved in a long, bloody war in Vietnam. American casualties were mounting. Antiwar protests were growing larger and louder on college campuses in the United States. Martin Luther King was assassinated in Memphis. Senator Robert Kennedy was running against Senator Eugene McCarthy for the presidency after the incumbent president, Lyndon Johnson, withdrew from the race. On the night that he won the California primary Bobby Kennedy was shot and killed. The Watts riots in Los Angeles were followed by other racial outbursts all across the country, in which businesses burned down and thousands of people were injured. Blacks were leading sit-ins, demanding black studies programs. The Youth International Party (Yippies) was a protest movement against the war. An organization was formed, Clergy and Laity Concerned about Vietnam, that broke the silence of religious communities. Every evening we sat in our living room in front of the TV, listening to the British Broadcasting Corporation (BBC) give its nightly reports of the scary bad news coming from America.

That was the year we were radicalized. Two Jesuit priests, Philip and Daniel Berrigan, were jailed for burning hundreds of draft records at a Selective Service Center in Maryland. Joan Baez and Pete Seeger were singing antiwar songs like "Where Have All the Flowers Gone?" The British public was totally opposed to the war, and we saw things their way. LaVonne and I enjoyed a weekly sherry hour with the Jensons, followed by dinner, either at our house or theirs. We reinforced each other's opposition to the Vietnam War. We let our hair grow long, then a symbol of identification with radical politics. When we returned to the States, we were ready to march in support of the antiwar movement.

The Turn to a Futurist Eschatology

We realized that we were not in Oxford for political reasons. Jens was writing books and articles, and so was I. We had lots to talk about; we rehearsed what we approved and disapproved of in theology. Jens was moving from a Barthian background toward certain aspects of the new eschatological theology; I was coming from a Tillichian background, but was now fully immersed in the writings of Wolfhart Pannenberg, Jürgen Moltmann, and Ernst Bloch. Jens was writing his book *The Knowledge of Things Hoped For,*[2] in which he used the British approach of linguistic analysis to make sense of the biblical-Christian language of faith and hope. Thus he was creating a synthesis of various streams of thought in American, German, and British theology. In the same year Jens wrote his book *God after God: The God of the Past and the God of the Future, Seen in the Work of Karl Barth.*[3] The book can be read as an answer to the "death of God" theologians William Hamilton, Thomas J. J. Altizer, and Dorothee Sölle. Here he goes beyond Barth's thinking to the futurist eschatology of Pannenberg and Moltmann to conceptualize his answer.

I was then writing what I called a "little dogmatic," *The Future of God: The Revolutionary Dynamics of Hope.*[4] Implicitly it was my answer to the "God is dead" thinking of the radical theologians like Hamilton, Paul van Buren, and Altizer. So Jens and I were crossing many of the same bridges in theology at the same time. The basic theme was the idea of the future — the future of God *in* history and the future *of* history in God. The rediscovery of the futurist tense in the apocalyptic eschatology of Jesus and early Christian writers gave new impetus to the language of Christian hope. God is viewed not only as "above us" or "within us" but also as "ahead of us." The loss of future hope precipitated the crisis of faith in the "death of God" move-

2. Robert W. Jenson, *The Knowledge of Things Hoped For* (Oxford University Press, 1969).

3. Robert W. Jenson, *God after God: The God of the Past and the God of the Future, Seen in the Work of Karl Barth* (Bobbs-Merrill, 1969).

4. Carl E. Braaten, *The Future of God: The Revolutionary Dynamics of Hope* (Harper and Row, 1969).

ment. The rebirth of eschatological faith — of the biblical vision of the kingdom of God — gives birth to a politics of hope and an ethic of change.

Wolfhart Pannenberg invited me to give two lectures to his theological students at the University of Mainz. I wrote the lectures in English and paid someone to translate them into German. The first lecture, entitled "Radical Theology in America,"[5] was a survey of the theologians who were then claiming that they could be Christian without believing in the living God. On its face it was an unbelievable hypothesis that I could have ignored, but it offered the occasion to present a convincing argument in favor of retrieving eschatology as the starting point of a new theology. I dealt with the thought of Gabriel Vahanian, van Buren, Hamilton, Richard Rubenstein, and Altizer. Harvey Cox was conspicuously missing from this lineup. In fact, he had reinvented himself since the days of his book *The Secular City* and was now jumping on the bandwagon of the new theology of hope. He wrote: "The only future which theology has is to become the theology of the future." I could not agree more. At one time I had been very critical of Cox; that was when he was the proponent of secular theology. Later I backed off when he latched on to the theology of hope as the answer to the "God is dead" theologians. Cox has since published several new versions of himself. I must confess that I have lost count of how many times Harvey Cox has reinvented himself.

My second lecture was entitled "Toward a Theology of Revolution."[6] Talk of revolution was in the air — in South America, in the colleges and cities of the United States, and especially among students in France, Italy, and Germany. What is the right Christian theological response to this phenomenon? I am not a Lutheran pacifist but neither was I about to espouse the Communist idea of revolution as a bloody struggle for world domination by the proletariat masses. My question was, "Is there any way to baptize the concept of revolution?" The common view is that Christianity deals with the way of salvation; rev-

5. Carl E. Braaten, "Radikale Theologie in Amerika," *Lutherische Monatshefte* (February 1968): 55-60.

6. Carl E. Braaten, "Zur Theologie der Revolution," *Lutherische Monatshefte* (May 1968): 215-20.

olution, with changing the world. The one is eternal, the other temporal; the one is spiritual, the other secular; the one is personal, the other political. Such dichotomies have often caused Christians to take sides with the counterrevolutionary forces in the modern world, pitting them against those who struggle for a new world order that expands the possibilities of freedom, peace, and justice. Some early Christians were accused of "turning the world upside down" (Acts 17:6). That sounds pretty revolutionary. But the question is, what kind? Christian or Communist? Jesus or Marx?

In order to baptize the concept of revolution, it must conform to the kind of eschatological revolution that Jesus envisioned in his message of the oncoming future of God's kingdom. Jesus did not have in mind a bloody revolution brought about by violence. Jesus was not trying to bring in the kingdom of God by worldly power. Jesus did not endorse the existing order, like the Herodians, nor did he propose its violent overthrow, like the Zealots. His kingdom was not of this world, but he did not flee to the wilderness and hide in the caves, like the Essenes. He took his revolution downtown, into the midst of things. He paid for it with his life; his crucifixion was a public event. Jesus was a unique kind of revolutionary. I am not sure that my eschatological concept of revolution was a successful experiment of thought. But I do believe that the cause for which Jesus lived and died is alive in the world today, and that it will outlast all the pseudorevolutionary movements led by people whose names are soon forgotten.

Theological Conversations at Oxford

Many American theologians came to Oxford for their sabbatical year of study. We counted nineteen the year we were there. We met many of them every Wednesday evening for dinner at High Table with the faculty of Mansfield College. The meal was preceded by sherry hour and then followed by port. Our polite and refined British colleagues seemed aghast at the loud and raucous style of the Americans, arguing theology and politics at high decibels. The Oxford dons were content to talk about their gardens or the weather, anything noncontroversial.

Dinner at High Table was a formal event. We dressed for a banquet. It was a multicourse meal elegantly served, with no limit on how many times the steward came around to refill our wine glasses. Then, all of a sudden the Breathalyzer was introduced by the police to test for intoxication. John Marsh, the principal of Mansfield College, used the new law as an occasion to limit each person to one glass of wine — not a popular decision with the Americans.

There was not much to do in Oxford, so I had a lot of uninterrupted time to write. That is what sabbaticals are for, and I was making good use of the opportunity. To break the monotony LaVonne and I would drive out into the countryside, visiting a few pubs on our way. We saw more plays than ever before. We attended a small Anglican church and though the sermon was weak, the liturgy was strong. We did host a few theological conversations at our house. One in particular was arranged for an evening of conversation with Paul van Buren.

Paul van Buren was a professor of religion at Temple University. He came to Oxford University as a visiting professor. He had become famous overnight as one of the radical theologians in America on account of his book *The Secular Meaning of the Gospel*. It bore a subtitle, *An Original Enquiry*. For one who claimed to be a Christian theologian, van Buren wrote some spectacularly stupid things, for example: "Today, we cannot even understand the Nietzschean cry that 'God is dead!' for if it were so, how could we know? No, the problem now is that the *word* 'God' is dead."[7] There are over two billion Christians in the world who don't believe that, plus a billion and some Muslims and almost that many Hindus. His book applied the method of language analysis to theological statements, with the result that "God-statements" must be translated into "man-statements." Statements about God are allegedly meaningless because they can be neither verified nor falsified by the empirical criterion of meaning. Yet, van Buren still claimed to be writing a new program for Christian theology. To me it seemed downright contradictory to call something theology *(theos-logos)* without reference to God. Van Buren said a Christian theologian is a person who has a historical perspective with Jesus of

---

7. Paul van Buren, *The Secular Meaning of the Gospel* (Macmillan, 1963), p. 103.

Nazareth at the center. The disciple of Jesus is one who personally accepts the moral perspective of Jesus; that is all that can be expected in a secular age.

Oxford students were eager to hear this newest wonder from the United States. At the first session van Buren lectured in a large assembly hall, filled to capacity. At each succeeding session the numbers dwindled. By the sixth session fewer than a dozen diehards showed up. They got the point; theology without God does not make sense.

The evening of conversation with Paul van Buren focused on his interpretation of the resurrection of Jesus. The consensus of New Testament theologians is that all the witnesses and memories of the historical Jesus have been handed down to us in the light of Easter. What is the meaning of Easter for us today? How do Christians witness to the resurrection of Jesus if it must be verified by empirical criteria? I do not remember much from the evening dialogue, except for one astounding statement that van Buren made: "Easter means to share the freedom of Jesus." Well, what about Easter as God's answer to the universally human destiny of death, the end of life? Van Buren said, "Modern man is not afraid of death. Death is a natural occurrence. It happens and that is all." What a farce! It may be that atheism in the West is on the rise, but it is now certain that the "God is dead" theology is dead. The happy sequel to this sad story of Paul van Buren in Oxford is that he later recanted and wrote a number of books on the living God of Israel in the context of the Jewish-Christian dialogue.

At Oxford LaVonne and I started an enduring friendship with Gabriel and Dorothy Fackre. Gabe was well embarked on a long and prolific journey of theological authorship. I have since regarded him as one of the most important twentieth-century Protestant theologians in America. He has not flip-flopped like so many others; he has kept alive the evangelical catholic perspectives of the old Mercersburg theology of Philip Schaff and John Nevin. He is a model of a truly ecumenical theologian for our day. We also met Paul Crowe, the head of COCU (the Consultation on Church Union), whose dream was to unite nine Protestant denominations, including Episcopalians, Presbyterians, Methodists, Disciples of Christ, members of the Reformed Church in America, and others. Crowe lamented that no Lutheran church was a member of COCU. I answered that it was because COCU was founded as a pan-Protestant union of churches in America. Lutheranism is a confessing theological movement oriented primarily to the Roman Catholic Church. That is how Lutheranism originated, and such an identity is deeply inscribed in our Lutheran confessional writings. The fact that in recent years the ELCA has entered into full communion agreements with a number of Protestant denominations may actually be a sign that it is drifting away from its historic Catholic identity. Tragically, the gap seems to be widening between the Roman Catholic Church and the Evangelical Lutheran Church in America.

Robert Jenson and I were invited to a late afternoon sherry hour with Norman Pittenger. Norman Pittenger was an Anglican theologian who had taught in the United States at General Theological Seminary in New York. He was a dyed-in-the-wool devotee of process theology, in the line of Alfred North Whitehead and Charles Hartshorne. As we entered his living room he turned to me and asked, "What do you think about process theology?" My spontaneous reply was, "It is the next best thing to Christian theology." It was not politic of me to say that, but it expressed my conviction that the God of process theology and the living God of the Bible are not on speaking terms. The idea of God in process thought is an imaginative construct of a few British and American philosophical theologians trying to square their under-standing of God and the world with modern scientific theories. I agreed with Paul Tillich's response to process theology: "A finite God is no God at all." Such a God is an idol, a thing, just one object among others.

Our Visit to the Holy Land

Within a year after the six-day war between Israel and the Arab states of Egypt, Jordan, and Syria in June 1967, our family made a one-week visit to the Holy Land. We joined a tour of Irish Catholic pilgrims led by a priest who kept them informed about how many indulgences they could earn by saying so many prayers at each of the holy sites. We never let the priest know that we were Lutheran interlopers, but he must have wondered why we passed up so many opportunities to cancel the temporal punishments we had coming for our sins. We visited the usual tourist sites, one after the other in rapid succession — Nazareth; Cana; the Sea of Galilee; the Mount of Beatitudes; Mount of Olives, for a panoramic view of Jerusalem; and the Garden of Gethsemane. It was Holy Week in the East, so we walked the Via Dolorosa along with the various processions of pilgrims from around the world; we took pictures in the Holy Sepulchre; we visited the Room of the Last Supper and the Garden Tomb. In Bethlehem we visited the Church of the Nativity and saw the Shepherds Field. Walking in the footsteps of Jesus makes a person unforgettably aware of the historical roots and geographical origins of the Christian faith.

The trip to the Holy Land was unforgettable in many ways and left a deep impression. This is the land that has witnessed the events that have shaped the world in which we live. This is the land that has played host to three great religions, Judaism, Christianity, and Islam. This is the land where many evangelical sharpshooters believe the battle of Armageddon will be fought and the world will come to an end. This is where the angels sang, "Glory to God in the highest, and on earth peace among men with whom he is pleased" (Luke 2:14). Jews and Christians and Muslims are still waiting for the promise of shalom to be fulfilled in the Holy Land.

Before returning to the United States our family traveled to Norway to visit our relatives and the old Braaten farm where my father, his three brothers, and his one sister grew up. My father often talked about the poverty and hard life they endured growing up in the mountains of Telemark. It was easy to understand why he and two of his brothers left Norway as soon as they scraped up enough money to cross the Atlantic. He had no fond memories to share about the good old days in Norway.

Late in July our family together with the Jenson family returned to the United States on the great ocean liner SS *France*. Robert Jenson had accepted a position as professor of systematic theology at the Lutheran Theological Seminary in Gettysburg, Pennsylvania. We were heading back to Chicago on the eve of the 1968 Democratic National Convention, not knowing what troubles to expect from the antiwar and countercultural activists. This was the occasion when Mayor Daley gave his infamous order to 12,000 police officers, "Shoot to kill!" Little did we then realize that the next years at Lutheran School of Theology at Chicago (LSTC) would be a stressful period of struggle in opposing dominant trends in our nation's politics (right-wing) and in American Christianity (left-wing).

CHAPTER TEN

Lutheran School of Theology at Chicago

1968–1991

Radical Politics and Vietnam

In the summer of 1968 we returned from England to a different America. Rioting was occurring in many cities across the country, including New York, Washington, D.C., and Chicago. Poverty and unemployment were increasing in African American communities; police were engaged in racially motivated brutality and excessive force in making arrests. American casualties in the Vietnam War passed the 30,000 mark. Antiwar protests were growing larger and louder, especially on college campuses. In response to the draft, students were shouting, "Hell, no, we won't go!" Some left for Canada. A few chose to dodge the draft by entering seminaries. The student enrollment doubled at the Lutheran School of Theology at Chicago (LSTC), and that was the prevailing pattern at most divinity schools. How did we know half of the students were draft dodgers? As soon as the war ended, the seminary enrollment shrank accordingly.

At the University of Chicago, students seized one of its buildings to protest the school's link to defense contracts. Senator Eugene McCarthy challenged incumbent president Lyndon Johnson over his conduct of the war. When Johnson withdrew from the race, Senator Robert Kennedy entered the fray, only to be shot dead the night he won the California primary. Eight leaders of demonstrations against the Vietnam War at the Democratic National Convention in Chicago were indicted, including Abbie Hoffman, Jerry Rubin, David Dellinger, Tom Hayden, Rennie Davis, John Froines, Lee Weiner, and Bobby Seale. The trial took place in Chicago in the courtroom of Judge Julius Hoffman. The defense attorneys were William Kunstler and Leonard Weinglass. The jurors selected to sit in judgment of these Yippies were mostly white, middle class, and middle age. It had all the makings of a kangaroo trial. After the trial one of the jurors commented that the defendants should be convicted for their appearance, language, and lifestyle. Another juror said they should have been shot by the police. The Chicago Eight became the Chicago Seven when Judge Hoffman separated Bobby Seale from the case and sentenced him to four years in prison for contempt of court.

We followed the bizarre events surrounding the Chicago Seven conspiracy trial because the radical students at the Lutheran School of Theology at Chicago invited several of the Seven, notably, Jerry Rubin and Tom Hayden, to come to the seminary and explain the philosophy of the Yippies and what the trial was all about. While the trial was going on, I was asked to preach during Lent at Kountze Memorial Church in Omaha, Nebraska. The sermon text dealt with the trial of Jesus before Caiaphas the high priest and the whole council of scribes and elders (Matt. 26:57ff.). I could not help but see some parallels between the court proceedings in Jerusalem and those in Chicago. Two other famous trials came to mind, the trial of Socrates four hundred years before Christ and the trial of Luther fifteen hundred years after Christ.

My sermon theme was "the trial of truth." Truth is always on trial in our world, facing fraudulent court proceedings, kangaroo courts, mock trials, the framing and condemning of innocent men, false swearing, stacked juries, dirty jails, and finally, the gallows, the cross, the gas chamber, or possibly years on death row. The Truth Incarnate in Jesus was treated like a criminal. Jesus suffered a criminal's fate and died a criminal's death. As the embodiment of Truth, Jesus was accused of committing crimes against the established religion, with its high priests and elders, or the sovereign state, with its governors and judges. It happened to Socrates and it happened to Luther. The powers that be charged Luther with inciting the German people to riot. It was said:

"Luther claims that the Germans should wash their hands in the blood of the papists." Luther would have to be killed and all his books burned. He was seen as a devil in the habit of a monk. In the Edict of Worms it was charged that his teachings were fostering rebellion, polarization, war, murder, robbery, and arson, and would bring about the collapse of Christendom. Words like that had the ring of contemporaneity; they were similar to some of the charges brought against the Chicago Seven. Were they trumped up, as we believe was the case with Socrates, Jesus, and Luther? Although I did not make a single reference in my Omaha sermon to the Chicago Seven conspiracy trial, the similarities were too close for comfort. After the service I could sense that my sermon had aroused opposition. In the end all the convictions handed down by Judge Hoffman were reversed. One need not approve of the theatrical antics of the Yippies, sometimes grotesque and ludicrous, to take a stand against the miscarriage of justice about to be perpetrated against the antiwar demonstrators. In the eyes of some, taking a stand against the war was itself a crime deserving of punishment.

The LSTC faculty was clearly divided over the Vietnam War. LaVonne and I made no secret of our opposition to the war. Only a few days after LaVonne opened the door to her health food store on Fifty-third Street, she and I took an overnight bus trip with a group of Hyde Park residents — including Bill and Jean Lesher and Axel and Fylla Kildegaard — to join the march on Washington, a mass gathering of antiwar protesters. Some of the leaders were the Berrigan brothers, Jane Fonda, Pete Seeger, Eugene McCarthy, Muhammad Ali, Eldridge Cleaver, Abbie Hoffman, Timothy Leary, Allen Ginsberg, and other celebrities. Through speeches and music the protesters expressed the anger and hopelessness that a growing number of Americans were feeling about the Vietnam War. LaVonne and I believed it was appropriate for us to be among them. What else could we do?

Students representing the peace movement organized a prayer service calling for an end to the war in Vietnam. The service was held outdoors in the courtyard of LSTC. They asked me to preach. It was an awkward situation. The students were restless and noisy, obviously in no mood to listen to a sermon. For my text I chose Revelation 13, which tells about the dragon and the beast. The dragon gave to the beast great power and authority. People worshiped the dragon and the beast, saying, "Who is like the beast and who can fight against it?" Out of the mouth of the beast came haughty and blasphemous words; it exercised authority for forty-two months, coincidentally about the length of the Vietnam War up to that time. The beast exercised its authority over every tribe and people and tongue and nation. The passage ends with these prophetic words: "If anyone slays with the sword, with the sword must he be slain."

I opened my sermon with these words: "We are living in convulsive times. Students are in the streets and soldiers are in the schools. American fighting men are pushed across another border, uttering obscenities against their commander in chief. Churches are confused, making an uncertain sound." I believed the churches had a theological problem. My sermon proposed that churches need to recover the apocalyptic symbols of the Bible to understand what is going on, the kind we find in the book of Revelation. The Seer of Patmos was confronting the massive persecution of Christians by imperial Rome. In his analysis the powers at work behind the scenes were the dragon and the beast. The fight is not against mere flesh and blood, or a handful of gutless politicians, faceless generals, or greedy corporations. The beast is a world imperialist; it exercises authority over every tribe and people and tongue and nation. It dominates the world's markets; it exports instruments of violence and vice; it sneers at the ways and customs of other peoples; its language is the Esperanto of the nations; and it forces all the poor people of the world to live off the crumbs that fall from its table. That was the empire of Rome in the first century. That was the America we saw behaving like an empire in the war against Vietnam. The response of Christians, I admonished the students, cannot be to add to the violence. I knew that a faction among the antiwar protesters aimed to incite riots and cause the police to overreact. But those who follow the Lamb who was slain will not be among those who resort to violence. We know there will be violence; that is the way of the wounded beast. Christians believe that we cannot get to peace by war. War begets more war. The only way to get peace is by doing it now. Followers of Jesus are called to be among the peacemakers, doers of peace.

Not long after this event I started receiving scatological letters and postcards in my campus mailbox. The message was clear; the author accused me of the chief heresy for Lutherans: confusing law and gospel and commingling the two kingdoms. I shared the communications with the president of the seminary, Stewart Herman, and the acting dean, Frank Sherman. There were one or two others receiving similar postcards, obviously from the same author, but not as many. Stewart Herman and Frank Sherman viewed the matter as very serious. The letters were a combination of accusations, threats, and sexual innuendos. How should we respond? Was the author mentally unstable? Was he (there were no women on the faculty) capable of an act of violence? Was this a faculty colleague doing this, or was it possibly a student prank?

We decided to consult with Elisabeth Kübler-Ross, a psychiatrist and a faculty member of the University of Chicago. She said it was impossible to discern from the letters the state of the person's mind, but that by all means we should try to find out who was doing it. Frank Sherman devised a plan. The postcards were written on an old-fashioned typewriter that caused some letters to appear regularly uneven. If we could locate the typewriter, we would know who the author was. Sherman acted the part of the sleuth. He called on a colleague at his home, a prime suspect in the case, and asked him to provide a sample of writing from his typewriter. He cooperated but it was clearly not the typewriter in question. So Sherman called on the wife of this colleague at her place of work and asked if she had a typewriter. She did. Then he asked if he could use it to get some samples of writing. He did, and it proved to be the one with the telltale keys. The next day the president of the seminary summoned this colleague to his office and gained both his confession and resignation from the faculty. I was told that some kind of deal was struck to the effect that both parties would keep it quiet and not publicize what had occurred. The colleague's reputation was not smeared; he went on to teach at other Lutheran institutions until his retirement a few years ago.

The anonymous letters and postcards forced me to consider whether I had in fact crossed over the line from theology into politics. Should they not be kept completely separate? Is not that what the Lutheran doctrine of the two kingdoms requires? During the Vietnam War the presiding bishop of the Lutheran Church in America wrote to all the parish clergy: "Don't say anything controversial." He wanted pastors to keep quiet about the war. No matter what they said, it would offend some of the laity, and that would have negative consequences at the bottom line. In a voluntary association — which is what a congregation is — disaffected laity can and do vote with their feet and their wallets. A recurrence of the dilemma is happening now during the war in Iraq. The issue of faith and politics is on the front burner as never before.

The Vietnam War provided a test case of whether the Lutheran doctrine of the two kingdoms was a help or a hindrance to the church and its ministry in a time of war and social unrest. To tell a minister of the Word not to say anything controversial is to gag him or her. I rejected the conservative dualistic interpretation of the two kingdoms that separates the church and the world, relegating the church to the realm of spiritual matters, and leaving the phenomena of law and justice, reason and power, war and peace to the secular world. Article XVI of the Augsburg Confession states: "If a command of the political authority cannot be followed without sin, one must obey God rather than human beings" (Acts 5:29). Luther expounded on this principle in his pamphlet *Temporal Authority: To What Extent It Should Be Obeyed*. I believed the Vietnam War was an unjust war and to engage in it was a sin. Many of those who protested the war were bound by their conscience to obey God rather than the secular government. To remain silent was not an option.

Theology of the Body and Foods of the Earth

While LaVonne and I were busy supporting the antiwar movement, we faced a challenge of quite a different kind. LaVonne had become interested in healthful foods, and found it necessary to drive rather long distances outside of Hyde Park to find a store that sold natural and organic foods, as well as a good loaf of bread. This went on week after week until one day the idea popped up: Why not open a health food store in Hyde Park? There was none, and yet Hyde Park seemed to be the kind of community whose residents would welcome an alternative to the local supermarkets. We surveyed the neighborhood and found a For Rent sign in the window of a vacant office space. After some delicate negotiating, we signed a one-year lease with the owner for use as a health food store. But now we had a real problem: How could we start a business without any money? My monthly income from LSTC was barely enough to live on, plus we had to pay the tuition for our son Craig at Augustana College and for our other three children — Martha, Maria, and Kristofer — attending Harvard–St. George, a private school in Hyde Park. LaVonne mustered the courage to apply for a $10,000 loan from a Hyde Park bank. The banker asked what kind of collateral she had to back up the loan. She answered that she had nothing but the watch on her wrist and her four children. Of course, we owned a house on Greenwood Avenue, but the seminary owned the second mortgage. So it was worthless as collateral.

The banker must have had a sense of humor and a good deal of trust; he agreed to make the loan. LaVonne and I went to work to transform the office space into a store. We painted the walls, purchased shelving and refrigeration from a North Side store selling used fixtures, and installed the plumbing. We were ready to open for business in record time. The store took off beyond our wildest expectations and was profitable from day one. That was the start of LaVonne's twenty years of doing business in merchandising natural and organic food products in the Chicago area. During those twenty years LaVonne owned and operated six stores at various times in Chicago and the suburbs. Upon our retirement to Northfield, Minnesota, in 1991, our son Kristofer purchased the business of Braaten and Braaten, Inc., and continues to operate a number of successful stores in the metropolis of Chicago.

LaVonne and I frequently reflected on the theological significance and wider ramifications of our new preoccupation with food. We read a lot of books that dealt with nutrition. We soon discovered a dilemma: people interested in religion and theology were indifferent to the quality of foods they ate; and people concerned about what they ate had no interest in religion and theology. To be sure, a few Hindus and Muslims were sensitive about what they ate and drank, but that was generally not the case with Christians, except for the Seventh-Day Adventists. We decided to write a book that would bring the two worlds together, faith and foods. In 1976 we published a book with Harper and Row entitled *The Living Temple: A Practical Theology of the Body and the Foods of the Earth.*

The themes of this book encompass our shared commitment to broader ecological concerns for the "whole person and the whole earth." Humanity and earth exist together in an interdependent relationship. A person cannot be whole without the whole earth. When the earth becomes sick, people become sick. A human being is part of the earth, and the earth is part of the human being. I was aware that the Christian tradition has been mostly indifferent to the health of the body and of the earth. That concern was left to sects, and they were mostly ridiculed. Ecology was not a word in the Christian lexicon. In giving an account of the drama of salvation from the beginning of creation to the last things (eschatology), traditional theology tilted toward spiritual matters that concerned chiefly the soul and the afterlife. In contrast, the biblical vision of reality is all-embracing; the earth goes together with heaven, and the body is united with the soul.

Nothing more exemplifies our human interconnection with the earth than the foods we eat. The German philosopher Ludwig Feuerbach coined the saying: "We are what we eat." Bread is one of the central religious symbols in the Bible. We pray in the Lord's Prayer, "Give us this day our daily bread." Bread and faith are intertwined in the Bible. The organic and natural food movement is the application of ecological wisdom to the things our bodies need for healthful living. Organic foods taste better and they are more healthful. After years of being accustomed to eating foods treated with chemical additives by a process of spraying, dyeing, and waxing to make them look good, we rediscovered the natural taste of vegetables and fruits.

A theology of the body brings together a number of movements that constitute an alternative lifestyle. The ecology movement deals with the external environment of the body, placing us invariably on the side of a politics that demands clean air and water. The natural food movement focuses on the interior ecology of the body, demanding pure foods good for the body. The peace movement is a protest against dehumanizing references to the victims of war in terms of "body count." The movement for holistic medicine is a challenge to the easy resort to drug therapies and surgery by modern medical practice.

Our new interest in the place of the body, foods, and the earth in a biblically grounded Christian theology led to various invitations to address organizations of various kinds. One such invitation was to address a conference on "Physical Activity and Human Well-Being" in Quebec, Canada, in connection with the Olympic Games of Montreal in 1976. Another invitation was to address an ecumenical conference on the environment in Mexico City; my talk was entitled "Caring for the Future: Where Ethics and Ecology Meet." To our disappointment but not to our surprise, the Lutheran organizations to which we belonged — seminary, congregation, synod, and denomination — showed little or no interest in a theology of the body and its related concerns — natural foods, the environment, and holistic medicine. All of these matters were regarded as fads that serious Christians should treat with indifference or disdain. In the meantime we have witnessed a growing receptivity in the mainline churches to alternative ways of caring for the body and the earth, so much so that sometimes we fear that the new (really ancient) perspectives on health and healing may be confused with the gospel of salvation.

One aspect of my interest in a theology of the body must be a mere footnote — my lifelong love for the sport of tennis. I got my first tennis racquet at the age of nine while my folks were on furlough in St. Paul from the mission field. Upon returning to Madagascar my interest in sports shifted from basketball and tennis to soccer and volleyball. During the years of World War II it was impossible to maintain the equipment for tennis, although we did have a tennis court for our use. With worn-out tennis balls and broken racquet strings, my love for tennis had to be put on hold. One of the first days after returning to America I bought a tennis racquet from a Minneapolis tennis pro, Norm McDonald, and tried to make up for lost time. By my junior year at St. Olaf College I had become good enough to make the varsity tennis team. For the next ten years in graduate school and parish ministry, I did not have time or money to play tennis or any other sport.

When I began teaching at the Lutheran seminary in Maywood, Illinois, I became serious about tennis again. I joined a local team and began to play in various leagues and tournaments. The rest is history. I have been playing ever since, with backaches, pulled muscles, and intermittent bouts of tennis elbow. Tennis has also become something of a family sport, bringing generations together for recreational fun.

Theology of Global Mission

After I had fulfilled the required six years of teaching to be eligible for a sabbatical, LaVonne and I were faced with a dilemma. She had a health food store in Country Club Hills to manage, which she could hardly abandon to join me for a year of overseas study. We had already been abroad three times on various study projects — a Fulbright in Paris, a Lutheran World Federation Scholarship in Heidelberg, and a Guggenheim in Oxford. What should we do this time, given our limited options? Out of the blue came a letter from the Lutheran Church in America informing me that I had been awarded a Franklin Clark Fry Fellowship worth $10,000 for sabbatical use — a lot of money at that time. That opened up the possibility of a different kind of sabbatical, teaching and lecturing at theological schools around the world, especially of the younger churches in Asia, Africa, and South America.

This sabbatical would provide the opportunity to do research for a book on a theology of the Christian mission in world history. I wanted to correlate the eschatological theology I was teaching with my existential origins on the mission field in Madagascar. I started with two elemental convictions: one, the eschatological beliefs of the first Christians launched the earliest gospel mission to the nations; and two, the apostolic mission to tell the story about Jesus was the "mother of all Christian theology," in the phrase of Martin Kähler. The plan we developed would have me go first to Japan for a month of teaching at the Lutheran seminary in Tokyo. Not wishing to go alone, we arranged for Kristofer to accompany me as my traveling companion and tennis partner. He was only ten years old but already a very good tennis player. At the end of October 1974 I put Kristofer on a return flight to

Chicago, and a few days later I met LaVonne at Tokyo's international airport. From there we traveled to Hong Kong, Singapore, Madras and Bangalore in India, Nairobi in Kenya, Dar es Salaam and Arusha in Tanzania, and finally Tananarive and Fort Dauphin in Madagascar. I gave lectures on various aspects of missiology at each place.

I was able to observe firsthand the huge success of the worldwide missionary movement that began with the pietists in the eighteenth century and reached its zenith in the early twentieth century. But now a new day was dawning. The former mission fields were fast becoming indigenous churches in their own right — self-governing and self-supporting. I tried to lay out the essentials of what it means to be the church of Jesus Christ wherever it is being planted by the Word and the Spirit. The younger churches will respond to the Great Commission of our Lord in their own way; perhaps some day they will send missionaries to reevangelize western Europe and North America, rapidly becoming secularized, neo-pagan, and post-Christian. The lectures I gave in Asia and Africa became the substance of my book *The Flaming Center: A Theology of the Christian Mission* (Fortress, 1977).

Our whirlwind tour that took us to cities and villages in Asia and Africa was bound to yield rather superficial impressions of the activity of the younger churches and of their theological endeavors. My most vivid impression was that the standard theology being taught in the seminaries and shaping the churches and their ministries — no matter where we went — was exactly what the missionaries left behind. It was the theology of low-church Protestant evangelical pietism, with a strong dose of biblicism and legalism. But there were signs of restlessness and dissatisfaction with the imported theology of the Western colonial missions. Some of the younger professors had been abroad, received their doctorates in Germany, Scandinavia, England, and the United States. When they returned to their native lands, they were eager to develop new theologies appropriate to their cultural situations, and yet faithful to the core principles of the gospel. But first of all, they had a massive amount of catching up to do, because the missionaries could not teach what they did not know. Missionaries were in general opposed to all modern theology from Friedrich Schleiermacher to Karl Barth. Younger theologians who had studied abroad got excited about various types of modern theology, whether neo-orthodox, dialectical, existentialist, or hermeneutical. They set about to translate the original documents of these movements into their native languages, as resources for their own constructive theological works. None did this better than the Japanese.

My chief interest was to discover what if anything new was emerging in theology from the Third World. Japanese theologians were busy translating the chief writings of Martin Luther, Karl Barth, Rudolf Bultmann, Emil Brunner, Dietrich Bonhoeffer, and many others. The Japanese made theology like they made cars, by copying Western models. Even the first book I wrote, *History and Hermeneutics,* was translated into Japanese. I was on the lookout for any truly indigenous theological constructions. In Japan I was privileged to have a conversation with Kazoh Kitamori, the author of *Theology of the Pain of God* (1946), the first book of theology conceived in the context of Japanese Buddhism and its social experience. His Western readers criticized Kitamori's book as patripassianism, which he vehemently denied. Greatly influenced by Luther's theology of the cross, Kitamori connected it to the Japanese Buddhist tradition of redemptive suffering initiated by love. He appropriated Luther's concept of the wrath of God in relation to the sinful world of humankind, a wrath that can be reconciled only by God's own suffering love. As a Lutheran I found little to quibble with in his idea of a suffering God. I thought, if Kitamori is guilty of patripassianism, in violation of the traditional understanding of orthodox dogma, then perhaps Luther's theology of the cross must be subject to the same indictment. However, if the Christ event is a God event, then on the basis of a proper doctrine of the Trinity, God must be said to suffer in the event of the cross of Christ. We have an echo of the same notion in Bonhoeffer's saying, "Only a suffering God can help."

In India all the denominational theologies of Western Christianity were on display, with one exception. M. M. Thomas was a creative thinker within the context of Indian society. He was a layman of the Mar Thoma Church, a church that claimed to have been founded by Thomas, the doubting disciple of Jesus. He was the most important Indian theologian of the twentieth century, a prolific writer of more than sixty books, in English and his native tongue Malayalam. I heard him lecture in Bangalore at the Christian Institute for the Study of Religion and Society (CISRS), of which he was the head. He championed the cause of the disadvantaged, the untouchables, and those who lived in the shadows of society, a stance for which he was at times accused of Communist sympathies. His theology was thoroughly christocentric, mounted on the concept of the cosmic lordship of Christ. As an ecumenical theologian and at one time the moderator of the World Council of Churches, his influence reached far beyond India.

African Christianity in the 1970s had reached the tipping point of developing its own contextual theology. African theologians were no longer content to live on prefabricated traditions imported from the outside. John Mbiti was the most important African theologian at the time we visited the churches and seminaries in Kenya and Tanzania. He interpreted African religious experience as a preparation for the gospel *(praeparatio evangelica)*, as a kind of "Old Testament" foreshadowing of the gospel of Jesus Christ. He said God was in Africa before the missionaries arrived. They did not bring God to Africa; God brought them so that the African people might come to know Christ as the crowning fulfillment of their prior history and experience. This idea was fully congenial to my way of thinking about religion and revelation. God's general revelation in the religious histories of humankind should not be separated from nor equated with his special revelation in the gospel of Jesus Christ. Mbiti's influence on mainstream African theology helps to explain why Karl Barth's mono-christological idea of revelation and his rejection of all natural theology found no fertile soil in African Christianity.

From Africa we traveled to Madagascar, first to the capital city of Tananarive and then to Fort Dauphin, located at the southernmost tip of the island. We had no grandiose plan to fulfill, no lectures to deliver, no theologians to interview, and no seminaries to visit. I was interested mainly in showing LaVonne the old watering holes where I grew up as a teenager. I had been away from Madagascar for almost thirty years. During that time I could not escape the question to what extent the missionary enterprise was a success or failure. Why should that even be a question? It had become commonplace in the academic community to criticize the missionary movement as an accomplice of colonial exploitation, cultural supremacy, and racial arrogance. Popular movies like *Hawaii* held up missionaries to ridicule. One African leader coined the pithy statement: "When the missionaries came to Africa they had the Bible and we had the land. They said, 'Let us pray.' We closed our eyes. When we opened them we had the Bible and they had the land." In the 1970s African churches were calling for a missionary moratorium. The mainline churches responded by slashing their support for missions in terms of money and personnel. The handwriting was on the wall. It was only a question of time before the foreign missions would give way to native churches. That would be the sure sign that the missionary enterprise had achieved its goal of planting churches where previously they did not exist.

Our trip to Madagascar in 1974 confirmed that the deepest roots of my faith and worldview were embedded in the missionary practice of preaching the gospel so that the Malagasy people might believe in Christ and become members of his church. I was asked to speak to the missionary community in Fort Dauphin. I spoke from the pulpit in the Malagasy Lutheran church where I had sat every Sunday for years, listening to long sermons in a language much of which I did not understand. My address did not go over very well with this missionary community. The mood was noticeably different from when I was living in the Missionary Children's Home. Everyone now seemed to be happy and content, a far cry from the way I felt during the war years of 1940-45 — feeling at times misplaced, deprived, and longing to return home to America, the place of my birth. Nevertheless, it felt good, very good, to revisit my boyhood haunts; it was like a homecoming.

When we returned to Chicago, I began to write my book *The Flaming Center*. This title represents the missionary commitment to what is central in the Bible, its witness to Christ. For Lutheran missionaries the hermeneutical principle — although they did not use the term — was expressed by Luther's phrase *was Christum treibt*. For them theology is not a speculative exercise of abstract thought; it is rather ongoing reflection on the ground of missionary praxis. This view was captured in a slogan coined by Martin Kähler: "Mission is the mother of Christian theology." This kind of christocentric theology that the missionaries left behind is now being taught by indigenous theologians, pastors, evangelists, and catechists. All the younger churches that we visited retained the missionary idea in their DNA. The result is that the Christians in the global South are now sending missionaries to the older churches of Europe and North America. For example, the churches in South Korea send more missionaries around the world than any other nation, except for the United States. The younger churches agree with what the missionaries taught them — evangelism belongs to the essence of Christianity because the gospel is a unique message of universal salvation rooted in a divine commission. For the most part they show no interest in the pluralistic theology that teaches that all religions are equally valid ways of salvation. They know better. Their conversion to Christ gave them the kind of freedom and peace they did not find in their native religious rituals.

Liberation Theology

Our sabbatical travels did not end with our return to Chicago from Madagascar. In the spring of 1975 LaVonne and I toured five countries in South America — Peru, Bolivia, Chile, Argentina, and Brazil. The tour's purpose was to learn what Latin American liberation theology contributes to a comprehensive theology of the Christian mission in a global perspective. I had read most of the Latin American liberation theologians, for example, Juan Luis Segundo, Gustavo Gutiérrez, Leonardo Boff, Jon Sobrino, Enrique Düssel, José Míguez-Bonino, and others. There was much in their writings to affirm. For the first time they had a sense of creating their own theology. Such a theology would engage the problems of their concrete situation, rather than merely pass on secondhand systems that bore the stamp of "made in Germany" or England, Sweden, Spain, Italy, or the United States. Heretofore converts to Christianity often became alienated from their own cultural situation in the process of learning a theology reflecting a foreign culture. Liberation theology starts with an analysis of the concrete situation, rather than imposing ready-made theologies from the outside. Hence, liberation theologians reflected the struggles of the poor, the oppressed, and other marginalized peoples — blacks, Chicanos, women, students, etc.

Liberation theologians were enthusiastic about what they claimed was a new way of doing theology. Their criticism of the old way was relentless; their target was the theology of the oppressors. They opposed the traditional pattern in which whites wrote theology for blacks, men for women, intellectuals for peasants, Spaniards for Indians, colonialists for the colonized, the rich for the poor, and Europeans for Third World peoples. Gutiérrez spoke for all the liberation theologians in stating: "The theology of liberation offers us not so much a new theme for reflection as a new way of making theology. Theology as critical reflection on historical praxis is thus a liberating theology."[1]

I went to South America with a positive attitude toward liberation theology. This new theology was particularly congenial to me because most of its practitioners had studied in Europe and reflected central themes of the post-Bultmannian theology of hope of Wolfhart Pannenberg, Jürgen Moltmann, and Johann Baptist Metz. Nevertheless, what I learned on the ground in discussing liberation theology with professors, pastors, and students raised some red flags and cautioned me against a wholesale endorsement of Latin American liberation theology. The biggest red flag was its conscious and uncritical adoption of the Marxist analysis of society. I was not opposed to its socialist bias that seeks to nationalize the means of production, overcome the classist society, and educate the masses to share in the political process that determines their living conditions. For a long time I had been convinced that one can be a Christian and a socialist at the same time. Christian socialism has been a lively political option in Scandinavia, Germany, France, and England. From a theological point of view the problem was not the socialism but the Marxism at the root of the popular versions of Latin American liberation theology.

The key concept of liberation theology is "praxis." As Gutiérrez says, theology is "critical reflection on historical praxis." The word "praxis" is not found in the lexicon of the classical Christian tradition. It was first introduced into philosophy by critics of Hegel, Karl Marx

---

1. Gustavo Gutiérrez, *A Theology of Liberation* (1988), p. 15.

chief among them. The concept of praxis made its way into liberation theology from the neo-Marxists of the Frankfurt School (Adorno, Horkheimer, and Habermas). Moltmann and Metz jumped on the bandwagon of this new definition of theology as critical theory of praxis. Moltmann wrote, "The new criterion of theology and of faith is to be found in praxis."[2]

My criticism of liberation theology was not that it adopted the idea of praxis. Theology has always accepted new concepts from philosophy into its vocabulary. That kind of process began when Christians first started doing theology in the Roman Empire, adopting Greek philosophical categories, amalgamating them with the Hebrew categories of the Bible. If Christian theology is to adopt the Marxist concept of praxis into its working vocabulary, it needs to baptize it. I proposed such a strategy at one time. I coined the word "eschatopraxis" — linking eschatology and praxis — to express the biblical notion that eschatological truth is not idle fantasy but something to be done here and now. The First Epistle of John speaks of "doing the truth" (1:6).

Theology is certainly free to adopt the concept of praxis into its lexicon, despite its Marxist provenance. I discovered during my South American tour that liberation theology is not sufficiently critical of the critical theory of praxis that stems from Marxism. Reluctantly I came to the conclusion that "praxis is the Trojan horse of liberation theology." I developed this critique of the critical theory of praxis in my book *The Apostolic Imperative*. It has often happened in the history of theology that the greatest threat to the Christian faith does not arise from those who explicitly attack it from the outside, but from those who invade Christianity in a Trojan horse. Only when the horse is inside the walls of Troy does the hatch open and Agamemnon and all the rest jump out and capture the city. The Marxist critique of the Christian religion from the outside was not able to succeed; but if its critical theory of praxis can spread inside the household of faith, it might be able to claim victory at last.

Traditional Christianity in South America was vulnerable to such an attack. The Marxist idea of praxis was welcomed by the liberation

---

2. Jürgen Moltmann, *Religion, Revolution, and the Future* (1969), p. 138.

theologians as a way of linking Christianity to a movement that promises to change the world for the better. Liberation theology has been relentless in its attack on traditional theology, Roman Catholic or Protestant, on account of its political ineffectiveness. The lure of Marxism was its promise to transform society by concrete emancipatory praxis. What does this mean? For Marxists it means revolutionary praxis, by means of violence if necessary. Liberation theology, at least at the beginning, did not come clean in disavowing the Marxist notion of revolutionary praxis by the use of violence.

The Marxist idea of praxis is responsible for the way in which liberation theology flattens out certain dimensions of Christian theology. The liturgical and mystical dimensions are brushed aside. The mystery of God as the power to inspire awe, prayer, and praise is given the silent treatment. Eschatology is reduced to ethics, the "already now" of the kingdom of God is surrendered to the "not yet" of a Marxist utopia. The motifs of mystery and transcendence are diminished in the radical reduction of everything to the dialectics of the historical process. The themes of sin and salvation, so central in Lutheran theology, are one-sidedly translated into social and political terms to the neglect of the personal and interior aspects. Structural changes in the world wrought by human praxis do not remove the roots of sin in the infrastructure of human life. A liberated society no longer marked by injustice, inequality, poverty, oppression, and disease would be a wonderful utopia to dream about, but that would do nothing to reconcile a person to God or to relieve a person of the existential problems of anxiety, guilt, dread, death, and meaninglessness. I had read too much of Kierkegaard to be duped by the Marxist dream of a classless society.

Nevertheless, in bidding adieu to Latin American liberation theology, at least as a model for North America, I have retained its suspicion of the hidden connections of traditional theology with the self-interest of ruling classes in society. Many New Testament scholars have correctly pointed out that traditional Christianity has downplayed the political facts involved in the struggles of Jesus with the ruling authorities. By neutralizing the political significance of Jesus' words and actions, the Constantinian churches thereby purchased a state license to operate freely without being harassed as a religion of subversion. There is little doubt that the picture of the historical Jesus has been spiritualized and his message voided of political implications. Jesus is usually portrayed as a very pious man kneeling in prayer and looking upward, meditating on an otherworldly kingdom. Such a person is a political eunuch and poses no threat to the establishment; it becomes hard to imagine why Jesus was crucified by the state. It makes no sense for the state to persecute those who follow a leader whose message is devoid of any social and political implications. A wall of separation between church and state has been erected to the detriment of biblical Christianity, reducing its message merely to matters of personal and private interest.

Not long after I had made my critical assessment of liberation theology, Rome's Congregation for the Doctrine of the Faith issued a written instruction on the theology of liberation, pointing out its many deviations from Catholic orthodoxy. When the announcement of this instruction was first released, liberation theologians understandably let out a howl. They were nervous about the possibility that the Vatican was ready to condemn their theology as heresy. But this did not in fact happen. Joseph Cardinal Ratzinger, head of the Congregation for the Doctrine of the Faith, produced a surprisingly fair and balanced analysis of certain aspects of liberation theology. His chief concern, as it was mine, had to do with the use of Marxist categories, particularly with the Marxist theory of class struggle.

The Vatican instruction did have a sobering effect on the liberation theologians. In 1988 liberation theologians from around the world gathered at the Maryknoll School of Theology in New York to mark the twentieth anniversary of the Medellín conference of South American bishops. At the Medellín conference the Catholic bishops issued a document that gave an official stamp of approval to key themes of liberation theology. Now they were meeting at Maryknoll to pay tribute to the Peruvian priest Gustavo Gutiérrez, the father of Latin American liberation theology. In an interview Gutiérrez acknowledged that liberation theologians viewed the world in more complex terms than they had twenty years earlier. He insisted that liberation theology does not reduce Christianity to politics, nor does it embrace the cardinal features of Marxism, its materialism, economic determinism, and athe-

ism. Liberation theologians were then emphasizing issues of spiritual-
ity and were much less doctrinaire in their use of Marxism as a tool of
social and economic analysis. Gutiérrez felt constrained to make one
thing clear: "I don't believe in liberation theology; I believe in Jesus
Christ." He had heard and heeded the Vatican warning. Liberation
theology was coming of age. There were welcome signs that it was
breaking with the Marxist dogma about class struggle and revolutionary violence.

Latin American liberation theology was mostly a project of Roman
Catholic theologians. But Lutherans found themselves exposed to the
same social and economic realities that gave rise to liberation theology
as a protest movement. We arrived in Chile two days after the Lutheran church there had split. The Evangelical Lutheran Church in
Chile was presided over by Bishop Helmut Frenz, a courageous de-
fender of human rights. The new church that separated from Frenz's
church called itself the Lutheran Church in Chile, presided over by
Bishop Richard Wagner. The schism was caused by two different interpretations of the Lutheran doctrine of the two kingdoms. The separat-
ist group accused Bishop Frenz and his German Lutheran pastors of
mixing the gospel with politics. Politics is the business of the kingdom
on the left hand of God, and salvation is the work of God's right hand.
The one is the responsibility of government, and the other is the function of the church's ministry of Word and sacraments. What do the
two spheres have to do with each other? Bishop Frenz was aware that
during the church struggle in Hitler's Germany, most of the bishops
and pastors chose to do nothing. He was determined not to let that
happen again. In General Pinochet's Chile the state was guilty of de-
taining, imprisoning, and torturing people with no regard for justice.
Should the pastors remain silent in the face of the government's violation of human rights? The schismatic group was made up of a colony
of German Lutherans who believed in a strict separation of the two
kingdoms; in their view the gospel has nothing whatsoever to do with
politics. They wanted their pastors to preach a nonpolitical gospel, in
such a way that the lay folks were free to pursue their own interests in
the economic and political realm (the left-hand kingdom). Bishop
Frenz and his pastors believed that the gospel generates Christian re-

sponsibility for every sphere of life, and that the acts of the state are legitimate targets of the prophetic critique of the church and its ministers. As we interviewed leaders on both sides of the church struggle, we realized that we were witnessing a classic exhibit of the Lutheran dilemma in modern history, how to relate the gospel and government, church and state, the sacred and the secular. The Chilean Lutherans were facing the same problem that Lutherans in the United States did during the Vietnam War, and that Lutherans later would regarding the preemptive strike of the Bush government against Iraq.

There is, to be sure, a danger of politicizing the gospel. It is all too tempting for us to grant the gospel a political relevance, so long as it supports our kind of politics, whether to the left or to the right or in the middle. However, between the option of linking the gospel to a partisan political preference, on the one hand, and voiding it of any political relevance at all, on the other hand, there is a lot of wiggle room for exploring anew the political implications of the gospel. This is a never-ending task.

Two of the Lutheran pastors in Chile were American missionaries, former students of mine when I was teaching at the Lutheran seminary in Maywood. They were James Savolainen and William Gorski. Both were involved in the very dangerous enterprise of helping Chilean refugees escape from government oppression, imprisonment, and torture. Gorski subsequently was elected bishop of the Lutheran Church in Chile. He was eventually accused of mishandling church funds and forced to leave Chile. After that I lost track of him. Savolainen was deeply into liberation theology, and made no apologies for its Marxist orientation. After he left Chile he entered the doctoral program at the Lutheran School of Theology, and I was assigned to be his supervisor. He wrote some brilliant seminar papers, including a massive doctoral dissertation on the theology of Karl Barth, exploring its connections with socialism. By the time he was awarded the degree of doctor of theology, he had reasoned his way out of the Christian faith and embraced Marxist atheism, hook, line, and sinker. There was no way he could get a job anywhere teaching theology. He worked for the Communist Party, distributing copies of its newspaper, the *Daily Worker.* He got a job removing asbestos insulation from old apartment buildings. It was very disheartening to witness Jimmy Savolainen's conversion from a robust missionary faith to the shallow ideology of communist atheism. I once read a book that explained atheism as a psychiatric problem. I suspected that there were psychological roots of Savolainen's embrace of atheism, but I had neither the expertise nor the interest in pursuing the matter. Jimmy once told me that his father was a socialist organizer among the Finnish workers in Michigan. Was this a case of Jimmy somehow returning to his roots of origin? Last year Jimmy Savolainen died. A mutual friend has told me that a Roman Catholic priest befriended him in his last days and that he died in the embrace of the church.

Theology of Hope and the Future

I became convinced that liberation theology functioned with a defective eschatology. Between my two sabbaticals, the one in Oxford (1967-1968) and the one on a global tour of Asia, Africa, and South America (1974-1975), I published a number of books that explored various aspects of eschatology, the most important being *The Future of God* and *Eschatology and Ethics*. These writings gave me a public identity as an American exponent of the eschatological theology of hope, widely associated with two German theologians, Jürgen Moltmann and Wolfhart Pannenberg. On account of this connection, I was invited to participate in a Conference on Hope and the Future of Man, held at the Riverside Church in New York City, October 8-10, 1971.

The conference was uniquely designed to bring together for the first time three theological currents — eschatological theology from Germany, American process theology, and the evolutionary thought of Teilhard de Chardin. Theologians representing the three schools of thought were chosen to address the conference, all dealing with the question, "What do you mean by the future?" This conference was the most interesting and dynamic I have ever had the privilege to attend.

The conference began with three position papers on the meaning of the future. John Cobb represented the process point of view; Philip Hefner spoke from a Teilhardian perspective; I spoke for the theology of hope from the point of view of eschatology. Three German professors followed with plenary lectures, Wolfhart Pannenberg, Jürgen Moltmann, and Johannes B. Metz. Two American theologians responded to each of their presentations, some of them well known in their own right, Schubert Ogden, Daniel Day Williams, Christopher Mooney, S.J., Joseph Sittler, and Lewis S. Ford. An estimated twenty-five hundred people attended the sessions. There occurred a vigorous exchange between three divergent approaches to theology and reflections about the future. The main result of the conference was to clarify the many ways in which process thought, biblical eschatology, and Teilhardian perspectives are radically incompatible. Even while they may use the same words, they are loaded with different meanings.

My lecture was entitled "The Significance of the Future: An Eschatological Perspective." It laid out my understanding of the future, the source and motive of the symbolism of hope, and the difference between utopian and eschatological images of the future. The utopian future is projected as another time *in* history; the eschatological future deals with the final fulfillment and end *of* history. My lecture described the various theological theories of biblical eschatology, from the Old Testament prophets, intertestamental apocalypticism, the eschatology of Jesus, and the transformation of eschatology in the early church on account of the resurrection of Jesus. It covered a lot of ground in succinct terms, and still stands as the clearest exposition of my thinking on eschatology in a nutshell.

In the 1970s I wrote and published many articles on eschatology, many of them relating eschatology to ethics. I was invited by Frank Sherman to address the American Society of Christian Ethics, which I did under the rubric "Eschatology: The Key to Christian Ethics."[3] The room was packed with Christian ethicists and moral theologians teaching in Catholic and Protestant seminaries, divinity schools, and departments of religious studies. My aim was to transplant the roots of Christian ethics into the ground of biblical eschatology where they

3. Carl E. Braaten, "Eschatology: The Key to Christian Ethics," in *Eschatology and Ethics: Essays on the Theology and Ethics of the Kingdom of God* (Augsburg, 1974), pp. 105-22.

belong. I was aware that almost all the leading ethicists in America completely ignored biblical eschatology and had no idea what it might have to do with Christian ethics. The lecture hit the room with a loud thud. The audience was completely uncomprehending of anything I had to say — so far had Christian ethics strayed from its biblical moorings in the teachings of Jesus and the early church. During the question-and-answer period Paul Ramsey, the dean of Christian ethics, rose to his feet to sound off on his favorite ideas but offered no clue that he had grasped a word I said about the connection between eschatology and ethics. Still, I was proud of the essay I had written about eschatological ethics and, after reading it decades later, believe it is on the right track.

In summary, this is what I argued and still believe. Christian ethics must be grounded in Jesus' message of the kingdom of God. The leitmotif is that the eschatological future of God's kingdom has become proleptically present in a definitive way in Jesus of Nazareth. This determines the *goal* of ethics — the kingdom of God as the highest good. Love is the material content of God's eschatological rule revealed throughout Jesus' ministry. That determines the *norm* of ethics — the *agapē*-love of God as the absolute standard underlying all principles of justice, equality, freedom, etc. The proleptic presence of the kingdom of God in Jesus and his ministry makes possible a real participation in the new reality that it brings. This determines the *motive* of ethics — the motivating force of the new being in Christ. Finally, there is the *context* of the ethical decision. Goals, norms, and motives converge upon a concrete context to challenge and to change the present conditions in the direction of a better approximation of the kingdom of God. The bottom line is that all the talk going on in the church today about moral deliberation — about war and peace, care of the earth, or issues of human sexuality — is all beside the point unless it is grounded in and directed by what God revealed of his will and purpose in Jesus and his ministry. Quoting Bible verses out of context and throwing them at each other like verbal hand grenades exhibit a completely un-Lutheran hermeneutic.

I dedicated my book *Eschatology and Ethics* to Wolfhart Pannenberg; his influence on my theological thought was second only to that of Paul Tillich. Both were Lutheran theologians, but with very different styles and accents. Eschatological theology, however, was not a specifically Lutheran phenomenon. Theologians of different confessional backgrounds — Reformed, Roman Catholic, Evangelical, as well as Lutheran — were drawn to the futurist interpretation of eschatology. The particular confession from which a person comes shapes the way in which the themes of eschatology are developed. Jürgen Moltmann wrote the classic document of eschatological theology, entitled *Theology of Hope*. He had a special ability to turn a phrase and to give lively expression to the groundbreaking ideas that Wolfhart Pannenberg had previously published in German theological periodicals. Pannenberg had good reason to feel that Moltmann had stolen his thunder. Yet, they presented quite different versions of eschatological theology. Moltmann came from a Reformed background, Pannenberg from a Lutheran. Pannenberg's theological mentor and doctor-father was Edmund Schlink, the author of a book that instructed an entire generation of students on confessional Lutheran theology.[4]

Although I learned a lot from Moltmann, I resisted certain Reformed characteristics in his way of construing eschatology. The main difference has to do with the old controversy on the Lord's Supper between Reformed and Lutheran theologians regarding the relation between the finite and the infinite. *Finitum non capax infiniti* (the finite is not capable of the infinite) is the Latin slogan for the Reformed view. *Finitum capax infiniti* (the finite is capable of the infinite) is the Lutheran view. Moltmann tends to interpret eschatology primarily in terms of crisis and judgment, whereas a Lutheran would emphasize the real presence of the eschatological future of God in the Word and the sacraments. Crisis and judgment are real and important, but so are the notes of grace in celebration and thanksgiving. Moltmann stayed with Barth's emphasis on the infinite qualitative distinction between God and man. God is in heaven and man is on earth, and ne'er the twain shall meet. But that cannot be, because the divine and human natures have already been united in the one person of Jesus Christ. The Reformed tradition tends to stress the ontological distinction between the

---

4. Edmund Schlink, *Theologie der lutherischen Bekenntnisschriften* (1948).

two natures, whereas the Lutheran tradition underscores their personal union in the incarnation. It is truly amazing how the ancient controversies find their analogues in the contemporary discussions.

Feminist Theology

In 1972 I wrote an article entitled "Untimely Reflections on Women's Liberation." My intention was to affirm the movement for the equality of women in marriage and family life, in society and the life of the nation, as well as in the ordering of the church and its ministry. From the moment the question of the ordination of women arose, I became a vocal supporter. Many conservative Lutherans, particularly in the Missouri and Wisconsin Synods, oppose women's ordination and profess to do so on biblical grounds. After all, Paul (or, rather, the author of 1 Timothy 2:12) said: "I permit no woman to teach or to have authority over a man; she is to keep silent." Should not that settle the matter? Apparently not; women do in fact teach in the church schools of the Missouri Synod and in that capacity exercise authority over men. If they were silent, they could not teach, and if they exercised no authority, they could not give a grade. Even a few in the ELCA opine that it was a mistake for Lutheran churches to affirm equal opportunity for women in the ordained ministry. They claim that it damages ecumenical relationships, say, with Roman Catholics and the Eastern Orthodox. To that I counter that we should not be willing to pay any price to please our ecumenical partners. No Lutheran can believe in unity at all costs. The theological arguments advanced by churches that deny ordination to women are unconvincing; I have examined them all. We will take our stand using the words of Luther: "Unless we are proved to be wrong by the testimony of Scripture or reason, we will not renounce or retract what we have done in good conscience."

Rosemary Radford Ruether did not appreciate my article on women's liberation. She wrote a stinging rejoinder to counter everything I wrote about the male-female relationships in the structures of sex, marriage, and family. My article was allegedly paternalistic, a sleight of hand, a covert affirmation of the status quo, a male-power play with moralistic overtones, ideological, and so forth. I had no idea that my rather modest opinions would have the power to generate such anger. She closed her essay with these words about love: "Women may indeed intend to 'love' men, but at this time such love can only appear in the form of wrath."[5]

The exchange with Rosemary Ruether marked the beginning of an awareness that traditional orthodox theology, mounted on the trinitarian and christological doctrines of the ancient church, was headed for a protracted struggle with various new forms of heresy emanating from radical theological feminism. The more accurate name for the movement is post-Christian feminism. Its leaders are Mary Daly, Carter Heyward, Rosemary R. Ruether, Sharon Welch, Sheila Davaney, Elisabeth Schüssler-Fiorenza, Sallie McFague, among a host of lesser lights. Not a single one of them happens to be a Lutheran, but it did not take long before Lutheran seminary professors and bureaucrats were introducing radical feminist ideology into Lutheran circles, with no regard whether it was consistent with confessional Lutheran theology. Its most conspicuous point of entry into the life of the church focused on God-language, especially its use in the liturgy.

One morning at our seminary in Chicago (LSTC) the liturgy for the chapel service was printed in a bulletin. Every reference to God as Father and Jesus as Son was edited out. Every reference to Jesus as Master, Lord, or King was deleted. Every masculine pronoun was treated like a dirty word. Other terms were substituted. This was the first time anything so blatant had occurred in our chapel. Wanting to make sure it was the last, I wrote a letter of protest to the president (Bill Lesher) and dean (Ralph Klein) of the seminary and to the dean of the chapel (Jay Rochelle) and the faculty leader of worship that day (Jean Bozeman). I made it clear that I could no longer attend a chapel service where such practices were tolerated and encouraged. So I quit going to chapel. Then I learned that many students had already beat me to it, which accounted for the fact that chapel attendance was reaching an all-time low. This was especially troubling for me, because I believed

---

5. Rosemary Radford Ruether, "On Women's Lib," *dialog: A Journal of Theology* 11 (Summer 1972): 226.

that daily chapel attendance should be expected of all future pastors. Seminary chapel should function not only as a place of daily prayer but also as a laboratory for the training of future worship leaders.

The outcome of this brouhaha was a faculty decision to hold a year-long seminar on God-language. Robert Bertram was the coordinator of the seminar; he chose the topics and assigned authors and respondents. The papers were accepted by Fortress Press for publication; I was asked to be the editor. The volume is entitled *Our Naming of God: Problems and Prospects of God-Talk Today* (1989). This exercise provided a splendid opportunity to tackle the problem of inclusive language in Christian worship and to develop a critique of radical theological feminism.

What follows is a brief summary of the views I expressed orally and in writing during the faculty seminar on God-language. In my view the feminist demand for inclusive language in the liturgy has nothing whatsoever to do with the liberation of women or with their demand for equality in every sphere of life, including the church. It has to do with how Christians ought to speak of God in the language of prayer and preaching. The question of what language to use in speaking of God is inseparable from the question of the identity of the God of whom we speak. What language to use is determined by which God we intend to invoke in our prayers and proclamation. Laypeople have a right to expect that their pastors have learned to speak appropriately about God in their seminary training. They are unprepared for the way in which some clergy, especially recent seminary graduates, mess around with the traditional liturgies. They notice that their ministers have a hard time reading the scriptural texts without using their own idiosyncratic emendations. Some ministers think they have the right and the duty to improve on the biblical authors. When the Bible says "father," it should also say "mother"; when it says "son," it should better read "child"; when it says "Jews," it really means just plain "people," so as not to offend our Jewish friends. Laypeople have noticed that some pastors stutter through the liturgy, trying to avoid all personal pronouns for God, or fumble around for neutered substitutes for masculine images that refer to God or Christ, terms such as "lord," "king," "master," "son of man," "son of God," and the like. The laity, many of them members of my family, observe the silliness of clergy replacing the holy name of the triune God, Father, Son, and Holy Spirit, with some other triadic formulae that fail to specify God by his proper name. The most common replacement is "Creator, Redeemer, and Sanctifier." One leading feminist theologian, Sallie McFague, has proposed "Mother, Lover, Friend." She thinks it means the same thing as "Father, Son, and Holy Spirit." In some places of worship invocations and benedictions have become shameful exercises in avoiding the trinitarian name of God.

Reports began to circulate that some clergy, some of them even Roman Catholic priests, were baptizing infants without using the triune name of God — Father, Son, and Holy Spirit. Supposedly the male-referring words pose an offense to women. At a pastoral conference in Minnesota, a woman in the audience asked me whether an infant who was not baptized in the name of the Trinity, Father, Son, and Holy Spirit, would be saved. I answered that "the baby would be saved but the pastor would surely go to hell." The audience erupted in laughter, indicating that they knew I was using humor to make a serious point. After the session the woman introduced herself as a pastor who was totally opposed to the malpractice of altering the name of the Trinity to pacify the feminists; she wanted to hear me say it for the record.

The issue of inclusive language was easily confused with some other items. In opposing the reckless tampering with the language of worship that was becoming increasingly common, especially at the seminaries, I tried to specify what the controversy was not about. The controversy is not about change in the liturgy per se. The liturgy did not fall from heaven. Conservatives tend to resist change in the church. I am not one of them. Some resisted change from the black book of worship to the red, then from the red to the green, and now they resist going from the green *Lutheran Book of Worship* to its new cranberry-colored replacement, *Evangelical Lutheran Worship*. In the latter case, however, the issue is more complicated. Some are opposing the new book of worship not because they are traditionalists standing against change, but because the radical feminists forced their ideology on the editorial process. As a result we now have bowdlerized versions of the

Psalms and Collects. Male pronouns have been removed, so as not to inflict deep wounds on the psyche of women. None of the women in my family look at it that way. I believe that the radical feminists, starting with Mary Daly, have created a myth that the removal of male gender language in worship is necessary to contribute to the liberation of women in church and society.

I am personally in favor of a lot of changes in the church. The church lives in history, and history is like a river that keeps moving forward. Heraclitus was right in saying, "You can never step into the same river twice." Moreover, Christians are called to be agents of change. That is what repentance *(metanoia)* and conversion are all about. Our struggle is not about change as such; it is about the criterion of change and by whose authority. Whose big hand is working behind the scenes manipulating the changes taking place in the church?

My opposition to radical theological feminism is not about the use of female imagery in depicting attitudes and activities of God. It is not about the role of women in the church, or women's ordination to the pastoral office. I have always been in favor of these things. Often those who advocate linguistic surgery on the Bible and the church's tradition, especially its trinitarian and christological formulae, pretend to occupy the moral high ground as champions of equality and justice for women. Such an equation does not stem from moral insight, but from bad theology. The majority of faithful women in the church do not want their ministers to sacrifice the trinitarian language of faith for the sake of their rights and privileges in church and society.

My contribution to the faculty volume, *Our Naming of God,* set forth my chief reason for objecting to the proposal of radical theological feminism to eliminate all male imagery for God. It boils down to one theological point. The God of Jesus Christ appeared in the religious history of humanity with a specific name. The Christian faith is inseparably and permanently bound up with Jesus and the One he called "Father." Jesus' Father is none other than the God of the Hebrews, the God of Abraham, Isaac, and Jacob, as attested in the Old Testament. Jesus called Yahweh his "Abba," the most intimate word for Father. This God was not his mother. He knew who his mother was; her name was Mary. Jesus' Abba can love like a mother and care like a mother, but he cannot be referred to as "she." What is there about these straightforward assertions that radical feminists do not understand? To be sure, there is nothing wrong in using feminine analogies, similes, and metaphors in speaking about God. The Bible and the Christian tradition offer many examples of this sort of speech. If that is the meaning of inclusive language, who would be against it?

When it comes to the name of God, however, that is a qualitatively different matter. The Christian God has a name, unlike that of any other religion. God's name is triune, Father, Son, and Holy Spirit. That is God's proper name, his *nom propre,* as the French say. Jesus revealed himself as having a special relationship with God, uniquely as his Father's Son. No possible change in the relations between male and female, in the family structure, or in the social order could justify a revision of God's name, without altering the faith itself. Any change in God's name, such as the radical feminists propose, points to a different religion and a different gospel. The name for such an alteration is heresy. That is what the controversy is all about. When it becomes bad taste to refer to Jesus as Lord and King, that is heresy. When the liturgy omits the name of Father, Son, and Holy Spirit in its salutations, benedictions, and sacramental performances, that is blasphemy. When my friend and colleague Robert W. Jenson declared at the St. Olaf College "Call to Faithfulness" Conference (June 1990), "A church ashamed of her God's name is ashamed of her God," he received an electric ovation from a chapel-packed crowd.

I received support for my critical views on radical theological feminism from a surprising source. A new book came to my attention entitled *Theology and Feminism,* authored by Daphne Hampson, a Scottish woman teaching systematic theology at the University of St. Andrews. She identifies herself now as a post-Christian. She was a convert to Christianity, became an Anglican, and led a campaign for women's ordination in the Church of England. She tells the story of her journey into the church and then out of it, and why she is no longer a Christian. She is now a radical feminist who believes in the one God at the base of all religions, but not in the biblical God of Israel who revealed himself in a special way in Jesus Christ. The basic argument of her book is that it is impossible to be a Christian and a radical feminist at the same time. One has to choose — either/or.

Daphne Hampson's argument against Christianity is twofold. The first argument is moral; Christianity is so locked into a patriarchal system that it has proved itself incapable of treating women in an equal and just manner. It stands guilty as accused. The second argument is theological; Christianity depends on belief in the uniqueness of Jesus, at the very least that it was he whom God raised from the dead. That is an assertion of fact that is simply untrue, she avers. Hers is a viewpoint fundamentally in line with Mary Daly's. Mary Daly was a Christian, became a feminist, and gave up her faith. If all she were doing was to tell the same story as Mary Daly, the book would hardly have drawn any attention. She dropped a bombshell with her thesis that the leading Christian feminist theologians — Elisabeth Schüssler-Fiorenza, Rosemary Radford Ruether, Sallie McFague, and Carter Heyward — have produced theology that is not essentially Christian. The reason she gives is that they have no Christology and no doctrine of the triune God. For them Jesus is not the Son of God confessed by Christians in the Nicene Creed. For them Jesus was a great human being who knew and loved God, but he was not unique. His greatness lay in thinking thoughts and saying things with which the radical feminists could agree. Daphne Hampson had the courage to cry out that the emperor has no clothes.

Out of the blue Daphne Hampson wrote me a letter asking for any help I could give on recent resources for understanding Lutheran theology and its distinctive differences from Roman Catholic theology. I conveyed to her information about the new Finnish interpretation of Luther coming from Tuomo Mannermaa and his Helsinki students. She ended up writing a book attempting to prove that the structures of Lutheran and Catholic theology are completely incompatible. The book is entitled *Christian Contradictions: The Structures of Lutheran and Catholic Thought*. She favored the Lutheran categories but did not believe a word of the gospel they intended to frame. Neither Lutheran nor Catholic theologians have found her treatments of their respective thought structures accurate and acceptable.

The Vanderbilt Group

In the 1970s I was invited to join the Workgroup on Constructive Theology, convened by Peter C. Hodgson and Edward Farley, hosted by Vanderbilt Divinity School. Its purpose was twofold: to promote collaborative work among systematic theologians and to identify the issues and tasks on which they might profitably work together. The original membership was virtually a Who's Who of academic theologians teaching at the leading Protestant seminaries and divinity schools, including Julian N. Hartt, David Kelsey, Walter Lowe, Robert W. Williams, John Cobb, Schubert Ogden, David Tracy, Francis Schüssler-Fiorenza, George Stroup, and Sallie McFague. The list represented a stellar cross section of prolific authors of books and teachers of future pastors for the mainline Protestant churches.

After meeting for three years, members of the workgroup collaborated on a textbook of systematic theology entitled *Christian Theology: An Introduction to Its Traditions and Tasks,* edited by Peter C. Hodgson and Robert King. This text was later accompanied by a volume of readings from classical and contemporary sources. I was assigned the chapter on eschatology, entitled "The Kingdom of God and Life Everlasting." The two volumes became a standard textbook of systematic theology taught in mainline Protestant seminaries. To my knowledge the textbook was never used in Catholic, Evangelical, and Lutheran seminaries. Even though I was one of the authors, I did not use it as the basic text in my teaching of Christian doctrine, because there was very little in it with which I agreed. I appreciated its use of the traditional loci method, covering the main doctrines of the Christian faith from creation to eschatology. However, I did not accept its underlying premise that everything written prior to the Enlightenment is antiquated and needs to be revised to conform to modernity. The Enlightenment was perceived as a watershed in the history of theology that called for a "paradigm shift." No Lutheran theologian worth his or her salt could accept a theology in which the doctrines of the Trinity and Christology are treated as fossils of an antiquated Christianity. Only one scant paragraph makes mention of the Reformation doctrine of justification by faith. In general, the great truths of the councils of

Nicea and Chalcedon and the powerful insights of the Reformers are relegated to the history of Christianity rather than being newly interpreted as foundational for contemporary theology.

Members of the Workgroup on Constructive Theology eventually became embarrassed by the fact that, when looking around the room, they saw only senior white males, except for one token woman, Sallie McFague, who could hardly be excluded since she taught theology at Vanderbilt Divinity School. In moving quickly to correct the situation, the leaders invited a group of younger scholars, male and female, mostly liberationist, feminist, postmodern, post-Christian, and pro the GLBT ideology. The conversation changed so drastically that none of the traditional topics of the theological agenda were considered worth pursuing anymore. The older scholars dropped out one by one, I among them.

The entire experience for me was an eye-opener. It became unmistakably clear to me that liberal Protestant theology had come to a dead end, and that for Christian theology in America to have a future, it would need to move in an entirely different direction. First of all, Christian theology cannot afford to cut off the legs on which it stands, and secondly, it must learn once again that its primary context is the church and not the academy.

The *Christian Dogmatics* Project

The collaborative model of doing theology adopted by the Vanderbilt group was an excellent one. Why not adapt it for use by a select group of Lutheran systematic theologians, with the aim of producing our own textbook of Christian dogmatics? I discussed the project with Robert Jenson and we agreed to be coeditors of a two-volume work of dogmatics. For years we had been teaching theology to American Lutheran seminarians, using mostly textbooks written in Europe. We had an impressive list of dogmaticians from which to choose — Emil Brunner, Karl Barth, Gustaf Aulén, Regin Prenter, among others. What we needed was a textbook that reflected the American situation and a variety of Lutheran perspectives. No single Lutheran perspective would be acceptable to the majority of professors of theology. So we decided to produce a textbook with multiple authorship.

We surveyed the field of Lutheran professors teaching systematic theology and chose six to make up the team. In addition to Robert Jenson and myself, four others were invited to complete the team: Gerhard Forde and Paul Sponheim, both of Luther Seminary in St. Paul, Minnesota; Hans Schwarz of Trinity Seminary in Columbus, Ohio; and Philip Hefner, my colleague at the Lutheran School of Theology at Chicago. The two-volume work would consist of twelve loci; each of the six of us would write on two major doctrines. Our first meeting was held in our apartment in Chicago, 5490 South Shore Drive. All six of us stood firmly within the Lutheran tradition, but not without considerable differences among us. We knew each other very well. Four of us were graduates of Luther Seminary. We knew all about our different points of view and areas of specialization. Hence, the process of assigning the twelve topics turned out to be easy.

I was happy to be assigned the First Locus, "Prolegomena to Christian Dogmatics," because I had been writing extensively on contemporary methods of doing theology. I was also pleased to be assigned the Sixth Locus, "The Person of Jesus Christ," because Christology had been the focal point of my writing theology. All the topics were assigned to the persons best able to treat them. Robert Jenson was assigned the Second Locus, "The Triune God," a subject on which he has written copiously, as well as the Eighth Locus, "The Holy Spirit," the third member of the Holy Trinity. Paul Sponheim was assigned the Third Locus, "The Knowledge of God," as well as the Fifth Locus, "Sin and Evil," both areas that call for considerable expertise in philosophical theology. Philip Hefner was assigned the Fourth Locus, "The Creation," as well as the Ninth Locus, "The Church." Gerhard Forde was assigned topics on which he concentrated throughout his career, notably the Seventh Locus, "The Work of Christ," and the Eleventh Locus, "The Christian Life." Atonement and justification became the two lifelong foci of Forde's teaching and writing. Hans Schwarz was assigned the Tenth Locus, "The Means of Grace," and the Twelfth Locus, "Eschatology."

We set deadlines for the writing process. We met to discuss and critique each other's work in progress. The process went smoothly with only a few bumps in the road. A question was raised about Schwarz's treatment of the sacraments. Some thought he did not adequately take into account recent ecumenical developments. Coeditor Jenson volunteered to pitch in and write the section on the sacraments. Twenty-three years later *Christian Dogmatics* is still in print and continues to be used in courses on Christian theology, mostly at Lutheran seminaries. Both volumes have been translated into the Portuguese language, published in Brazil, with a preface by Walter Altmann. Altmann is a former professor of systematic theology at the Lutheran seminary in São Leopoldo, and since 2002 he has been the president of the Evangelical Church of the Lutheran Confession in Brazil.

Seminex Joins LSTC

The faculty of the Lutheran School of Theology at Chicago was a microcosm of ethnic pluralism in American Lutheranism. The school was a product of a series of mergers. The Lutheran seminary in Maywood belonged to the United Lutheran Church. In the late 1950s it merged with Grand View Seminary in Des Moines, Iowa, of the American Evangelical Lutheran Church (the Happy Danes), with the Suomi Seminary of the Finnish Evangelical Lutheran Church in Hancock, Michigan, and with a sister seminary of the United Lutheran Church in Fremont, Nebraska. Then in the 1960s this united seminary in Maywood merged with Augustana Seminary of the Augustana Lutheran Church in Rock Island, Illinois. The Lutheran School of Theology at Chicago (LSTC) was the result of these mergers, and as a united seminary it began operation in 1967 on a new site in Hyde Park, Chicago. The ethnic pluralism that made up the LSTC faculty was its most distinctive characteristic; it included two of Danish background, four of Swedish, one of Finnish, one of Estonian, one of Norwegian, two Hispanics, one African American, and half a dozen of German background. Three women were on the faculty.

That all changed in the fall of 1983 with the arrival of Seminex — nine faculty members plus Paul Manz, the majority of its students,

President John Tietjen, and four administrative staff. The name "Seminex" stands for "seminary in exile." Seminex began in 1974 as a result of a conflict in the Lutheran Church–Missouri Synod between the faculty of Concordia Seminary in St. Louis and Jacob Preus, the president of the synod. Preus campaigned for the presidency on the promise that he would get rid of all liberal tendencies in the Missouri Synod, particularly at its seminaries. He accused the St. Louis faculty of false doctrine, of using historical criticism in biblical interpretation, and of violating the principle of *sola Scriptura*. Preus got the Board of Control to suspend the seminary president, John Tietjen. The students and the faculty walked off the campus in protest, and set up a seminary in exile at an off-campus site. The LSTC faculty was sympathetic with the cause of the Concordia faculty. Since Seminex was not yet an accredited school, LSTC offered to grant diplomas to its first class of graduates.

Eventually the conditions for the survival of Seminex were such that they needed to look for other options. A final decision was reached to disperse the Seminex faculty to seminaries of the Lutheran Church in America. The majority were assigned to LSTC, and a few went to Pacific Lutheran Theological Seminary. I was involved in the negotiations led by President Bill Lesher and Dean Frank Sherman at LSTC. Offering hospitality to Seminex seemed like the churchly thing to do. Naturally we had some worrying questions about the effect the coming of Seminex would have on LSTC. Our faculty was being asked to welcome ten new faculty members all from the same ethnic group. The administrations of the two seminaries gave the LSTC faculty the proper assurances to relieve any doubts that its members might have had about the coming of Seminex. Who would pay for this influx? Seminex would, we were told. They would raise a million dollars annually to pay their own salaries and all of the overhead. What would be their teaching responsibilities? Their faculty members would teach courses in the core curriculum as needed, plus seminars in their respective areas of specialization. When a vacancy would occur on the LSTC faculty, a nationwide search for a successor would be undertaken, with the stipulation that a member of the Seminex faculty would be eligible for consideration. It seemed like a fair deal.

Sad to say, none of the assurances were met. In due course Seminex became part of the LSTC family. The annual support of a million dollars diminished with each passing year. All the Seminex faculty merged into the LSTC faculty, with one exception. The Seminex professor of homiletics, David Deppe, was discontinued on charges of homosexual promiscuity. He left his wife with five children for a male partner. The irony is that some members of the Seminex faculty — I do not know how many — later expressed support for same-sex partnerships, maintaining that the biblical prohibitions to homosexual behavior under certain circumstances are not relevant to the contemporary discussion.

The end result of the merger of Seminex and LSTC faculty was a radical transformation of the ethos and modus operandi of the school. Members of the Seminex faculty were all of German background. Most if not all had attended Missouri parochial schools from kindergarten through college and seminary. They were all intelligent and well educated, with an impressive work ethic. Together they had weathered the storm of heresy charges in the Missouri Synod, and they stood together as brethren leading a confessing movement in a contemporary church struggle. Dietrich Bonhoeffer was frequently quoted. As like-minded colleagues, they formed a voting bloc strong enough to dominate the political process of a small faculty. Soon the day-to-day administration of LSTC was firmly in their hands. The old guard at LSTC was marginalized. Frank Sherman was replaced as dean by Ralph Klein. Bob Conrad took over the doctor of ministry program. Kurt Hendel became chairman of Division Two, Church History and Christian Theology. These things happened not because of any conspiracy, but simply because of the personal competence and energetic leadership of these Seminex colleagues.

The unexpected consequence of such a strong contingency of Seminex personnel was to move the faculty and student body to the left on social, cultural, and theological issues. Having been condemned as liberals and heretics in their home church, they became advocates of progressive agendas in their new ecclesial setting. The poison of political correctness spread into every aspect of seminary life. The LSTC practice of having social gatherings exclusively for faculty members and spouses was changed to include nonacademic staff — secretaries, janitors, and kitchen help. Committees on every conceivable matter were expanded beyond the faculty to include an equal number of students and staff. The cult of egalitarianism drove out every remnant of elitism. Orwellian shades of 1984 had arrived: we were all equal, but some were "more equal than others." This was not unilaterally the work of the Seminex faculty; the entire faculty was involved in contributing to the transformation of LSTC into a modern Protestant seminary, hospitable to the many isms of American culture.

The theology that backed up the "paradigm shift" at LSTC was either antinomian or a close relative. Robert Bertram and Edward Schroeder were founders of Crossings, an educational institution whose purpose was to relate the gospel to daily life. Both were greatly influenced by the law/gospel theology of the German Lutheran theologian Werner Elert of Erlangen University. They followed Elert in rejecting the third use of the law. Elert maintained that the title of Article VI of the Formula of Concord, "Third Use of the Law," mislabeled what it really affirmed. The question was debated among first-generation Lutherans whether the law applies to regenerated Christians; that is, whether they are to live in obedience to the Ten Commandments.

The first use is the public law that everyone must obey or else face the punishment. The second use is the law that accuses and leads to the knowledge of sin. The third use is the law that shows believers how to order their lives. Do Christians need the guidelines of the third use of the law, or is the gospel sufficient of itself to provide moral guidance for the Christian life? Traditionally Lutherans have affirmed the necessity of the third function of the law; even the saintliest believers are sinners who need to be guided by the moral wisdom enshrined in the laws and commandments of God. Many modern Lutherans have set aside the third use; thereby, they have jumped from the frying pan of legalism into the fire of antinomianism.

The ideology of Crossings moved in a straight line from the rejection of the third use of the law to the support of the gay/lesbian agenda that has since taken the ELCA by the throat. Does the gospel by itself offer any rules or restrictions regarding the sexual behavior of Christians? To say that it does is to legalize the gospel, that is, to make the gospel of God's love and forgiveness do what the law is designed to do.

Antinomianism is thus pernicious in theology and the church, not only because it truncates the law but also because it subverts the gospel.

We will never know what would have happened to LSTC if the merger with Seminex had not occurred. Was it a mistake for LSTC to bring Seminex on board? Would it possibly have been better for all the churches involved if the dissenters had remained within the Missouri Synod and carried on their struggle there? If they were truly confessors for the sake of the gospel, as some of them claimed to be, what is the meaning of their confession once they have run away from their Missouri oppressors? In any case, the presence of Seminex was so powerful and far-reaching in its effects that LSTC was radically transformed in the process. This is merely the opinion of one faculty member who taught at LSTC for thirty years.

The New Lutheran Church

The Association of Evangelical Lutheran Churches (AELC), numbering around 100,000 members, less than 4 percent of the membership of the Missouri Synod, served as a catalyst to bring the American Lutheran Church (ALC) and the Lutheran Church in America (LCA) into merger negotiations. Those three bodies — AELC, ALC, and LCA — united as one church in 1988, thereby creating the Evangelical Lutheran Church in America. The AELC received a lot of the credit — or the blame — for creating a new church that moved to the left on the spectrum of Christianity in the United States, resembling more than ever just another liberal Protestant denomination. The Commission for a New Lutheran Church (CNLC) that drafted the constitution for the ELCA rammed through a quota system modeled on the principles of the left wing of the Democratic Party. Polls indicated that 80 percent of the membership of these Lutheran churches were not in favor of the quota system.

The new church began its life on the basis of a defective ecclesiology. The ex-Missourians pushed for greater democracy in the church and they got it, with all its virtues and liabilities. The upshot was that the church was destined to be governed by a lay majority vulnerable to the manipulation of an unelected bureaucracy at liberty to use the organs of the church to promote its own liberal agendas. Edgar R. Trexler, editor of the *Lutheran* magazine, wrote an account of the formation of the ELCA. His opening sentence reads: "No one ever tried to put a church together the way the Lutheran Church in America, the American Lutheran Church, and the Association of Evangelical Lutheran Churches did in the mid-1980s."[6] From the start I was opposed to the methods used and the results achieved in forming the new Lutheran church. During its twenty some years of existence the church has been mired down in one controversy after the other. Its membership has declined steadily; its annual budget is much lower than expected. It has suffered a number of defections and schisms.

Would the merger of the ALC and the LCA have turned out differently without the presence of the AELC to provide the swing votes in merger negotiations? During the deliberations of the CNLC, the AELC representatives together with the representatives of minorities, blacks, Hispanics, and Asians, and the representatives of women, formed a coalition to emasculate the "old boys," as they were called, the veteran leaders from the ALC and the LCA, people like James Crumley, Robert Marshall, Herbert Chilstrom, Reuben Swanson, William Lazareth, John Reumann, David Preus, Albert Anderson, Lowell Almen, Gerhard Forde, and the like. One example was the notorious vote on an amendment to the statement of faith proposed by Elwyn Ewald, a lay leader of the AELC. In the interest of inclusive language he moved to delete "Father, Son and Holy Spirit" from the statement and instead have it read "triune God." The amendment was defeated by a narrow margin, 33-30. That vote sent a message that the CNLC was not to be trusted with the faith and doctrine of the Lutheran church.

I had been an outspoken advocate of Lutheran unity in America. When David Preus, president of the ALC, published a letter in the *Lutheran Standard* (1980) opposing the merger of the ALC and the LCA, I responded with "An Open Letter to David Preus" that I published in *dialog,* challenging his flimsy reasons. Preus had argued that he was all in favor of Lutheran unity, but that there was no biblical mandate for

---

6. Edgar R. Trexler, *Anatomy of a Merger* (Augsburg Fortress, 1991), p. ix.

an organizational form of unity. I acknowledged that he was right about that, and also that denominational Lutheran unity was of a lesser order than universal Christian unity. Nevertheless, there were good reasons to advance the cause of Lutheran unity in America, even if it meant going forward without our Missouri brothers and sisters. The ALC had its strength in the Midwest and the LCA in the East; merging them would produce more of a national church body, possibly — not inevitably — good for the gospel and its mission in North America and around the world.

On account of the quota system it became clear from the start that theologians would not have much say in the formation of the new Lutheran church. The coalition of minorities and feminists would see to that. To them the issue of race and gender was far more important than dotting the i's and crossing the t's in matters theological and ecclesiological. Will Herzfeld, leader of the black caucus, put it succinctly: "My blackness is a part of my competence."[7] Theologians were regarded as one of many categories of people to fit into the quota system, along with people of color and people whose primary language was not English. Still, I thought it would be wise and useful to bring theological perspectives to bear on the process of forming a new church, for those who would be interested. I proposed to Bill Lesher, the president of LSTC, that our seminary should sponsor a weeklong conference on the theme "How New Can the New Church Be?" The seventy members of the Commission for a New Lutheran Church were meeting concurrently in Chicago, whether by design or luck, I do not know. In hindsight we were naive to expect that the commissioners, many of them theologically uneducated, would welcome the opportunity to hear lectures given by the most distinguished Lutheran theologians in the United States on the very topics that would be front and center in their deliberations. Some 700 people attended some or all of the sessions, debating the theological issues facing American Lutheranism: Lutheran identity, authority in the church, the doctrine of the ministry, the role of bishop, the vocation of the laity, church polity, ecumenical relations, mission objectives, quotas and inclusiveness. Why

---

7. Trexler, *Anatomy of a Merger*, p. 68.

did the commissioners not bother to listen to what the best theologians of the church were saying on these topics? Perhaps it was the perception that the speakers were mostly a bunch of white males spouting their own elitist ideology in the name of theology. The hermeneutics of suspicion had arrived, poisoning the wells of theology in the church. Augsburg Publishing House published the papers given at the conference with the title *The New Church Debate: Issues Facing American Lutheranism*, 1983, which I edited and for which I wrote a lengthy introduction.

The CNLC was ill equipped to deal with the most controversial issues on the nature of the church and the ordained ministry. Instead, the commissioners tried to solve serious theological matters in pragmatic terms, looking for resolutions on which a majority could agree. Not being able to come to any agreement on the doctrine of the ministry, the CNLC agreed to recommend that the new church enter into a six-year study. Seventeen members were appointed to this Task Force on the Ministry, all chosen on the basis of the quota system. Given all the possible categories to choose from, this meant that there would be room for only one systematic theologian who had any experience in teaching the doctrine of the church and its ministry. I was chosen to be that one lone professor. Jack Reumann was chosen as the only biblical theologian; he had written on the church and the ministry from a New Testament perspective. For the next six years the group met twice a year, listened to numerous experts on every conceivable subject, spent over a million dollars of the church's funds, and deliberated and debated the issues on which historic Lutheranism has always been divided, going back to deep ambiguity in Luther's own teaching on the church and the ministry.

Almost predictably nothing of any lasting value came of our study. All the old divisions and disagreements remain in American Lutheranism on the nature of the church and its office of ministry. The only new thing that came of the study was a recommendation that the church should have not only ordained ministers in the traditional sense but also "diaconal ministers" whose auxiliary functions remained unspecified. The word *diakonia* is Greek for service; the word *minister* is Latin for service. So now we have a new office of ministry in the ELCA. They are "serving servants." It struck me as a rather silly outcome of our rather expensive commission. The task force refused to take up the topic of episcopacy, leaving it to fester in the new church, until it flared up in full force over the CCM (Called to Common Mission) agreement between the ELCA and the Episcopal Church USA.

The only really new thing in the new Lutheran church is the commitment to inclusiveness. One pundit suggested that its new name should be the Inclutheran Church. Robert Jenson wrote an editorial in *dialog* saying that if the commissioners knew anything about ecclesiology, they would know that the only way for the church to become more inclusive is to become more catholic. "Catholicity" is the church's theological word for inclusivity. But the commissioners were not interested in theology. The politically correct word is "inclusiveness." That is a code word for quotas. The problem with quotas is that they exclude more categories of people than they include. Alongside of Jenson's editorial I wrote one entitled "Quotas: The New Legalism." When the church of Christ can no longer trust the operations of the Word and the Spirit, it must resort to the law. I ended my editorial with these words: "Unless we are prepared to declare spiritual bankruptcy, we must reject the quota system as a dreadfully Spirit-less affair." Twenty years of quota-mongering later, those with eyes to see will be able to read the handwriting on the wall. We were promised that with the quota system the new church would number 10 percent of blacks in its congregations by the end of the decade. Blacks would be so impressed with the new quotas that they would pour into our white Lutheran congregations asking to be included. What a farce. After two decades the percentage remains the same. Why? Because the only way to get blacks into a predominantly white Lutheran church is through the hard work of evangelism, not by playing the "black power" game of quotas.

I have written my assessment of the new Lutheran church from a theologian's perspective. Of course, I am biased. I studied to become a theologian of the church and have served in that capacity for half a century. I do believe that theology is one of the lifelines of the Christian faith. From my perspective theology is no longer considered a lifeline but a liability in the church of which I am still a member. I am waiting for someone to prove me wrong. The teaching theologians in the Evangelical Lutheran Church in America have little or no credibility outside the walls of their own diminishing denomination. Some who agree with that negative assessment have jumped ship and are plying other waters.

Why I Left LSTC

In 1991 I submitted my resignation to the administration and board of LSTC. I left for two reasons: one, because I had had enough of what was going on in Chicago, both in the ELCA and at LSTC, and two, because I envisioned the possibility of doing something that might be more useful for the church and its theology. I was sixty-two years old, in good health, and not at the age of retirement. One afternoon LaVonne picked me up at school after I'd had a long day of frustration. Out of the blue I popped the question: "Do we have enough money to retire?" That started a long evening of intense reflection and discussion. Did we have enough, with no salary and no promise of another job? Where would we go? What would we do? I had been teaching at LSTC for thirty years. I had turned down opportunities to teach elsewhere. I could not dream of a better place to teach theology than LSTC. However, by 1990 I sensed a profound change had taken place.

My friend and colleague Robert Jenson wrote a *dialog* editorial in which he answered the question many were asking, "So why did Braaten do it?" He hit the nail on the head: "What made Carl Braaten overturn his life is a judgment: seminaries of the ELCA are now institutions emphatically inhospitable to theological work and instruction, and are likely to remain so for the foreseeable future." Like Gaul, a seminary is made up of three parts: students, faculty, and administration (everybody from the president and deans to the janitors and secretaries). The seminary had a good administration; I had no quarrel with it. Bill Lesher was not only an excellent president but a good friend. Don Palmquist was the vice president for development (chief fundraiser); he and Dorothy (Dot) were our best friends both at the seminary and after. Students were admitted with no adequate pretheological requisites. Academic standards were lowered. One example: the faculty periodically examined the records of students with failed grades. I had given an F to a student who could not read or write, judged by his tests and term papers. He received an A from another faculty member who said he was one of the best students in her class in social ethics. How come? Because he was good at going into the neighborhood and interviewing people. Yes, his verbal skills were good; he could talk a blue streak. But his writing skills were zilch. The seminary was admitting many second-career persons who had attended college years ago with no appropriate higher education for serious theological studies. The upshot was that it became increasingly less interesting to teach the required courses in systematic theology and advanced seminars in contemporary theology.

The faculty of LSTC had been strong. New faculty members were invariably elected after a lengthy search for the most qualified candidate. Now something disastrous for theological education interrupted that procedure — the quota system of faculty appointments. There was an opening in theological ethics, after the departure of Frank Sherman. I was appointed the chairman of the search committee. We advertised the position in the usual places, received many nominations, and scheduled a number of interviews. The committee interviewed a young man at the American Academy of Religion who met all the stated qualifications. He was Reinhard Hütter of Erlangen University. Some students and faculty started to rally against the decision of the search committee to submit Hütter's name to the faculty for an up or down vote. Their rallying cry was "anybody but a white male." The search committee really did believe in equal opportunity for minorities and women, and had tried extremely hard to find such qualified candidates. Finally, the committee did agree to interview Elizabeth Bettenhausen, a Lutheran woman who had studied theology and ethics under George Forell at the University of Iowa and had an earned doctorate. She had been a member of the Commission for a New Lutheran Church and had gained a church-wide reputation as a radical feminist. She was a teacher of religion at Boston University, a school in the Methodist tradition. Word was out that she was having difficulty getting tenure because she had not written any books.

Elizabeth Bettenhausen was invited to interview for the position in theological ethics at LSTC. She met with all segments of the student body and made a good impression. Her candidacy was being taken seriously, no doubt about it. Then she met for the faculty interview. This was always a sink-or-swim occasion. Ralph Klein asked her this question: "What is the significance of the resurrection of Jesus for your understanding and teaching of Christian ethics?" She responded with a blank stare, for once at a loss for words. The search committee was divided on her suitability for the position. Yet, the majority believed that Reinhard Hütter was by far the stronger candidate. A noisy campaign was waged among students, again voicing the slogan, "Anybody but a white male." One colleague observed that, besides, this guy was a German.

As chairman of the committee, I was pressured from all quarters. I could foresee that the outcome would be a no-win situation. The committee decided to submit both names with résumés to the faculty for deliberation and decision. Many true and foolish things were said at the following faculty meeting. One colleague who spoke in criticism of Bettenhausen observed that she seemed to have no confessional center in her theology, certainly not the kind one would expect of a Lutheran theologian. Another colleague countered with the remark that Bettenhausen represented a postmodern worldview for which there is no such thing as a center. The result of the ballots cast for Hütter and Bettenhausen was dead even, 15 to 15. President Lesher could have broken the tie but he realized that the faculty was so badly split that a different approach would be needed to deal with the problem. A compromise was proposed by a small group of faculty members. Hütter would be called, not for the usual three-year term as assistant professor but for a two-year term, after which he would be eligible for continuation. It was a slap in the face and was inevitably interpreted as such. I called Hütter long distance at his home in Erlangen and urged him to accept the call in spite of the insult. Hütter was gracious enough to join the faculty. He turned out to be everything we expected, a very popular and productive scholar whose work ethic put most other faculty members who voted against his appointment to shame.

That experience more than anything else was the straw that broke the camel's back. I could no longer conceal my disappointment with the colleagues whose judgment on such an important faculty appointment was beneath contempt. After I resigned I agreed to continue to teach and advise the dozen graduate students under my supervision. I called Robert and Blanche Jenson to talk about my desire to establish a Lutheran center for theological renewal. LaVonne was supportive from the start. The Jensons endorsed the idea with enthusiasm and suggested that we locate the center in Northfield, Minnesota. We could work together, the four of us. We sold our condo in Hyde Park and bought a large beautiful house in Northfield. Immediately after we moved we launched the Center for Catholic and Evangelical Theology in the spring of 1991.

The "Call to Faithfulness" Conferences at St. Olaf College

It was clear from the day of its birth that things were not working out well in the new Lutheran church. Many people from coast to coast were voicing their unhappiness. Some wished they could turn back the clock and rescind the decision to merge. Already in its infancy the new church needed to be reformed and renewed. Herbert Chilstrom called for a new start and settled for restructuring the bureaucracies of the church. Dark clouds were hanging over the church; the atmosphere was charged with rancorous criticism of almost everything going on: quotas, multiculturalism, radical feminism, political correctness, inclusive language, homosexuality, episcopacy, and ecumenism. Not everyone was mad about the same things, but neither was anybody happy with everything.

The editors of three independent Lutheran journals decided to join forces in sponsoring a free conference, open to anyone wishing to attend, to deal with the neuralgic issues facing American Lutheranism, especially within the fledgling ELCA. The three journals were *dialog*, *Lutheran Forum*, and *Lutheran Quarterly*. Richard J. Neuhaus suggested we name the conference "A Call to Faithfulness"; it was held at St. Olaf College in June 1990. I was appointed the coordinator to plan the program, and St. Olaf College agreed to handle the advertising and registration. More than 900 pastors and laypeople attended. The three journals shared equally in selecting the plenary speakers: Robert W. Jenson, James M. Kittelson, Gerhard O. Forde, Joseph A. Burgess, George Lindbeck, Paul R. Sponheim, Richard John Neuhaus, Larry Rasmussen, and myself. The conference received mixed reviews. Some reported that the majority of those in attendance were older white male pastors. That was natural, because they were the ones in the position to know from firsthand experience that the new church was drifting away from its traditional moorings. A few complained that the roster of speakers did not match the ELCA quota system — no women, no minorities, and no persons whose primary language was other than English. Uffda!

The speakers did not all speak from the same script. The major division in the ELCA between denominational Lutherans and evangelical catholics was clearly in evidence, especially on the topics of church, ministry, and ecumenism. It did not happen without notice and comment that a large bloc of pastors from the East showed up in black shirts and clerical collars, while Midwest pastors walked around in casual clothes, looking cool and comfortable. The irony is that while these two parties were at odds with each other on ecclesiology and ecumenism, they were united in opposing the main trends in the ELCA, its revisionism bearing on Christology and the Trinity, its abandonment of world missions and evangelization, its exchange of catholicity as a mark of the church for inclusivity, its confusing of law and gospel (and of the two kingdoms) in social statements, its failure to discipline clergy breaking the rules, and its treatment of the gospel as a marketing product. That is only a partial list.

We did not expect that our call to faithfulness would engender a serious response from the ELCA headquarters in Chicago, its seminaries, and its synodical judicatories. Nevertheless, we decided to sponsor a second "Call to Faithfulness" conference at St. Olaf College, in June 1992. It drew over 600 registrants, mostly pastors, very few bishops and seminary professors. The presiding bishop of the ELCA was invited to speak. His message was "Love This Church." He attended only his own session, so if there was anything not to love in the new church, he would not have heard about it. His opening remark was to congratulate the Center for Catholic and Evangelical Theology for sponsoring this conference. In fact, the Center had nothing to do with it; this "Call to Faithfulness" conference was a function of the same three independent journals that sponsored the first one. The confusion in Chilstrom's mind was understandable because by this time the Center for Catholic and Evangelical Theology was already up and running in Northfield. Robert Jenson and I were its cofounders, and at the same time we were among the planners and speakers at both "Call to Faithfulness" conferences.

The lesson I learned from the two highly popular and successful "Call to Faithfulness" conferences was that the voices and opinions of pastors and theologians in the new church would be marginalized. The quota system made sure of that. The new church would be guided by opinion polls and cultural trends. This does not mean that theologians would not be heard, only that they would be used as tools of selective manipulation by those who manage the quota system. Nobody who bucks the system gets elected to any office in the ELCA. This is why only retired bishops dare to speak out against the ordination of gay clergy in partnered relationships and the blessing of same-gender unions in the church. Even theological professors have become muted for fear of appearing out of sync with the rising trends in church and society. So much for the "here I stand" courage of the founding father of the Lutheran movement. Not even faint echoes of that are to be heard in the church establishment and its publications, for example, the *Lutheran Magazine, Lutheran Partners,* as well as books published by Augsburg Fortress Publishing House. Censorship is massive, complete, and effective, however it works.

CHAPTER ELEVEN

The Center for Catholic and Evangelical Theology

1991–2005

When LaVonne and I decided to leave Chicago for Northfield, Minnesota, we did not have a well-thought-out plan. We knew two things for certain. LaVonne was leaving her flourishing health food business, uncertain about how to manage it from week to week from a distance and at the same time arrange for its future. Our son Kristofer had started working his way into the business as an apprentice under LaVonne's supervision. That relationship developed and prospered until he not only managed the stores in Hyde Park and Country Club Hills, but also opted to purchase the entire business over a ten-year period. I was leaving the seminary after thirty years as a professor of systematic theology — which involved classroom teaching, faculty meetings, graduate students, and a monthly salary, such as it was — uncertain whether our combined retirement income would be able to support us in a new but as yet undefined venture.

We were clear about what we were leaving behind but not so sure of what we were getting ourselves into. We were going to Northfield to set up housekeeping in a new place, as we had done a dozen times before, and to start talking with the Jensons about the kind of theological center we wanted to establish and what steps to take to make it become a reality. We felt comfortable embarking on this undertaking with the Jensons because of our many years of friendship and collaboration on many projects. We had become lifelong friends in Heidelberg (1957-1958), after that first awkward encounter on Hauptstrasse the first Sunday we were there, which I have already written about. Jens helped me with my translation of Kähler's book on the historical Jesus, since he was fluent in German and I was not. We worked together in founding *dialog: A Journal of Theology;* Jens was the journal's first book review editor and I was its first editor in chief. Jens later served as editor in chief for nine years. LaVonne and I spent a lot of time with the Jensons in Oxford, England, during our sabbatical year of study, 1967-1968. Jens and I had collaborated in publishing a number of theological works, including the two-volume textbook *Christian Dogmatics.* It seemed as though the foundation stones were perfectly laid for a new venture in creating theology in the service of the church.

Our plans for the new center developed quickly. We named it the Center for Catholic and Evangelical Theology. The name conveys our conviction that the original intent of Martin Luther and his fellow reformers was to be a gospel-centered movement within the western branch of Christianity. It was not Luther's intention to be the founder of a new church named after him. Lutherans are evangelical catholics. For some Lutherans the term "evangelical catholic" is an oxymoron; not for us. They feel more comfortable being called "protestant"; for them Lutheranism is one of the Protestant denominations. Sociologically, they are right. However, they would be hard put to find any basis for that in the Lutheran *Book of Concord.*

Immediately after signing the legal documents on May 24, 1991, to form a nonprofit corporation in the state of Minnesota, we created an all-Lutheran board of directors and appointed ourselves to various staff positions. LaVonne became the treasurer, a natural move, because she had twenty years of business experience, and also had invested her money on the start-up costs of the Center. Blanche became the planning coordinator; she was an idea person involved in every discussion regarding conferences and projects. Jens became the associate director and I, the executive director. The following persons, well known in Lutheran circles, agreed to serve as directors: Harley C. Carlson (a medical doctor at Mayo Clinic, Rochester, Minnesota), Walter D. Carlson (pastor of Grace Lutheran Church, Lancaster, Pennsylvania), James R. Crumley (bishop emeritus, Lutheran Church in America), Karl P.

Donfried (professor of biblical literature, Smith College), William H. Lazareth (bishop of the Metropolitan New York Synod, ELCA), George A. Lindbeck (professor of historical theology, Yale University), and Robert L. Wilken (professor of the history of Christianity, University of Virginia). It would be hard to assemble a more distinguished group of Lutheran church leaders and theologians.

Prior to launching the Center for Catholic and Evangelical Theology, I sent a proposal of our plan to many bishops of the ELCA, to notify them of this new venture and to solicit their comments. Here are a few of the responses we received.

From Herbert W. Chilstrom, Bishop, Evangelical Lutheran Church in America

I have some mixed feelings and a good deal of uncertainty about how to respond to your request for an evaluation. On the one hand, I have always championed free movements in the life of the church. I believe they have filled a useful purpose. The church cannot cover all the bases. There are times when these movements have met those needs. If they are positive and if they help build up the church, they ought to have our encouragement. The governing documents of the ELCA make provision for such support.

As I read your statement of purpose, however, I find myself wondering why we need such a center for theological studies. It occurs to me that everything you envision should, in fact, be among the purposes our theological seminaries seek to fulfill. In my judgment, these areas of concern are already being addressed by competent faculty at our seminaries. Furthermore, as you mount concerted efforts to support the center at Northfield, you will be contacting the same persons who are now among the faithful supporters of our seminaries.

Since you are determined to move ahead, I can only wish you the very best and join in the hope that the Center can, indeed, be a very positive blessing and enhancement of the mission of the church.

From William H. Lazareth, Bishop, Metropolitan New York
Synod

*I want to commend you and Jens as you together embark on
this new venture. I am convinced that it will prove to be a blessing for this church and beyond, and I therefore commend you for
your courageous commitment to do theology as a function of the
church. It will certainly meet intentionally the theological needs
of this church and its ministries.*

From Glenn W. Nycklemoe, Bishop, Southeastern Minnesota
Synod

*I definitely believe there is a place for such a Center. . . . I am
excited about the Center sponsoring colloquies for significant
questions of theology affecting the life and ministry of the church
today. . . . As a Bishop of the church, I would have a deep concern that even though this would be a free movement in the life of
the church, it would not become a Center that fostered or even
promoted any bashing of church leaders, the ELCA approved
constitution, policies, social statements, etc.*

From Gerhard Knutson, Bishop, Northwest Synod of Wisconsin

*I recognize that down through history there have been free
and independent movements, organizations, and theological
journals that have addressed the church both in critique and in
affirmation. I was surprised to see that nowhere in the statement
of purpose is the word "Lutheran" mentioned, though it does
talk about Reformation Confessions. I would hope that such a
place would not become a church-bashing place, such as Forum
Letter has become, but rather an educational resource place. . . .
Is it your intention that this be an ecumenical center, not just a
Lutheran center? And what will be its relationship to the Evangelical Lutheran Church in America and to St. Olaf College?*

From Harold C. Skillrud, Bishop, Southeastern Synod

*I definitely have heard about your plan to move to Northfield
and to found a center for theological studies. I was quite sur-*

prised by this because somehow I had envisioned you remaining at LSTC through retirement, but I certainly recognize the need for what you are proposing and would support you in it. I am terribly bothered by what seems to be a perceptible drift away from our traditional confessional commitments, especially in the use of language with reference to a Triune God in worship and theological formulations. . . . It is good to know that you will be doing this, and I certainly wish you every success and blessing in it. Thank you for what I know will be a significant contribution to the life of the church.

Paull E. Spring, Bishop, Northwestern Pennsylvania Synod

To be candid, I regret that it seems necessary for you and Professor Jenson to found such a Center. Properly speaking, the theological seminaries of the church are called to fulfill many of the functions that you list for the Center. In that sense, and for the sake of the church's seminaries, I am sorry that you feel you cannot continue your work at LSTC. . . . At the same time, given our present situation, I applaud the effort you are engaged in. Perhaps a free-standing theological center will help the church to come to a fresh understanding of its life and mission.

Kenneth H. Sauer, Bishop, Southern Ohio Synod

I surely wish you and Jenson the best of success in this new work. It is sorely needed for the church, and will help us all to serve better, and smarter. My concern is that we not do theology in abstract but think through how it impacts the church where I am called and how to be faithful within the structures of that church. If the work that you and Jenson are embarking on can assist us to begin to make connections between our hearts, our heads, and our actual concrete churches, it could be very exciting. I wish you well.

Lowell O. Erdahl, Bishop, Saint Paul Synod

The ELCA and its leadership, beginning with bishops like me, need confrontation and correction, and I hope your Center will help to provide it. At the same time, I also hope that it will not become a center for the cynical, sarcastic smashing of persons or positions that are perceived and presented as the enemy. We are called in Christ to encourage and upbuild as well as to correct each other. If the Center fulfills all of those many functions it will be worthy of praise and will be a source of information, insight, and inspiration for many and a ground for gratitude even for generations yet to be. I wish you wisdom and compassion to help make that happen.

The responses from many influential bishops of the ELCA were on the whole cautiously encouraging. The Center would be operating within the boundaries of their jurisdictions, so they had good reason to be concerned. Since Jens and I had written numerous highly critical editorial opinions in the pages of *dialog,* many suspected that we would use the Center to the same effect. Jens and I agreed that our role as critics of the ELCA was mainly a thing of the past. Our focus would shift to a broader set of concerns. In our first announcement of the founding of the Center to the wider church public, we wrote these words:

> The Center for Catholic and Evangelical Theology is a new and independent theological enterprise whose goal is to promote faithfulness throughout the church to the Word of God in Jesus Christ. It will seek to advance the knowledge of God's revelation, as authoritatively mediated by Holy Scripture and normatively interpreted by the church's creedal and dogmatic tradition.
>
> The Center will challenge the church to reaffirm its identity. It will seek to retrieve, in the light of the Reformation critique, neglected treasures — doctrinal, institutional, and liturgical — of the catholic tradition. Serving the mandate of churchly unity, it will pursue ecumenical research and conversation. And it will seek to reclaim the normative application of the biblical ethic of obedient faith in Christian life and in the church's social witness.
>
> In pursuit of these goals, the Center will sponsor seminars and colloquia on dogmatic and biblical theology, publish books and a

new journal PRO ECCLESIA, dedicated to the interpretation and study of classical Christian theology, and offer courses for continuing theological education in the classical disciplines.

There is not a single hint about bashing the ELCA and its leadership to be found in these affirmations and promises. As editors of the new journal *Pro Ecclesia,* we were often tempted to comment on strange things going on in the ELCA. But we had turned a corner and were not going back. We had set our sights on the future of the ecumenical church, and to the extent Lutheranism would be in a position to contribute something positive to that end, it would certainly be involved as an important player.

The Center for Catholic and Evangelical Theology was only a year old when controversy erupted, starting with a letter that Bishop Herbert Chilstrom wrote to Bishop James Crumley, who had just been elected as chairman of the Center's board of directors. It all started with an article that appeared in a Faribault newspaper, covering an interview that I provided to its religion editor. A copy of this article was sent to Bishop Chilstrom by the bishop of the Southeastern Minnesota Synod, Glenn Nycklemoe. Chilstrom took umbrage at some of my criticisms of the church reported in the newspaper. Indeed, I did express many criticisms. I did not refer specifically to the ELCA but to "Christian churches in America." But neither did I say anything to exempt the ELCA from my general critique. In Chilstrom's letter to Crumley it was obvious that he was confused about the identity of the Center in relation to the two "Call to Faithfulness" conferences and to St. Olaf College. Chilstrom also wrote a letter to Melvin George, president of St. Olaf College, because the college had hosted the "Call to Faithfulness" conferences and, besides, Robert Jenson was a member of the religion faculty of St. Olaf College. Whatever their intent, Chilstrom's letters were interpreted as an attempt to put pressure on Crumley and George to rein in — and possibly discipline? — those "two loose cannons" with whom they had associated their good names.

Bishop Crumley did not take kindly to Chilstrom's reprimand. Crumley defended my criticisms as accurate descriptions of the mainline churches, of which the ELCA was one. Crumley pointed out the independence of the Center from St. Olaf College and from the two "Call to Faithfulness" conferences, which were sponsored by three journals, *dialog, Lutheran Forum,* and *Lutheran Quarterly.* Moreover, Crumley made no apology to Chilstrom for his strong support of the Center and its programs and rather resented having his loyalty to the church impugned. Jens and I, in turn, wrote a letter to Chilstrom complaining of his going behind our backs, rather than confronting us directly as ordained ministers of the ELCA, in criticizing our attitudes and actions, while sending blind copies to many officials of the church. Chilstrom was apparently still smarting from the "Higgins bashing" that certainly went on at the "Call to Faithfulness" conferences. It was more serious than mere bashing; dissidents were naming various heresies in the church. Chilstrom was standing up for his administration; there was no heresy. He defended the seminaries of the church; there were no "mutations of the gospel," a phrase I had used rather than the word "heresy." Chilstrom complained about my frequent use of what he called "inflammatory rhetoric, innuendo, and misleading accusation." He asked for documentation to the charge that radical feminist and liberationist theologies were supplanting confessional Lutheran principles in many quarters of the church. He concluded his letter, "In many ways, you are an eminent theologian of our church. When you speak, many people in the ELCA pay attention. You owe it to us to be specific in your charges." Then he pleaded for reconciliation. From my side I harbored no ill feelings against Chilstrom. I had supported his candidacy to be the first president of the ELCA. I respected and admired him. But from where he was sitting, he could see no serious theological problems facing Lutheranism. Considering his office, he could not afford to admit that the confessional core of Lutheranism was vanishing before our eyes. From where I was sitting, the handwriting on the wall was so clear, I felt a person had to be blind not to see it.

For me it seemed hardly necessary to provide chapter and verse to prove: (1) that the triune identity of God as "Father, Son, and Holy Spirit" was being challenged by radical theological feminism; (2) that the uniqueness of Jesus Christ as the one and only way of salvation was being challenged by the pluralistic theology of religion; (3) that the authority of Scripture was being challenged by an unchurchly hermeneutic based on postmodern historical relativism; (4) that the proper distinction between law and gospel was being challenged by the twin tenets of American culture religion, gnosticism and antinomianism; (5) that the church as the body of Christ was being challenged by a supposedly democratic quota system that owes its soul to the cult of egalitarianism; (6) that the doctrine of two kingdoms of God was being challenged from two sides — from the right, which wants to separate them, and from the left, which tends to equate them — so that the unique gospel mission of the church was being sidetracked by or confused with a plethora of worthy social causes. The common denominator of all these challenges and the underlying crisis in the church is one that H. Richard Niebuhr identified as the "church conforming to culture."

The strategy of the Center for Catholic and Evangelical Theology, as we conceived it, was to reclaim the great tradition of evangelical, catholic, and orthodox theology by bringing together the best theological minds in all the churches to join its colloquies, speak at its conferences, and write for its journal. From the start the Center struggled to define itself. It faced a certain ambiguity regarding its identity. Was it Lutheran, as suggested by the composition of its board of directors? Was it ecumenical, as announced in its mission statement? As the Center for Catholic and Evangelical Theology, what do we intend to convey by "Catholic" and "Evangelical"? Most people understand "Catholic" to mean Roman Catholic and "Evangelical" to mean conservative Protestant. The Center's name was obviously a tour de force, since we did not intend it to mean "Roman," though Roman Catholics would be included, nor "Protestant," though theologians from all Protestant denominations would in some ways be represented. Jens and I received the following letter from Father Avery Dulles, S.J. (now a cardinal), whom we had invited to serve on the advisory council of *Pro Ecclesia*. His remarks deal with the identity of the journal, but they are equally applicable to the Center.

Dear Carl and Robert:

I congratulate you on your initiative in founding the new journal, PRO ECCLESIA. Although I suspect you and the Board of the

Center are quite clear about the meaning of the term "Catholic and Evangelical Theology," it may be desirable in the course of time to give some descriptive definition of these terms for the benefit of the advisory council and possibly also for future readers. Does the term "Catholic" include "Roman Catholic"? Does the term "Evangelical" include Reformed? Does it mean "Protestant" or can it also include Roman Catholics? Is the Center essentially a Lutheran Center? If so, should it include the word "Lutheran" in its title? Questions such as these might arise out of the wholly Lutheran character of the Board and the broader membership of the Advisory Council. I am sure that you have good answers, but others might need some further explanation than is already given. These questions do not raise any real difficulties for me at the present time, and I do not expect that they will. I therefore accept with pleasure your invitation to be a member of the Advisory Council.

Sincerely yours
Avery Dulles, S.J.

Since its inception the Center has gradually evolved into a more explicitly ecumenical organization. Non-Lutherans have been elected to the board; it includes Roman Catholics and Protestants from across the denominational spectrum. Our policy was always to strive for an ecumenically balanced roster of speakers at all our conferences, and the same thing was true of the authors we invited to write for our publications. I believe that Jesus' saying holds true for the Center, "You will know them by their fruits" (Matt. 7:16). The Center's track record has removed the initial ambiguity that attended its early years of operation. The terms "Catholic" and "Evangelical" have no denominational reference but point to the sacred substance of the great tradition that all orthodox communities and Christians claim as their common inheritance. In this sense Roman Catholics may be as "evangelical" as any Protestants, and Protestants may be as "catholic" as any Romans. Our claim is that a Lutheran should aim to be both "evangelical" and "catholic" at the same time.

To make good on the promise of the Center, we laid down three tracks on which the initial programs of the Center would run: colloquies and seminars for theologians, theological conferences for clergy and laity, and an ecumenical journal of catholic and evangelical theology (small *c* and *e*).

Colloquies and Seminars

The Dogmatics Colloquium

In our first year of operation Jens and I invited a group of younger theologians to join us in forming what we called "The Dogmatics Colloquium." The group met regularly twice a year from 1992 to 1995 in Northfield. The following persons attended some or all of the sessions:

James Buckley (Loyola University)
Ellen T. Charry (Princeton Seminary)
David S. Cunningham (Hope College)
J. A. DiNoia (Congregation for the Doctrine of the Faith, Vatican City)
Reinhard Hütter (Duke Divinity School)
L. Gregory Jones (Duke Divinity School)
Bruce D. Marshall (Perkins School of Theology)
Paul McGlasson (First Presbyterian Church, Sullivan, Indiana)
Steven Paulson (Luther Seminary)
William Placher (Wabash College)
Eugene F. Rogers, Jr. (University of Virginia)
Theodore Stylianopoulos (Holy Cross Greek Orthodox Seminary)
Paul Wesche (St. Herman's Orthodox Church, Minneapolis)
Anna N. Williams (Cambridge University)
Susan K. Wood (St. John's University, Collegeville, Minnesota)
David S. Yeago (Lutheran Theological Southern Seminary)
Randall Zachman (University of Notre Dame)

The theological conversations and papers produced by the group resulted in the publication of a book, *Knowing the Triune God,* edited by James Buckley and David Yeago. The editors dedicated the book "To the Braatens and Jensons for their generosity, hospitality, and patience." By hospitality they undoubtedly had in mind the special role that LaVonne and Blanche played in providing for the coffee breaks, the happy hours, the gourmet cuisine, as well as bed and breakfast to many participants. Overall, the dogmatics colloquium was an enjoyable and fruitful experience of bringing such a stellar group of younger theologians together, providing the occasion for them to form close bonds of friendship and enduring collaborative relationships. In a certain sense they became the brain trust of what might be called the "*pro ecclesia* movement*" in American theology.

Finnish Luther Research Seminar

In 1996 the Center sponsored a seminar on new Finnish Luther research. We invited Dr. Tuomo Mannermaa and three of his closest associates from the Institute for Systematic Theology of the University of Helsinki to lead the seminar. Mannermaa was professor of ecumenics at the Institute and the leader of a Finnish school of Luther research that developed a new paradigm of interpretation. His associates at the seminar were Dr. Simo Peura, research scholar in ecumenics (now a bishop); Dr. Antti Raunio, research scholar in systematic theology; and Dr. Sammeli Juntunen, assistant in ecumenical theology. Those who attended the seminar were there by invitation only. The new Finnish paradigm centered on Luther's idea of the real presence of Christ in faith. This led to an understanding of the doctrine of justification that is more mystical and ontological, rather than purely forensic and juridical.

Mannermaa and his fellow Finns entered into ecumenical dialogue with theologians of the Russian Orthodox Church. In the process they became convinced that Luther's view on justification approximates the Orthodox concept of *theosis*. This Finnish interpretation has provided not only a fresh approach in Luther research but also a new opening for considering the relationship between the Reformation and Eastern Orthodoxy. Not being a Luther scholar myself, I have reached no independent conclusion on whether the Finnish paradigm is right or wrong. My hunch is that Luther can be quoted in favor of both the forensic and the ontological understandings of justification. The former is more on the side of Melanchthon and the latter more on the side of Osiander, two of Luther's followers who opposed each other. We published a gem of a book of the seminar papers entitled *Union with Christ: The New Finnish Interpretation of Luther* (Eerdmans, 1998).

A Study Tour

The Center organized a special kind of seminar involving a study tour of Rome, Greece, and Turkey that took place September 27–October 13, 1998. The theme was "Christianity and Culture: East and West." About twenty were in the group. I made the arrangements and contacts; Jens provided the background lectures as we moved from site to site. The purpose of the study tour was to learn something about the encounter of Christianity with the culture of Mediterranean antiquity. Perhaps the catastrophes and opportunities confronting the church in modern times can be better understood in light of the meeting of the gospel and classical culture during the early centuries.

The tour took us to Greece, the birthplace of Mediterranean culture, as well as to the eastern and western capitals of the ancient and medieval church, Constantinople (now Istanbul) and Rome. We viewed architectural monuments and works of art that displayed examples of the synthesis of the gospel and ancient culture. The tour also provided the occasion to reflect on the deeply rooted division between the Eastern and Western branches of Christendom, what caused the great schism of A.D. 1054, and what is being done ecumenically in modern times to heal the breach. To prepare for this trip I reread the great book written by Charles Cochrane, *Christianity and Classical Culture*.

Theological Conferences, 1992–2008

Here is a list of the theological conferences sponsored by the Center over a period of fifteen years.

1992   "Facing the Challenge of the Future: Ecumenism and Mission." The Archer House, Northfield, Minn.

1993   "Either/Or: The Gospel or Neopaganism." St. Olaf College, Northfield, Minn.

1994   "Reclaiming the Bible for the Church." St. Olaf College, Northfield, Minn.
      "The Catholicity of the Reformation." St. Olaf College, Northfield, Minn., and Grace Lutheran Church, Lancaster, Pa.

1995   "The Church as a Communion of Churches." St. Olaf College, Northfield, Minn.
      "The Left Hand of God: The Church's Agenda for the World." St. John's Lutheran Church, Northfield, Minn., and Grace Lutheran Church, Lancaster, Pa.

1996   "Reformation and Ecumenism: At the Threshold of the Third Millennium." Central Lutheran Church, Minneapolis
      "Orthopraxy for the Secular City: On Being the Church in the City." Immanuel Lutheran Church, New York City
      "The God Who Saves: Models of Salvation — Deification/Justification/Liberation." St. Olaf College, Northfield, Minn.

1997   "Who Is Jesus? On the Identity and Meaning of Jesus of Nazareth." Augsburg College, Minneapolis
      "Marks of the Body of Christ." St. John's Lutheran Church, Northfield, Minn., and Grace Lutheran Church, Lancaster, Pa.

1998   "Sin, Death, and the Devil." St. Olaf College, Northfield, Minn.

1999   "Church Unity and the Papal Office." University of St. Thomas, St. Paul, Minn.
      "The Last Things: Biblical and Theological Perspectives on Es-

chatology." Central Lutheran Church, Minneapolis, and Grace Lutheran Church, Lancaster, Pa.

2000 "The Crisis of Christian Worship." St. John's University, Collegeville, Minn.

"The Strange New Word of the Gospel: Re-evangelizing in the Post-modern World." Immanuel Lutheran Church, New York, and St. Luke's Lutheran Church, Chicago

2001 "Jews and Christians: People of God." Augsburg College, Minneapolis

2002 "Mary, Mother of God." St. Olaf College, Northfield, Minn.

2003 "The Ten Commandments: On the Law of God." St. Paul's Cathedral, Charleston, S.C., and St. Olaf College, Northfield, Minn.

2004 "In One Body through the Cross: The Princeton Proposal for Christian Unity." Notre Dame University and Beeson Divinity School, Birmingham, Ala.

2005 "In One Body through the Cross: The Princeton Proposal for Christian Unity." Center of Theological Inquiry, Princeton, N.J.

"What Is Marriage?" St. Olaf College, Northfield, Minn.

2006 "Preaching, Teaching, and Living the Bible: A Challenge to the Church." Duke Divinity School, Durham, N.C.

2007 "Freedom and Authority in the Christian Life." St. Olaf College, Northfield, Minn.

2008 "Christian Theology and Islam." Loyola College, Baltimore

The topics indicate the scope of the Center's theological vision for the ecumenical church. All of them dealt with the substantive convictions of the Christian faith, interpreted by the most creative minds in contemporary theology. Some observers commented that the Center conferences were one-sided and scarcely politically correct. They did not give equal time to heretics and apostates, of which there are plenty to choose from in American Christianity and theology, and the choice of speakers did not measure up to the quota guidelines enforced in our Lutheran denomination (ELCA). The registrants were mostly pastors accustomed to attending conferences sponsored by their synods and seminaries, featuring theology-lite, updated information on the pension plan, and how-to techniques for successful ministry.

Publications

All the Center publications resulted from our theological conferences, but not all the conferences yielded papers. For one reason or another, we deemed some not worthy of publication. We discovered that some speakers used materials they had already published, and a few were off the topic or did not meet our standards. But on the whole the conference speakers gave their best efforts. The Center books have all been published by Eerdmans Publishing Company. Why Eerdmans? Eerdmans traditionally represented the Dutch Reformed tradition. Why not Augsburg Fortress Publishing Company, a more natural choice for us, since it was the publishing house of the ELCA? After all, Jens and I had published many books with Augsburg Publishing House and Fortress Press prior to their merger. To tell the truth, the decision was not exactly of our own choosing. In fact, we did meet with the editors of Augsburg Fortress, Marshall D. Johnson and Michael West, to present a prospectus of a plan to publish a series of *Pro Ecclesia* monographs in theology. They turned us down flat, with the explanation that they were going in a different direction. We got the point; they were indeed going in a different direction. The new editorial policy of Ausburg Fortress, judging from what they proceeded to publish, was to favor liberal, left-wing, liberationist authors who were either ignorant of or indifferent to the mainstream of the Christian tradition. We chose to send our Center manuscripts to Eerdmans. Bill and Sam Eerdmans not only accepted all the titles we sent their way but have also become good friends of all of us who work for the Center.

Only rarely does a book written by a confessional Lutheran theologian slip through the editorial censorship at Augsburg Fortress. Absent from the current academic book catalogues of Augsburg Fortress are the names of such prominent Lutheran theologians as, to mention just a few that come to mind: Roy A. Harrisville, Gerhard Forde, Robert W. Jenson, Karl Donfried, Steve Paulson, Walter Sundberg, Robert Benne, Robert Bertram, Marva Dawn, Richard Lischer, Gilbert Meilaender, Paul Rorem, and Hans Schwarz. On the other hand, books whose contents clearly exceed the limits of the Lutheran confessions and classical orthodoxy have become the trademark of the ELCA's publishing house. That is a widespread perception. Is it fair? Unfortunately, I think it is, and there is abundant evidence to support it. This is especially painful for me to acknowledge because Augsburg and Fortress have together published almost all of my books. Augsburg Fortress could have been the publishers of the books Jenson and I have coedited and published with Eerdmans. We are not unhappy about going with Eerdmans, yet it is a sad commentary on the fact that Augsburg Fortress has become the signature expression of just another liberal Protestant denomination.

Below is a list of the Center books published by Wm. B. Eerdmans Publishing Company.

1995   *Either/Or: The Gospel or Neopaganism*

1995   *Reclaiming the Bible for the Church*

1996   *The Catholicity of the Reformation*

1997   *The Two Cities of God*

1998   *Union with Christ: The New Finnish Interpretation of Luther*

1999   *Marks of the Body of Christ*

2000   *Sin, Death, and the Devil*

2001   *Church Unity and the Papal Office*

2001   *The Last Things: Biblical and Theological Perspectives on Eschatology*

2002   *The Strange New Word of the Gospel*

Pro Ecclesia: A Journal of Catholic and Evangelical Theology

When Jens and I decided to found a new journal very different from *dialog*, we came up with a bold idea. Why not propose at the next meeting of the editorial council of *dialog* (October 1991) that we, Jens and I, take over the journal, have the entire membership of the council resign, and transform the journal into one that promotes churchly theology? The members voted, and we lost by a margin closer than we had a right to expect. Most people do not like to vote themselves out of business. The group decided to continue to publish *dialog* as it was, so we went ahead with our plans to found the churchly journal we had in mind. Our hearts were no longer into doing the kind of ping-pong theology we had fostered for years in *dialog*. What had changed? We were convinced that all the churches in the United States were losing their doctrinal foundations and were sliding into a postmodern kind of neo-pagan gnosticism. We believed that the times called for a different response from the one we made at the founding of *dialog* thirty years before.

The Center for Catholic and Evangelical Theology entered into a partnership with the American Lutheran Publicity Bureau (ALPB) to publish an ecumenical quarterly journal of theology. Sixteen years later *Pro Ecclesia* has acquired an international reputation of being a serious journal of theology in the service of the church. Its first issue was published in the autumn of 1992.

The mission statement of *Pro Ecclesia* reads as follows:

> *Pro Ecclesia* is a journal of theology published by the Center for Catholic and Evangelical Theology. It seeks to give contemporary

expression to the one apostolic faith and its classic traditions, working for and manifesting the church's unity by research, theological construction, and free exchange of opinion. Members of its advisory council represent communities committed to the authority of Holy Scripture, ecumenical dogmatic teaching and the structural continuity of the church, and are themselves dedicated to maintaining and invigorating these commitments. The journal publishes biblical, liturgical, historical and doctrinal articles that promote or illumine its purposes.

In 1995 I decided that it was time to look for a new editor of *Pro Ecclesia*. I had been out of the academic loop for fifteen years and was no longer circulating among the younger theologians who must be the future of the journal. Jens and I lost no time in identifying the right person to succeed us as the editor. That would be Reinhard Hütter, formerly my colleague at the Lutheran School of Theology at Chicago, indeed, the one who prevailed in the final faculty vote for the position of professor of theological ethics. In addition, he was a professor of theology at Duke Divinity School, and in the perfect position to assume the editorship of the journal.

After serving two years as editor in chief of *Pro Ecclesia*, Hütter resigned, presumably to have more time to prepare himself to become a Roman Catholic theologian in a full sense, learning the nuts and bolts of the complex Thomist tradition that runs from Aquinas to Rahner. Hütter brought a lot of new energy and ideas to the journal and succeeded in reorganizing its editorial structure. Joseph Mangina, a professor of theology at the Toronto School of Theology, was elected by the board of directors to succeed Hütter as editor of *Pro Ecclesia*. The associate editors and members of the advisory council are a solid, ecumenically representative group. The journal is now published by Rowman and Littlefield Publishers, Inc. Jens and I have good reason to be proud of the journal we created and coedited for fifteen years. We continue to serve the journal in a new capacity as senior editors, more or less an honorary title. We believe the journal has found an important niche for itself among theological journals, and we expect it to flourish in the years to come.

Colloquium on Robert W. Jenson's Systematic Theology, Volumes–
1 and 2 (Oxford University Press, 1997 and 1999)

I took it upon myself to organize a colloquium to honor the occasion
of the publication of my colleague's magnum opus, the two volumes of
his systematic theology that he wrote in his spare time in the 1990s. He
was teaching full time at St. Olaf College, and he gave unstintingly of
his time to the Center's programs and to editing *Pro Ecclesia*. This was
the fitting culmination of a career of teaching dogmatics and systematics over three decades. I invited six persons to deal with different facets
of Jenson's theology: David S. Yeago, Gabriel Fackre, Susan Wood,
Vigen Guroian, Gerhard Forde, Christopher Seitz, and Anna Williams.
The responses were both laudatory and illuminating. My deep regret is
that we never received the papers in proper shape to publish them as a
symposium in *Pro Ecclesia*.

The Study Group on the Ecclesiology of Ecumenism

In 1999 the Center sponsored a consultation on the future of ecumenism that was attended by members of the board of directors and a select number of ecumenical theologians. Jens and I were proposing that
the Center undertake a major study on ecclesiology and ecumenism,
and we were inviting feedback. The consultation supported the plan
and urged us to proceed. We formed a task force of sixteen members,
not as fully representative of Christianity as would have been ideal.
The group consisted of two Roman Catholics, two Orthodox, two
Episcopalians, two Reformed, two Methodists, one Pentecostal, and
five Lutherans. Two of the Lutherans were ex officio, George
Lindbeck and Bill Rusch. The group met in Princeton twice a year,
three days at a time, and for three and a half years. Jens and I were
moderators of the sessions and finally the editors of the manifesto
composed by the group. We modeled the study on the Francophone ecumenical Groupe de Dombes, founded in 1937 by Paul Couturier of
Lyon, which produced a number of statements on controversial issues
that had an enormous influence on the subsequent course of ecumeni-

cal dialogues. The document that our study group published is entitled *In One Body through the Cross: The Princeton Proposal for Christian Unity*. It contains fifty pages of text, set forth in seventy-two paragraphs, with seven sections.

The statement focuses first on the realities of church division and the crisis of the ecumenical movement, and then proceeds to propose new and practical ways to be faithful to the founding ecumenical imperative of our Lord "that all may be one . . . so that the world may believe" (John 17:21). Since members of the study group were not officially appointed by their churches, they were not only not obligated to speak *for* their churches, but were also free to speak without restraint *to* all the churches. The statement is an indictment of conciliar ecumenism whose so-called "new ecumenical paradigm" subordinates the concern of the "faith and order" movement for the visible unity of Christians to divisive social and political agendas alien to Scripture and the common Christian tradition.

The members of the study group and signatories of the Princeton Proposal are:

William Abraham (Perkins School of Theology)
Mark Achtemeier (Dubuque Theological Seminary)
Brian Daley, S.J. (Notre Dame University)
John H. Erickson (St. Vladimir's Orthodox Theological Seminary)
Vigen Guroian (Loyola College of Baltimore)
George Lindbeck (Yale Divinity School)
R. R. Reno (Creighton University)
Michael Root (Lutheran Theological Southern Seminary)
William Rusch (Faith and Order Foundation)
Geoffrey Wainwright (Duke Divinity School)
Susan Wood (St. John's University, Collegeville, Minn.)
Telford Work (Westmont College)
Robert Wright (General Theological Seminary)
David S. Yeago (Lutheran Theological Southern Seminary)

The Princeton Proposal for Christian Unity was the subject at three national conferences organized by the Center. The first one was co-sponsored by the University of Notre Dame and held on its campus May 30–June 1, 2004. The second one was jointly sponsored with Beeson Divinity School in Birmingham, Alabama, a seminary representing southern conservative evangelical traditions. The third one was held at the Center of Theological Inquiry in Princeton, at the very site where the study group held its meetings. All in all, the document was thoroughly examined and critiqued by many of the most experienced ecumenists and ranking theologians in the United States. It has been reviewed in leading publications on the left and on the right.

My impression is that the Princeton Proposal is somewhat out of joint with the times. The ecumenical movement is suffering from its own success. Most denominations have placed ecumenism on the back burner. They are more worried about their identity, declining membership, and how to be relevant in a culture that is too secular to care. Faith and Order has been pushed aside. Christians and churches seem to accept each other in friendly competition and have learned to be tolerant of each other's differences. A few churches oppose ecumenism as a threat to their exclusive claim of being the only true Christianity. No conceivable invitation will attract them to the table. Thus, ecumenism is currently in a state of stagnation. Nevertheless, I believe that our commitment to ecumenism is based on a faith imperative and not on what the culture beckons. As long as the churches are divided and do not welcome each other's members to share the holy meal of which Christ is the host, the ecumenical quest for unity is not an option that we can take or leave. Working for Christian unity is an essential spiritual commitment, because disunity is a nasty wound in the body of Christ. I am pleased that the Center invested so much energy, time, and money to bring forth *The Princeton Proposal for Christian Unity*.

CHAPTER TWELVE

Postretirement Years: Sun City West, Arizona

2005–2008

In 2005 I retired for the second time. My first retirement was from teaching theology at the Lutheran seminary in Chicago in 1991. My chief regret at the time was leaving my graduate students. I thought we offered a strong doctoral program in theology and ethics at the Lutheran School of Theology at Chicago. Four professors taught at the level of graduate studies: Robert Bertram, Philip Hefner, Reinhard Hütter, and myself. I was the program director and dissertation adviser of thirteen students who received doctorates from LSTC. For the record I will list them here along with their dissertation titles, and indicate where they are serving.

Dr. James M. Childs, Professor of Theology and Ethics, Trinity Lutheran Seminary, Columbus, Ohio ("The *Imago Dei* and Eschatology: The Ethical Implications of the Image of God in Man within the Framework of an Eschatological Theology" [1974])

Dr. Steven M. Hutchens, Senior Editor, *Touchstone: A Journal of Mere Christianity*, Chicago ("Knowing and Being in the Context of the Fundamentalist Dilemma: A Comparative Study of the Thought of Karl Barth and Carl F. H. Henry" [1977])

Dr. David Lowry, Pastor, St. Thomas Lutheran Church, Chicago ("Toward a Theology of Prophecy: The Prophetic Element in the Church as Conceived in the Theology of Karl Rahner" [1986])

Dr. Alberto L. Garcia, Professor of Theology, Concordia University,

Mequon, Wisconsin ("Theology of the Cross: A Critical Study of Leonardo Boff's and Jon Sobrino's Theology of the Cross in Light of Martin Luther's Theology of the Cross as Interpreted by Luther Scholars" [1987])

Dr. José David Rodriguez, Professor of Theology, Lutheran School of Theology at Chicago ("Fellowship of the Poor: A New Point of Departure for a Lutheran Ecclesiology, Taking the Poor as a Theological Focus" [1987])

Dr. Faye Schott, Professor of Systematic Theology, the Lutheran Seminary Program in the Southwest, Austin, Texas ("God Is Love: The Contemporary Theological Movement of Interpreting the Trinity as God's Relational Being" [1990])

Dr. Michael Hoy, Pastor, Holy Trinity Lutheran Church, St. Louis ("The Faith That Works: Juan Luis Segundo's Theology of Liberation in Comparison with Some Contemporary Catholic and Protestant Theologies and the Theologies of Paul and Luther on the Relationship of Faith and Works" [1990])

Dr. Ronald B. MacLennan, Professor of Religion, Bethany College, Lindsborg, Kansas ("The Doctrine of the Trinity in the Theology of Paul Tillich" [1991])

Dr. Randall R. Lee, former Director, Department for Ecumenical Affairs, ELCA, Chicago ("The Use of Experience in the Theology of Eduard Schillebeeckx from the Perspective of a Lutheran Understanding of the Doctrine of Justification" [1992])

Dr. Steven D. Paulson, Professor of Systematic Theology, Luther Seminary, St. Paul, Minnesota ("Analogy and Proclamation: The Struggle over God's Hiddenness in the Theology of Martin Luther and Eberhard Jüngel" [1992])

Dr. Arnfridur Gudmundsdottir, Professor of Theology, Lutheran Theological Seminary, Reykjavík, Iceland ("Meeting God on the Cross: An Evaluation of Feminist Contributions to Christology in Light of a Theology of the Cross" [1995])

Dr. Richard Bliese, President, Luther Seminary, St. Paul, Minnesota ("Bonhoeffer as Confessor: The Nature and Presence of Confession in Dietrich Bonhoeffer's Life and Writings" [1995])

Dr. Guillermo Hansen, Professor of Systematic Theology, Luther

Seminary, St. Paul, Minnesota ("The Doctrine of the Trinity and Liberation Theology: A Study of the Trinitarian Doctrine and Its Place in Latin American Liberation Theology" [1995])

Retirement Reflections

When Robert Bertram retired from the faculty, it was announced that the position he held in systematic theology would be terminated. That signaled to me that the seminary was shifting its priorities away from the program of graduate studies and diverting Bertram's salary to other causes. I was the adviser at that time of a dozen active doctoral candidates, and with Bertram's departure that number was bound to swell. The future looked bleak. With a full load of courses in the master of divinity program, seminars for graduate students, plus supervising many doctoral dissertations, I could foresee no time left for research, writing, and speaking, as I had been accustomed to doing for thirty years. This happened soon after the Hütter/Bettenhausen brouhaha over a faculty appointment in theological ethics. Since I had lost all enthusiasm for teaching any longer at LSTC, retirement seemed like the preferable option.

My second retirement took place in 2005, when I realized that it was time to pass the leadership of the Center for Catholic and Evangelical Theology to a younger generation. Dr. Michael Root, dean and professor of theology at Lutheran Theological Southern Seminary, accepted the board's invitation to become the executive director of the Center, and Dr. Joseph Mangina, professor of theology at the Toronto School of Theology in Canada, was elected editor of *Pro Ecclesia,* following the resignation of Reinhard Hütter. Organizing twenty-some theological conferences, publishing fourteen Center books with Eerdmans, and coediting with Robert Jenson fifteen years (sixty issues) of *Pro Ecclesia* took a heavy toll on the time and energy I had left for other things.

Thus, relieved of my official positions with the Center, what have I done with the available time for reading and writing? The advantage of retiring as a professor of theology is that one can go on working in the realm of ideas; nothing needs to stop until the neurotransmitters in the brain come to a halt. Of course, it is unlikely that at a ripe old age one will change one's mind and head off in a different direction. At least, I have not done that. In the last several years I have returned to the topic of my doctoral dissertation, the modern quest of the historical Jesus. The report of the first quest was written by Albert Schweitzer; the second quest was conducted by the pupils of Rudolf Bultmann; and now the third quest has been launched predominantly in the United States by Robert Funk, John Dominic Crossan, and Marcus Borg. These are the leaders of the "Jesus Seminar." Its methods and results are being thoroughly challenged by a number of scholars who pursue the quest in a more positive manner, such as N. T. Wright, James Dunn, Marcus Bockmuehl, Ben Witherington, Timothy Luke Johnson, and others. In reading all these recent Jesus books, I have become convinced that it is time to renew Kähler's judgment that, whether from a conservative or from a liberal point of view, we are dealing with a "so-called historical Jesus," not the real Jesus, but a reconstructed figure shaped by and expressing the individual historian's religious beliefs and moral values. The question needs to be asked again, why is it that these modern historians "discover" a Jesus who just happens to agree with them? That was Kähler's suspicion, and it is mine.

Belief in the historicity of Jesus' resurrection continues to be a major concern of mine. The new interest in discovering who Jesus really was, establishing what he said and did, is quite irrelevant for the Christian faith if Jesus did not really rise from the dead. Yet, some contemporary theologians treat the resurrection as a predicate of faith rather than as a statement about Jesus. I believe that such a view spells the death of the faith founded on the witness of the New Testament evangelists and apostles.

The area of missiology is also still of great importance to me. In 2006 I was invited to contribute an essay to a volume entitled *Shaping a Global Theological Mind*, edited by Darren C. Marks. My chapter is entitled "The Missionary Enterprise in Cross-Cultural Perspective." Its focus is on the missionary experience of planting the Malagasy church in the context of animistic religion, with its witch doctors (diviners) and ancestral worship.

Christianity in the Far East

From a completely different direction — and out of the blue — I received an invitation to deliver the keynote address at the Sixth International Symposium of the Graduate School of Practical Theology in Seoul, South Korea. Why me? I had never been to Korea, and I did not know a soul in Seoul. From conversations, I discovered to my surprise that my theological ideas were quite well known in Korea, especially my writings on missiology. How could that be, since I had never had any Korean doctoral students, and to my knowledge none of my books had been translated into the Korean language? Some of my books had been translated into Japanese, French, Spanish, and Portuguese, but I knew of none translated into Korean. But in fact, some had been translated without my knowledge. The publishers of my books would have informed me. One of my hosts told me that prior to the 1980s Korean publishers did not bother with copyright laws, and simply translated whatever they wished without worrying about trivial niceties like permissions and royalties.

In May 2008 LaVonne and I traveled to South Korea by way of Japan, a return visit for me, since I had been a guest professor at the Japan Lutheran Theological Seminary in Mitaka, Tokyo, in 1974. President Naozumi Eto, whom I knew from the years he studied for a doctorate at the Lutheran School of Theology at Chicago, invited me to deliver a guest lecture at the seminary and to preach at a downtown Tokyo Lutheran church. My lecture was entitled "Revisiting Dietrich Bonhoeffer's Question: 'Who Is Jesus Christ for Us Today?'" The occasion had been well advertised. The lecture hall was filled to capacity. Professors and students attending from near and far evinced a keen interest in the relevance of Bonhoeffer's theology for current christological questions. On Sunday I preached a sermon entitled "The Church as the House of God." Afterward the leaders of the congregation hosted a luncheon for us and gave us gifts.

The outpouring of appreciation and gracious hospitality extended to us by these Japanese Lutheran Christians was deeply moving and unforgettable. It warmed our hearts to witness the living fruits of the heroic labors of last century's Christian missionaries. The professors of the Japan Lutheran Seminary all held graduate degrees in theology from abroad, two from the Lutheran School of Theology at Chicago, four from Luther Seminary in St. Paul, two from Concordia Seminary in St. Louis, one from the Lutheran seminary in Philadelphia, and two from Germany. My host was an ELCA missionary, Dr. Timothy McKenzie, who teaches church history. His colleagues told us that he was a linguistic genius, and from what we could observe of his fluency in Japanese, such an accolade was no exaggeration. He took us sightseeing in Tokyo, most notably to the Edo-Tokyo Museum and the Jindai-ji Temple and Arboretum. In meeting so many highly educated and cultured Japanese people, it was hard to believe that once in our lifetime their military leaders were so misguided as to bring their nation into an ignominious war against the United States they were bound to lose.

From Tokyo we flew to Seoul, where we were met by Dr. Jong Hwan Park, who would be my chief translator for the various occasions at which I spoke. Like so many Korean intellectuals, he had studied at a number of graduate schools in the United States, such as Chicago Divinity School, Candler School of Theology of Emory University, and the Graduate Theological School in Berkeley. His grasp of the English language, even of my colloquial expressions, and of theological issues in general was truly impressive. The president of the Graduate School of Practical Theology, Dr. Joon Kwan Un, was the person who invited me to speak at the Sixth International Symposium of the school. It was a new school he had founded to train pastors from all denominations to integrate all theological disciplines with the arts and skills of the church's ministries of leadership. He was a Methodist and once served a Korean Methodist church in Chicago. He spoke impeccable English. Wondering why he invited me to give this lecture, I jokingly asked him if he just happened to pick my name out of a phone book, since I did not know him and we had never met. He said he used some of my writings as source material for a doctoral dissertation he wrote on the biblical idea of the kingdom *(basileia)* of God. He was referring to my argument, following Wolfhart Pannenberg, that Jesus' idea of the kingdom of God was the key to unite biblical and systematic theology, thus overcoming their long-standing separation. Wishing to speak on a topic I knew something about, I volunteered the title "Current Trends in

American Christianity and Theology." Dr. Un said fine, but please do it from the perspective of eschatology. He was quite convinced that the eschatological interpretation of the kingdom of God, rather than the reductionistic ethical interpretation of liberal Protestant theologians (from Ritschl to Rauschenbusch), held the greatest promise to promote the spread of Christianity in Korea. I did not know if that was true, but I was inclined to agree.

The next day I gave a lecture at Yonsei University, the largest and most prestigious Christian educational institution in Korea. The topic was "Reclaiming the Missionary Nature of the Church." This proved to hit a raw nerve. On July 19, 2007, twenty-three South Korean missionaries were captured and held hostage by members of the Taliban in Afghanistan. Two of the hostages were executed before a deal was reached between the Taliban and the South Korean government. South Korea promised to withdraw its 200 troops from Afghanistan by the end of 2007, and was reported to have paid the Taliban $20 million. The group of missionaries was composed of sixteen women and seven men on a mission sponsored by a Presbyterian church. After my lecture I was asked what I thought about sending missionaries to a foreign country, a Muslim one at that, where they were not wanted and would be risking their lives. Korean government officials and many Christian leaders, including Dr. Un and members of his faculty, were intensely critical of the practice of sending missionaries into dangerous situations. This had become a major controversy both among Christians and in the public media. How was I to respond?

I had learned that South Korean churches send more missionaries around the world than any other country except the United States. Sending missionaries is what churches have done since apostolic times, and it is what all churches should be engaged in today, one way or another. So I admired the missionary zeal and courage of the Korean missionaries. I said that, although the tragedy of the Korean missionaries was widely reported in the Christian news in America, I did not know enough about this concrete incident to offer a definitive judgment. However, I said that there is a long, illustrious history in Christianity of missionaries going to places where they were not invited, of turning the world upside down, and getting martyred in the process. It was

Tertullian who said, "The blood of the martyrs is the seed of the church." The word "martyr" comes from the Greek *martyria,* which means "witness." Not seldom does a missionary get martyred for his or her witness. The apostle Paul described his missionary experience in terms of "imprisonments, countless floggings, often near death, receiving forty lashes minus one, three times beaten with rods; once I received a stoning, three times shipwrecked, adrift at sea for a night and a day, on frequent journeys, in danger of rivers, danger from bandits, danger from Jews, danger from Gentiles, danger in the city, danger in the wilderness, danger at sea, danger from false brothers and sisters, in toil and hardship, through many a sleepless night, hungry and thirsty, often without food, cold and naked" (2 Cor. 11:25-27). Many missionaries since have told similar stories of what happened to them as they witnessed to Christ in foreign places. My sympathies were with the Korean missionaries and not with the murderous Taliban who rejected their witness. What happened to these Korean missionaries is not dissimilar to what has happened to missionaries wherever the gospel has been preached and the church has been planted in foreign fields. It happened in Madagascar when the pagan Queen Ranavalona expelled the missionaries, killed the Malagasy Christians, burned their Bibles, and forbade them to assemble for worship. And in some mysterious way by the providence of God, that persecution triggered the spread of Christianity throughout Madagascar in later years.

We spent the weekend with the small contingent of Lutherans in Seoul. The Lutheran Church in Korea was started by the Lutheran Church–Missouri Synod and still retains an affiliation with its mother church. However, it is also a member of the Lutheran World Federation and, unlike the Missouri Synod, is ecumenically engaged with other Christian denominations in Korea. I preached at Central Lutheran Church on Sunday, and on Monday I gave a lecture to the seminary community entitled "The Ten Principles of Lutheran Identity." The president of the Lutheran seminary and university is Dr. Il Young Park, who was our gracious host and expert translator. Unbeknown to me, he had published a number of substantial articles on my theology in Korean periodicals.

On Sunday afternoon we were taken to the largest Christian congregation in the world, the Full Gospel Pentecostal Church in Seoul, numbering over 800,000 members, founded and pastored by Dr. David Yonggi Cho, famous as a world-renowned preacher and charismatic healer. We arrived in time for the youth service, held in a huge auditorium with a seating capacity of at least 10,000. The music was earsplittingly loud; people clapped their hands, swayed to and fro, and danced in the aisles. To us this was more of a spectacle, not a worship service, a musical extravaganza with not even half a gospel. But young people were there en masse, staying off the streets, not doing drugs, and seemingly enjoying a rocking good time. Who are we to judge?

We left Korea with some vivid impressions. The people are beautiful and healthy. Everywhere women would carry parasols, to prevent the sun from darkening their skin. The whiter the better. We did not take readily to the Korean cuisine — too many unfamiliar ingredients, some of which appeared and smelled fishy. Cars were everywhere, but the drivers seemed to feel their way through the traffic. The rules for the road are definitely not what we are used to observing. The people are incredibly polite. Like the Japanese, Koreans are scrupulously clean and neat. They remove their shoes and put on slippers upon entering their houses. Almost every Korean is named Kim, Lee, or Park. So it is not surprising that most of the young women at the top of the leaderboard playing professional golf in the United States are named either Kim, Lee, or Park. And there is no mistaking that South Korea is without peer as a high-tech society. Almost every car is equipped with a GPS navigation system, and cell phones are everywhere in use.

After one week in Seoul LaVonne and I flew to China, where we spent one week as sightseers in Beijing and Shanghai. We had our own tour guide along with a van and driver. Our guide in Beijing was a secularized Buddhist who knew virtually nothing about Christianity, so she was unable to tell us anything about its growing influence in Chinese society. In Shanghai we insisted that our guide take us to both a Protestant church and a Catholic church on Sunday morning. The two large churches had been recently refurbished and were filled with worshipers.

Accurate statistics are hard to come by, but according to the most reliable estimates, there are between forty and sixty million Christians in China. The ecumenical movement has not yet reached China; Protestantism and Catholicism are regarded as two different religions. Under Communist rule the denominational identities of Protestant churches, established by Western missionaries, were removed to form one official, state-sanctioned Protestant church in China. What is called the Three-Self Patriotic Movement formulated three principles to ensure the indigenous character of Christianity in China free of foreign influence: self-governance, self-support, and self-propagation. The jury is still out on whether the death of denominationalism in China will be a blessing in the long run. The traditional church-dividing differences, having to do especially with the marks of the church and the ministry of Word and sacraments, are permitted to exist in a state of tolerant pluralism. In other words, differences remain but are not permitted to divide. Can this model of church union be exported to other parts of the world where churches coexist in a state of unreconciled differences?

Struggles in the ELCA

The life of a retired Lutheran theologian isn't all that tranquil and serene. Like other mainline Protestant churches, the ELCA is embroiled in controversy the outcome of which will determine its future. And I have not succeeded in remaining neutral. As a retired pastor on the roster of the Grand Canyon Synod of the ELCA, I have for the last twelve years been only remotely in touch with what goes on at church headquarters in Chicago. I read the *Lutheran Magazine* and occasionally log on to http://www.elca.org to get the news from officialdom on Higgins Road. Sometimes I am asked to comment on this or that, but for the most part I have shared my views about the ELCA with only a handful of people. The bubble of relative obscurity burst in 2005 when I sent an open letter to Bishop Mark Hanson regarding my theological concern about what is happening within the Evangelical Lutheran Church in America. Many people who agreed with the letter placed it on the Internet, and like a flash it made its way to the far corners of the world. I am including this letter in these memoirs because it reflects some of my concerns for the ELCA.

The Reverend Dr. Mark Hanson
Bishop, Evangelical Lutheran Church in America
8765 West Higgins Road
Chicago, Illinois 60631

Dear Bishop Mark Hanson:

Greetings! I am writing out of a concern I share with others about the theological state of affairs within the Evangelical Lutheran Church in America. The situation might be described as one of "brain drain." Theologians who have served Lutheranism for many years in various capacities have recently left the ELCA and have entered the Roman Catholic Church or the Orthodox Church in America. Why?

When Jaroslav Pelikan left the ELCA and became a member of the OCA, I felt it was not terribly surprising. After all, he had been reading and writing about the Fathers of Eastern Orthodoxy for so many years, he could quite naturally find himself at home in that tradition, without much explanation. A short time before that Robert Wilken, a leading patristics scholar teaching at the University of Virginia, left the ELCA to become a Roman Catholic. Then other Lutheran theological colleagues began to follow suit. Jay Rochelle, who for many years was my colleague and the chaplain at the Lutheran School of Theology at Chicago, joined the Orthodox Church. Why? Leonard Klein, pastor of a large Lutheran parish in York, Pennsylvania, and the former editor of *Lutheran Forum* and *Forum Letter*, last year left the ELCA to study for the Roman Catholic priesthood. Why? Bruce Marshall, who taught theology for about fifteen years at St. Olaf College and was a long-standing member of the International Lutheran-Orthodox Dialogue, has left the ELCA to enter the Roman Catholic Church. Why? David Fagerberg, formerly professor of religion at Concordia College, although coming from a strong Norwegian Lutheran family, left the ELCA for the Roman Catholic Church, and now teaches at the

University of Notre Dame. Reinhard Hütter, a German Lutheran from Erlangen University, came to the Lutheran School of Theology at Chicago fifteen years ago to teach theology and ethics, now teaches at Duke Divinity School, and this year became a Roman Catholic. Why? Mickey Mattox, a theologian who recently served at the Lutheran Ecumenical Institute in Strasbourg and now teaches at Marquette University, has recently begun the process of becoming a Roman Catholic. In all these cases the transition involves spouses and/or children, making it incredibly more difficult. Why are they doing this? Is there a message in these decisions for those who have ears to hear?

All of these colleagues have given candid explanations of their decisions to their families, colleagues, and friends. While the individuals involved have provided a variety of reasons, there is one thread that runs throughout the stories they tell. It is not merely the pull of Orthodoxy or Catholicism that enchants them, but also the push from the ELCA, as they witness with alarm the drift of their church into the morass of what some have called liberal Protestantism. They are convinced that the Evangelical Lutheran Church in America has become just another liberal Protestant denomination. Hence, they have decided that they can no longer be a part of that. Especially, they say, they are not willing to raise their children in a church that they believe has lost its moorings in the great tradition of evangelical (small *e*) and catholic (small *c*) orthodoxy (small *o*), which was at the heart of Luther's reformatory teaching and of the Lutheran Confessional Writings. They are saying that the Roman Catholic Church is now more hospitable to confessional Lutheran teaching than the church in which they were baptized and confirmed. Can this be possibly true?

I have decided, without any doubt about it, that I could not reinvent myself to become something else than I was raised to be by my Madagascar missionary parents — an heir of the Lutheran confessing movement. Through theological study and ecumenical engagement I thought I learned something about what it means to be Lutheran. I have written many books and articles, preached and published many sermons — leaving a long paper trail — over a period of five decades, explaining what it means to be Lutheran. There is nothing in all of those communications that accommodates liberal Protestantism, which Karl Barth called a "heresy," an assessment with which I fully agree. If it is true that the ELCA has become just another liberal Protestant denomination, that is a condition tantamount to heresy. The most damning thing in my view that can be charged against the ELCA is that it is just another liberal Protestant denomination. Are all these theologians wrong in their assessment of the ELCA? I wish I could deny it. I have been looking for some convincing evidence to the contrary, because I am not about to cut and run. There is no place I know of where to go. I do know, however, that the kind of Lutheranism I learned — from Nygren, Aulén, Bring, Pinomaa, Schlink, P. Brunner, Bonhoeffer, Pannenberg, Piepkorn, Quanbeck, H. Preus, and Lindbeck, not to mention the pious missionary teachers from whom I learned the Bible, the Catechism, and the Christian faith — and taught in a Lutheran parish and seminary for many years is now marginalized to the point of near extinction. In looking for evidence that could convincingly contradict the charge that the ELCA has become just another liberal Protestant denomination, it would seem reasonable to examine what is produced by its publishing house, theological schools, magazines, publications, church council resolutions, commission statements, task force recommendations, statements and actions by its bishops. The end result is an embarrassment; there is not much there to refute the charge. As Erik Petersen said about 19th century German Protestantism, all that is left of the Reformation heritage is the aroma of an empty bottle. A lot of the pious piffle remains, but then, so was Adolf von Harnack a pious man. All of the heretics of the ancient church were pious men. Our pastors and laity are being deceived by a lot of pietistic aroma, but the bottle is empty. Just ask these fine theologians — all friends and colleagues of mine — who have left the ELCA. They are not stupid people; they don't tell lies; they don't make rash decisions. They are all serious Christians. What is happening is nothing less than a tragedy. The ELCA is driving out the best and the brightest theologians of our day, not because it is too

Lutheran, but because it has become putatively just another liberal Protestant denomination. I would think that this is a situation that ought to concern you immensely as well as all the leadership cadres of the ELCA. But might it also be the case that the very persons who ought to be troubled by this phenomenon will say to themselves (perhaps not out loud), "good riddance, we won't be bothered by those dissenting voices anymore? We wish more of their ilk would leave."

I must tell you that I read all your episcopal letters that come across my desk. But I must also tell you that your stated convictions, punctuated by many pious sentiments, are not significantly distinguishable from those that come from the liberal Protestant leaders of other American denominations. I do not disagree with your political leaning to the left. I am a life-long political liberal, unlike many of my friends. My wife and I opposed the unjust war against Vietnam in the 60's and 70's, and we have with equal conviction opposed the foolhardy invasion of Iraq by the Bush administration. We also supported the ELCA in its ecumenical decisions to re-institute the episcopal office by means of passing the CCM as well as to adopt the Joint Declaration on the Doctrine of Justification with the Vatican. But none of that equates with transforming Lutheranism into a liberal Protestant denomination, in terms of doctrine, worship, and morality.

When I finished my graduate studies at Harvard and Heidelberg, I was ordained by the ELC and served a parish in North Minneapolis, simultaneously teaching at Luther Seminary. At that time I was instrumental in founding *dialog*, a journal of theology, together with Robert Jenson, Roy Harrisville, Kent Knutson, James Burtness, and others, in order to draw midwest Lutheranism into the world-wide orbit of Lutheran theology. We were not ecumenically oriented at the start. At that time no Luther Seminary professors were dealing with the issues posed by Bultmann, Tillich, Bonhoeffer, Barth, Brunner, Aulén, Nygren, and many others. *Dialog* got the reputation of being a journal edited by young upstarts who thought they knew better. It seemed to us then that most of our professors were not well informed. But they were good Lutherans, not a single heretic among them. Heresy was not the problem at that time. The journal that our group founded in 1961 has now become the voice of a liberal Protestant version of Lutheranism. Robert Jenson and I resigned from the journal as its editors in 1991 to found a new journal, PRO ECCLESIA, A JOURNAL OF CATHOLIC AND EVANGELICAL THEOLOGY. In the last fourteen years we have published the articles of theologians of all traditions — Lutheran, Anglican, Catholic, Evangelical, and Orthodox — exhibiting the truth that we all share common ground in the Great Tradition. The same cannot be said of *dialog* anymore. It has become a function of the California ethos of religion and morality, nothing seriously Lutheran about it anymore, except the aroma of an empty bottle. Too bad. I was its editor for twenty years and Jenson for ten years, but now in our judgment it has become, perhaps even unwittingly, the very opposite of what we intended. The journal now expresses its belief that to be prophetic it is to become the mouthpiece of the denominational bureaucracy, that is, to attack the few dissenting voices in the ELCA.

One day a church historian will write the history of Lutheranism in America. There will be a few paragraphs trying to explain that the self-destruction of confessional orthodox Lutheranism came about around the turn of the millennium and how it underwent a metamorphosis into a liberal Protestant denomination. Recently in an issue of the *Lutheran Magazine* you expressed your hope that Lutherans could some day soon celebrate Holy Communion with Roman Catholics. My instant reaction was: it is becoming less and less likely, as the ELCA is being taken hostage by forces alien to the solid traditions Lutherans share with Roman Catholics. The confessional chasm is actually becoming wider. So much for the JDDJ [Joint Declaration on the Doctrine of Justification]! The agreement becomes meaningless when Lutheranism embarks on a trajectory that leads into rank antinomianism.

Where do we go from here? I am going nowhere. Meanwhile, I am hearing rumors about a possible schism or something about the formation of a dissenting synod. None of that will redound to the benefit of the one, holy, catholic and apostolic church we confess in the Creed. Each person and each congregation will do what they deem fitting and appropriate in view of the apostasy that looms on the horizon of our beloved Lutheran Church. My friend Wolfhart Pannenberg has stated that a church that cannot take the Scriptures seriously is no longer a church that belongs to Jesus Christ. That is not an original statement of his or mine, but one said by every orthodox theologian in the Great Tradition, including Athanasius and Augustine, as well as Martin Luther and John Calvin. Does the ELCA take the Scriptures seriously? We will soon find out. Whoever passes the issue off as simply a hermeneutical squabble is not being honest — "we have our interpretation and you have yours." Who is to judge who is right? The upshot is ecclesiastical anarchy, sometimes called pluralism. To each his own. *Chacun à son goût!*

I am extremely sorry it has come to this doctrinally unstable situation in the church I was ordained to serve almost a half century ago. My father and two of his brothers served this church in Madagascar and China. My brother and sister served this church in Cameroun and Madagascar. My cousins have served this church as ordained ministers in this country and abroad for decades. Knowing them as well as I do, I am confident in stating their belief that this church in some of its expressions is not remaining truly faithful to the kind of promises they made upon their ordination to the Christian ministry.

Can the situation which I have described in stark terms be remedied? Have we reached the point of no return? Are we now hopelessly mired in what Karl Barth identified as *"Kulturprotestantismus"?* I know of about a dozen Lutheran renewal groups desperately trying to call the ELCA back to its foundational texts and traditions. Would they exist if there were no problem that needs to be addressed? How many congregations and pastors have left or are leaving the ELCA for other associations?

One day we will have to answer before the judgment seat of God as to what we have done for and against the Church of Jesus Christ. There will be no one by our side to help us find the words to use in response. All of us will have many things for which to repent and to implore God's forgiveness. And we'll all cry out, "Lord, have mercy!"

> Sincerely in Christ our Lord,
> Carl E. Braaten

Bishop Mark Hanson responded in a letter nearly as long as mine; he asked that it be received as a personal and not as a public response. I have honored that request. However, the comments I made about *dialog* elicited a response from its editor, Ted Peters. I should say here that Ted and I have been friends for many years, decades in fact. He was one of the most helpful contributors to the journal when I was its editor. He was my first choice to be my successor, and has kept the journal alive ever since, even though subscriptions have declined considerably. He asked some members of the editorial council to respond to the proposition that the ELCA is becoming "just another liberal Protestant denomination." The responses of my Lutheran critics were a mixed bag. Only Bob Benne expressed agreement with what I wrote. The others were negative, but for different reasons.[1] Some defended the ELCA against the charge that it was sliding toward liberal Protestantism. Granted, there may be differences of opinion on matters *adiaphora* in the ELCA, but certainly no such thing as heresy. Others said, in effect, so what if the ELCA is becoming more like liberal Protestantism; what is wrong with that? That means we are becoming more relevant to modern culture, shedding some of our old scholastic baggage. One way or another, these theologians were saying that there is nothing wrong with the ELCA; their views seem to be typical of the majority of Lutheran theologians teaching at our colleges and seminaries. That is part of the problem, from my perspective.

---

1. The responses to my "Open Letter to Bishop Mark Hanson" appeared in *dialog: A Journal of Theology* 44, no. 4 (Winter 2005), written by Ernest Simmons of Concordia College, John Benson of Augsburg College, John Hofffmeyer of the Lutheran Seminary in Philadelphia, Marc Kolden of Luther Seminary, Risto Saarinen of the University of Helsinki, Klaus Nürnberger of the University of KwaZulu-Natal, Pietermaritzburg, South Africa, and Robert Benne of Roanoke College. My response to my Lutheran *dialog* responders appeared in *dialog: A Journal of Theology* 45, no. 2 (Summer 2006).

Most of the e-mail letters I received from church people who read my letter on the Internet responded with profuse thanks, praise, and commendation. But not all. Some read it as a personal attack against everything they stood for. They said my assertions were "unfair, unkind, un-Christian, and ignorant." Ouch! The letter was a lightning rod. The responses underscored the fact that the ELCA is badly divided between those who wish to accelerate its rush toward liberal Protestant American culture-religion, spouting Lutheran slogans to grease the skids, and those who are trying to reclaim the biblical, creedal, and confessional roots of classical Lutheran identity within the new post–Vatican II ecumenical context.

A number of commentators smelled a rat. Though my letter made no mention of the ELCA preoccupation with the issue of homosexuality, they jumped to the conclusion that that was its underlying concern. Since my letter was written a few weeks before the 2005 ELCA churchwide assembly in Orlando, Florida, which was scheduled to vote on various resolutions bearing on the ordination or blessing of gays and lesbians living as married couples, it is likely that everyone, including me, had to have that in mind. But my letter did not clarify my views on the issue of homosexuality. Rarely have I addressed the subject. Recently, however, I accepted an invitation to write an article on the law of God for the online *Journal of Lutheran Ethics*. I wrote an article with the title "Reclaiming the Natural Law for Theological Ethics." After explaining the concept of natural law and why I think it is indispensable in Christian ethical theory, I wrote a few words about homosexuality in a concluding section entitled "Where the Rubber Hits the Road." This is what I wrote.

What is the cash value of these ruminations about natural law for Christian theology and ethics? We could choose any number of issues with which to demonstrate the applicability of a theological understanding of natural law in Christian ethics. Space does not permit us to deal with a full deck of controversial topics, such as capital punishment, pacifism, just war theory, weapons of mass destruction, contraception, abortion, euthanasia, eugenics, cloning, stem cell research, universal health care, and all the rest. The one topic on which the mainline churches seem prepared to impale themselves is homosexuality, including the ELCA of which I am a member, and with that I conclude with an untimely postscript of sorts.

Homosexuality has become a critical moral issue facing almost all churches today. In the light of natural law and the Bible, the practice of homosexuality can easily be seen as a disordering of God's creation, contrary to nature and knowable by reason to be morally wrong. I will not attempt to explain why or how the churches have managed to work themselves into a corner where modern cultural trends hold greater sway than two thousand years of Christian consensus on the matter, informed by the Scriptures and natural law. When post-Enlightenment movements in philosophy and theology rejected the natural moral law and post-modern hermeneutics applied its techniques to the Bible, the way was paved for moral relativism. Theology followed along with some kind of *agapē* ethics, giving rise to antinomianism. The dike was broken. Previously condemned patterns of Christian behavior were now considered licit in some situations, all depending on the quality of relationships. The twin authorities of human reason and revealed truth collapsed, creating great uncertainty whether, even among Christians, we can tell the difference between right from wrong, good from evil, and truth from the lie.

We know by reason what the natural law tells us — the sexual organs are designed for certain functions. God made two kinds of humans, "male and female created he them" (Gen. 1:27). By the light of reason human beings the world over, since the dawn of human civilization and across all cultures, have known that the male and female organs are made for different functions. Humans know what they are; they are free to act in accordance with them or to act in opposition to them. The organs match. What is so difficult to understand about that? Humans learn these things by reason and nature; no books on anatomy, psychology, or sociology are needed.

Nor do people first learn what the sexual organs are for from the Bible. Scholars say there are seven explicit passages in the Bible that condemn homosexual acts as contrary to the will of God. This is supposed to settle the matter for a church that claims its teachings are derived from Scripture. But for many Christians this does not settle the matter. Why not? The answer is that they don't believe what the natural law, transparent to reason, tells us about human sexuality. In my view the biblical strictures against homosexual acts are true not because they are in the Bible; they are in the Bible because they are true. They truly recapitulate God's creative design of human bodies. The law of creation written into the nature of things is the antecedent bedrock of the natural moral law, knowable by reason and conscience.

The ELCA has spent more than a million dollars to discern what to teach on matters of human sexuality. It's unbelievable. If the church would have spent a million dollars to educate its membership regarding what is true and false, right and wrong, good and bad on issues of sex, marriage, and family, that would have been money well spent. But to spend a million dollars trying to figure out what should be said in a social statement on sexual ethics is tantamount to moral bankruptcy. Is the ELCA morally bankrupt? We will have to wait and see what comes out in the end.

I dealt with the issue of homosexuality again in a chapter I contributed to a 2007 book, *The Ten Commandments for Jews, Christians, and Others*.[2] My chapter was on the seventh commandment, "Thou shalt not commit adultery."[3] After a section entitled "Human Sexuality in the Order of Creation" and another named "Sex and the Dimensions of Love," I wrote one headlined "Deviations of Sexual Behavior." There are, of course, many deviations, like exhibitionism, rape, incest, and zoophilia. I chose to limit my discussion to prostitution and homosexuality. Since what I wrote is relevant to the current controversy on homosexuality in the ELCA, I will include it here.

2. Roger E. Van Harn, ed., *The Ten Commandments for Jews, Christians, and Others* (Eerdmans, 2007).

3. The numbering of the commandments in the Reformed tradition is different from what I am accustomed to from Luther's *Small Catechism*.

It is still a matter of scientific debate whether homosexuality has a biological basis or is the result of cultural conditioning traceable to early childhood experiences. Christian ethics is in no position to take sides on this psychological question. Its chief concern is not to explain homosexuality but to lay the theological basis for the pastoral care of homosexuals. Yet, the psychological question does have direct social consequences. The widespread acceptance of the biological explanation of homosexuality is behind current attempts to justify it and to make it socially acceptable. If homosexuals are made that way, the reasoning goes, they have a moral right to express what is natural to them. Within recent decades this way of thinking has been gaining ground not only in society at large but also among theologians and within Christian circles.

On the basis of the Christian view of the polarity of the sexes grounded in the "image of God," homosexuality must be regarded as contrary to the divine intention for human sexuality. This statement is ethically normative even though one might accept the biological theory of homosexuality. The mere fact that some homosexuals may be born with such a predisposition does not necessarily mean that it is God's design for humanity. What we often call "natural" is the good creation in the state of its fallen condition. Homosexuality, however natural it might seem in the biological sense, is not rooted in the order of creation in the theological sense. It was not as a biologist but as a theologian that the apostle Paul regarded homosexuality as absolutely contrary to the ordering of human relations intended by God. On account of sin God's intention is being frustrated in the sexual dimension as well as everywhere else.

It is much easier to demonstrate that homosexuality is physiologically, psychologically, socially, and ethically abnormal than to heal the condition. It is, moreover, not merely a question of healing the homosexual; society itself needs to be healed. Many homosexuals would not think of going to their pastor, for instance, for fear of being rejected by moralistic indignation. Most homosexuals have already accepted the fact of their abnormality; their life is a continual round of struggle and defeat; they know they need help.

Because of traditional repugnance of homosexuality, widespread ignorance of the problem, moralistic attitudes in the church, and legal hazards in society, the homosexual is often far removed from easy access to the ministrations of healing.

For Christians the ethical problem soon becomes a matter of pastoral care. How can the church help homosexuals to be "cured" so far as that is possible, to accept their condition for what it is, to sublimate their sexual urges, and to live by forgiveness in this aspect of life too? Homosexuals are not helped at all by anyone pretending that their condition is normal after all. The burden on the church today is not to revise its belief that homosexuality is a deviation from the divine purpose of sex, to which the Scriptures abundantly testify, but more to change its attitude toward those afflicted by this condition and to open up channels to help them. From the point of view of the church's ministry of healing, it makes no real difference whether homosexual practice is theologically spoken of as "sin" or psychiatrically spoken of as "sickness." The grace of love and compassion is needed in either case.

My chapter also contained the sections "A Theological Perspective on Marriage," "The Structure of Marriage," "Premarital and Extramarital Intercourse," "Marriage and Celibacy," and "Divorce and Remarriage." The book was organized so that each chapter was followed by a response from a person of a different faith. Rabbi Elliot N. Dorff wrote a nine-page response from a Jewish perspective. He has written extensively on the Jewish tradition's perception of sex and marriage in a book, *Love Your Neighbor and Yourself: A Jewish Approach to Personal Ethics*. The rabbi acknowledges that he is offering *one* and not *the only* Jewish perspective on sex and marriage.

There are differences in Judaism just as in Christianity on the ethics of sex. Orthodox Jews regard homosexual acts as sinful. Reform and Reconstructionist movements now ordain openly homosexual Jews as rabbis. The Conservative movement is in the middle and continues to debate the issue. Rabbi Dorff stands in the Conservative tradition but takes a progressive position; he advocates that homosexual unions be publicly celebrated and consecrated. I asked Rabbi David Novak, who holds the chair in Jewish studies at the University of Toronto, what he thought about Rabbi Dorff's views. They are both rabbis in the Conservative tradition. His comment was that on this debate Christians and Jews are in the same boat; their opinions run the gamut from left to right.

I intended that that would be the last word I would write on the issue of sexuality. That was not to be. Bishop Paull Spring, chair of *Luther Core — Coalition for Reform,* invited me to serve as a member of a newly formed advisory council for the group seeking to promote faithfulness to the confessional standards of the ELCA, as spelled out in its constitution. In that capacity I wrote "A Critique of the 'Draft Social Statement on Human Sexuality' Prepared by the Task Force for ELCA Studies on Sexuality, Church in Society." This social statement was presented to the 2009 convention of the ELCA to determine whether the ELCA will change its policy and guidelines for clergy so as to permit the ordination of practicing gays and lesbians as well as to approve a rite of blessing of same-gender unions. My critique was given wide circulation on a number of Web sites and published in the online *Journal of Lutheran Ethics,* July 2008. This issue of the journal includes essays written by other Lutherans, most of whom explicitly approve of the ordination of practicing homosexuals and the blessing of same-sex marriages.

My critique of the "Draft Social Statement" is that it fails to apply distinctively Lutheran principles of theology and ethics in formulating its positions on sexuality, marriage, and family. The statement is so badly written and theologically flawed that I could not offer any helpful suggestions for revision. Those Lutherans who approve of the statement operate on a different theological foundation, one that more or less supports "situation ethics" and its antinomian consequences, and they do it in the name of love and justice. The idea that there are moral laws, principles, norms, and standards that are grounded in the way God created and ordered the world and human existence is trumped by the overarching appeal to the love of God. "Love God and do as you please!" Since Augustine said that, shouldn't that settle the matter? Situation ethics is alive and well in the ELCA, and its chief advocates have their hands on the wheel that steers the ship. It seems that the ELCA is not learning any lessons from what is going on in the Anglican Communion as it rushes like the Gadarene swine toward the cliffs of potential schism.

Dr. Kristin Largen is the new editor of *dialog,* the theological journal of which I was the founding editor in 1962. She teaches systematic theology at the Lutheran Theological Seminary at Gettysburg. In planning an issue to mark the twentieth anniversary of the ELCA, she asked me to contribute an essay of reflections for the occasion. I submitted an article with the title "On Flunking the Theological Test in the ELCA." The test I administered dealt with four subjects: (1) the naming of God; (2) the uniqueness of Christ; (3) the authority of the Bible; (4) and the distinction between law and gospel. I could have added a dozen others, but I was told to keep the article short. The voices that speak for the ELCA in all its expressions — church bureaucrats from the presiding bishop on down, editors of its official publications, synodical bishops, seminary professors, whatever — have been muted by the collective impact of radical feminism, religious pluralism, historical relativism, and moral antinomianism. The exceptions to this pessimistic generalization are few and far between. For the most part they cower in the shadows, feeling outnumbered and outmaneuvered, subject to marginalization and humiliation. How do I know? Because they have told me so.

LaVonne and I now belong to Lord of Life Lutheran Church, a congregation of over 1,000 members in Sun City West, Arizona. We settled in Arizona for our retirement years on account of its beautiful weather, except for the hot summer months, and because I continue to be an active tennis player and golfer. The members of Lord of Life are all senior citizens who, like us, moved to Arizona for its warm sunny weather. At the invitation of Pastor Kautz I have given three series of lectures to members of the congregation. The first one was "Lutheranism: Its Core Beliefs and Practices," presented in the spring of 2007. A revised and expanded second edition of my book *Principles of Lutheran Theology* was published in 2007, so its contents were fresh in my mind. The second series was "Who Is Jesus? Disputed Questions," in which I used the infamous "Jesus Seminar" as a convenient foil. This is the subject of a book I am currently writing. The third series was presented in the spring of 2008, "The Church and Ecumenism:

What Unites and What Divides." I have always enjoyed the challenge of teaching theology to laity without dumbing it down.

As I bring these memoirs to a close, my hope is to continue to write and publish as long as God gives me strength of mind and body. In 2008 my latest book, *That All May Believe: A Theology of the Gospel and the Mission of the Church,* was published by Eerdmans. This is a book of essays written in recent years on various dogmatic, ecumenical, and missiological topics. I have also edited a book of sermons preached in recent years, *Preaching Christ in a Pluralistic Age.* This will be my third book of sermons. The previous two were *The Whole Counsel of God* (Augsburg, 1974) and *Stewards of the Mysteries: Sermons for Festivals and Special Occasions* (Augsburg, 1983). I always admired theologians who published their sermons, particularly those who have influenced me very much, Paul Tillich, Karl Barth, Helmut Thielicke, and Wolfhart Pannenberg. Sermons yield the cash value of a person's theology, and I hope that mine do. For me the acid test of a good theology is whether it leads to sound preaching.

The sad thing about growing old is not growing old; it is seeing lifelong friends and colleagues make the final transition into the church triumphant, leaving the rest of us to soldier on in the church militant. From the old gang that started *dialog* in the early sixties, we no longer have with us Kent Knutson, Jim Burtness, and Lavern Grosc. The three of us who dreamed up the idea of founding *dialog* — Roy Harrisville, Robert Jenson, and I — are still busy doing theology for the church we love.

But theology isn't everything. As heads of a growing Braaten tribe, LaVonne and I keep watch over an ever-expanding calendar of birthdays and anniversaries, not only as parents and grandparents but now as great-grandparents. As they say, it doesn't get any better than this. LaVonne has found a new love for the Norwegian folk art of rosemaling. I continue to do as much damage as possible to my opponents on the tennis court, singles and doubles; and in golf, well, with every passing year I come closer to shooting my age. I am writing these final words looking forward to celebrate my eightieth birthday. LaVonne and I are grateful for every year that the good Lord is pleased to add to our lives together.

Bibliography of the Publications of Carl E. Braaten

_____

1962–2009

Books Authored

History and Hermeneutics: New Directions in Theology Today. Volume 2. Westminster, 1966.

The Ethics of Conception and Contraception: Studies in Man, Medicine, and Theology. Board of Social Ministry, Lutheran Church in America, 1967.

The Future of God: The Revolutionary Dynamics of Hope. Harper and Row, 1969.

Spirit, Faith, and Church. Coauthored with Wolfhart Pannenberg and Avery Dulles. Westminster, 1970.

The Futurist Option. Coauthored with Robert W. Jenson. Paulist, 1970.

Christ and Counter-Christ: Apocalyptic Themes in Theology and Culture. Fortress, 1972.

Eschatology and Ethics: Essays on the Theology and Ethics of the Kingdom of God. Augsburg, 1974.

The Whole Counsel of God. Sermons by Carl E. Braaten. Fortress, 1974.

The Living Temple: A Practical Theology of the Body and the Foods of the Earth. Coauthored with LaVonne Braaten. Harper and Row, 1976.

The Flaming Center: A Theology of the Christian Mission. Fortress, 1977.

Stewards of the Mysteries: Sermons for Festivals and Special Occasions. Augsburg, 1983.

Principles of Lutheran Theology. Fortress, 1983.

The Apostolic Imperative: Nature and Aim of the Church's Mission and Ministry. Augsburg, 1985.

Justification: The Article by Which the Church Stands or Falls. Fortress, 1990.

No Other Gospel! Christianity among the World's Religions. Fortress, 1992.

Mother Church, Eschatology, and Ecumenism. Fortress, 1998.

That All May Believe: Theology of the Gospel and the Mission of the Church. Eerdmans, 2008.

Books Edited

Kerygma and History: A Symposium on the Theology of Rudolf Bultmann. Translated and edited by Carl E. Braaten and Roy A. Harrisville. Abingdon, 1964.

The Historical Jesus and the Kerygmatic Christ, by Rudof Bultmann. Translated and edited by Carl E. Braaten and Roy A. Harrisville. Abingdon, 1964.

The So-Called Historical Jesus and the Historic Biblical Christ, by Martin Kähler. Translated, edited, and with an introduction by Carl E. Braaten. Fortress, 1964.

Perspectives on Nineteenth and Twentieth Century Protestant Theology, by Paul Tillich. Edited with an introduction by Carl E. Braaten. Harper and Row, 1967.

A History of Christian Thought, by Paul Tillich. Edited and with a preface by Carl E. Braaten. Harper and Row, 1968.

The New Church Debate: Issues Facing American Lutheranism. Edited with an introduction by Carl E. Braaten. Fortress, 1983.

Christian Dogmatics. Volumes 1 and 2. Edited by Carl E. Braaten and Robert W. Jenson. Fortress, 1984.

The Theology of Wolfhart Pannenberg. Edited by Carl E. Braaten and Philip Clayton. Augsburg, 1988.

Our Naming of God: Problems and Prospects of God-Talk Today. Edited by Carl E. Braaten. Fortress, 1989.

A Map of Twentieth Century Theology: Readings from Karl Barth to Radical Pluralism. Edited and introduced by Carl E. Braaten and Robert W. Jenson. Fortress, 1995.

Either/Or: The Gospel or Neopaganism. Edited by Carl E. Braaten and Robert W. Jenson. Eerdmans, 1995.

Reclaiming the Bible for the Church. Edited by Carl E. Braaten and Robert W. Jenson. Eerdmans, 1995.

The Catholicity of the Reformation. Edited by Carl E. Braaten and Robert W. Jenson. Eerdmans, 1996.

The Two Cities of God: The Church's Responsibility for the Earthly City. Edited by Carl E. Braaten and Robert W. Jenson. Eerdmans, 1997.

Union with Christ: The New Finnish Interpretation of Luther. Edited by Carl E. Braaten and Robert W. Jenson. Eerdmans, 1998.

The Marks of the Body of Christ. Edited by Carl E. Braaten and Robert W. Jenson. Eerdmans, 1999.

Sin, Death, and the Devil. Edited by Carl E. Braaten and Robert W. Jenson. Eerdmans, 2000.

Church Unity and the Papal Office. Edited by Carl E. Braaten and Robert W. Jenson. Eerdmans, 2001.

The Strange New Word of the Gospel: Re-evangelizing in the Postmodern World. Edited by Carl E. Braaten and Robert W. Jenson. Eerdmans, 2002.

The Last Things: Biblical and Theological Perspectives on Eschatology. Edited by Carl E. Braaten and Robert W. Jenson. Eerdmans, 2003.

Jews and Christians: People of God. Edited by Carl E. Braaten and Robert W. Jenson. Eerdmans, 2003.

In One Body through the Cross: The Princeton Proposal for Christian Unity. Edited by Carl E. Braaten and Robert W. Jenson. Eerdmans, 2003.

Mary, Mother of God. Edited by Carl E. Braaten and Robert W. Jenson. Eerdmans, 2004.

The Ecumenical Future. Edited by Carl E. Braaten and Robert W. Jenson. Eerdmans, 2004.

*I Am the Lord Your God: Christian Reflections on the Ten Command-
ments.* Edited by Carl E. Braaten and Christopher R. Seitz. Eerdmans,
2005.

Articles and Chapters

1962

"The Crisis of Confessionalism." *dialog: A Journal of Theology* 1, no. 1
(Winter 1962): 38-48.

"Radical Laicism." *Koinonia* (Journal of the Chicago Lutheran Theological Seminary Student Association) (March 1962): 3-5.

"Grace." *Resource* 3, no. 7 (April 1962): 2-6.

"Jesus and the Kerygma in Rudolf Bultmann's Theology." *Koinonia*
(Journal of the Chicago Lutheran Theological Seminary Student Association) (December 1962): 11-13.

"Paul Tillich as a Lutheran Theologian." *Record* (Chicago Lutheran
Theological Seminary) 67, no. 3 (August 1962): 34-42.

"The Correlation between Justification and Faith in Classical Lutheran
Dogmatics." In *The Symposium on Seventeenth Century Lutheranism,* Selected Papers, vol. 1, pp. 77-90. St. Louis, 1962.

"New Frontiers in Theology." *Record* (Chicago Lutheran Theological
Seminary) 67, no. 4 (November 1962): 29-40.

1963

"A New Order of Relations." *Frontiers* 14, no. 6 (February 1963): 14-19.

"Christ Today: The Lord of History." *Lutheran World* 10, no. 3 (July
1963): 257-66.

"Christus Heute: Der Herr der Geschichte." *Lutherische Rundschau* 13,
no. 3 (July 1963): 183-298.

"Modern Interpretations of Nestorius." *Church History* 32, no. 3 (September 1963): 251-67.

"The Context and Scope of Theological Education." *Record* (Chicago
Lutheran Theological Seminary) 68, no. 4 (November 1963): 22-27.

"Incarnation and Demythologizing." *Koinonia* (December 1963): 1-6.

1964

"The Interdependence of Theology and Preaching." *dialog: A Journal of Theology* 3, no. 1 (Winter 1964): 12-20.

"The Dynamics of a Responding Church in a Changing World." In *The Challenge of Change*. Luther College Press, 1964.

"Obedient Love in Human Relations." *National Lutheran* 32, no. 3 (March 1964): 6-8.

1965

"Comment on Caemmerer's Paper" (A Theological Examination of the Concepts of the Church and the Church's Educational Institutions — Richard R. Caemmerer). In *Educational Integrity and Church Responsibility*, Papers of the 51st Annual Meeting of the National Lutheran Educational Conference, January 1965, pp. 9-11.

"The Tragedy of the Reformation." *Bell* (Thiel College Bulletin, Greenville, Pa.) 55, no. 3 (March 1965): 3-5.

"The Current Controversy on Revelation: Pannenberg and His Critics." *Journal of Religion* 45, no. 3 (July 1965): 225-37.

"How New Is the New Hermeneutic?" *Theology Today* 22, no. 2 (July 1965): 218-35.

"The Lordship of Christ in Modern Theology." *dialog: A Journal of Theology* 4, no. 3 (Summer 1965): 259-67.

"The Tragedy of the Reformation and the Return to Catholicity." *Record* (Chicago Lutheran Theological Seminary) 70, no. 3 (August 1965): 5-16.

"Un 'Sic et Non' Protestant." *Lumière et Vie* 24, no. 74 (August-October 1965): 12-20.

1966

"Reflections on the Lutheran Doctrine of the Law." *Lutheran Quarterly* 18, no. 1 (February 1966): 72-84.

"Rome, Reformation, and Reunion." *Una Sancta* 23, no. 2 (1966): 3-8.

"Reunion, Yes; Return, No." *Una Sancta* 23, no. 3 (1966): 27-33.

"The Theme of the Future in Current Eschatologies." *Record* (Chicago Lutheran Theological Seminary) 71, no. 3 (August 1966): 5-10.

Bibliography of the Publications

1967

"The Reunited Church of the Future." *Journal of Ecumenical Studies* 4, no. 4 (1967): 611-28.

"Toward a Theology of Hope." *Theology Today* 24, no. 2 (1967): 208-26.

"Speaking of God in a Secular Age." *Context* 1, no. 1 (Autumn 1967): 3-17.

1968

"Toward a Theology of Hope." *Theology Digest* 16, no. 2 (Summer 1968): 151-54.

"Radikale Theologie in Amerika." *Lutherische Monatshefte*, no. 2 (February 1968): 55-59.

"Zur Theologie der Revolution." *Lutherische Monatshefte*, no. 5 (May 1968): 215-20.

1969

"The Church on the Frontier of History." *Lutheran Quarterly* 21, no. 1 (February 1969): 12-16.

"Ecumenism and Theological Education in the United States." *Oecumenica* (1969): 199-208.

"The Phenomenology of Hope." In *Christian Hope and the Future of Humanity*, edited by Franklin Sherman. Augsburg, 1969.

1970

"Who Is Bernard Lonergan?" *Lutheran World* 17, no. 4 (1970): 372-76.

"Wer Is Bernard Lonergan?" *Lutherische Rundschau* (October 1970): 372-76.

"American Historical Experience and Christian Reflection." In *Projections: Shaping an American Theology for the Future*, edited by Thomas F. O'Meara and Donald M. Weisser, pp. 86-108. Doubleday, 1970.

1971

"The Future as the Source of Freedom." *Theology Today* 27, no. 4 (January 1971): 382-93.

"Untimely Reflections on Women's Liberation." *dialog: A Journal of Theology* 10, no. 2 (Spring 1971): 104-11.

"Ecumenism: Where Do We Go from Here?" *dialog: A Journal of Theology* 10, no. 4 (Autumn 1971): 288-91.

"The Significance of Apocalypticism for Systematic Theology." *Interpretation* 25, no. 4 (October 1971): 480-99.

"Theology of Hope." In *Philosophical and Religious Issues*, edited by L. Miller. Dickenson Publishing Company, 1971.

1972

"Ambiguity and Hope in the Ecumenical Movement." *dialog: A Journal of Theology* 11, no. 3 (Summer 1972): 209-15.

"Die Bedeutung der Zukunft." *Evangelische Theologie* 32, no. 4 (July/August 1972): 209-15.

"A Theological Conversation with Wolfhart Pannenberg." *dialog: A Journal of Theology* 11, no. 4 (Autumn 1972): 286-95.

"A Lutheran View of the Catholic Dialog with Luther." *dialog: A Journal of Theology* 11, no. 4 (Autumn 1972): 299-303.

"Theology and Our Common World." *Worldview* 15, no. 9 (September 1972): 22-27.

"Theology and Welfare." *Lutheran Social Concern* 12, no. 3 (Fall 1972): 31-38.

"A Response to a Critique of Braaten's Review of Pannenberg's *Basic Questions in Theology*." *Worldview* 15, no. 2 (December 1972): 56-57.

"The Significance of the Future: An Eschatological Perspective." In *Hope and the Future of Man*, edited by Ewert H. Cousins, pp. 40-54. Fortress, 1972.

"Religion as Patriotism or Protest." *Event* 12, no. 10 (November 1972): 4-7.

1973

"Die Botschaft vom Reiche Gottes und die Kirche." In *Evangelium und Geschichte. Das Evangelium und die Zweideutigkeit der Kirche*, vol. 3, edited by Vilmos Vajta, pp. 11-54. Vandenhoeck & Ruprecht, 1973.

"A Theology of the Body." *Lutheran* 2, no. 7 (April 1973): 12-15.

1974

"A Decade of Ecumenical Dialogues." *dialog: A Journal of Theology* 13, no. 2 (Spring 1974): 142-48.

"The Gospel of the Kingdom of God and the Church." In *The Gospel and the Ambiguity of the Church,* edited by Vilmos Vajta, pp. 3-26. Fortress, 1974.

"Response to Professor Carl Peter" (Carl Peter, *The Quest of a Credible Eschatology*). In *The Catholic Theological Society of America, Proceedings of the 29th Annual Convention, Chicago, Illinois, June 10-13,* vol. 29, pp. 273-78. 1974.

"From Apocalyptic to Somatic Theology." *dialog: A Journal of Theology* 13, no. 4 (Autumn 1974): 279-301.

"Caring for the Future: Where Ethics and Ecology Meet." *Zygon* 9, no. 4 (December 1974): 311-22.

"The Cancellation of Hope by Myth." In *Philosophy of Religion,* edited by Norbert O. Schedler. Macmillan, 1974. (Excerpted from *The Future of God,* pp. 42-46.)

1975

"Theology of Mission and Service." *Contact* (Lutheran Social Services Chaplaincy Newsletter) 8, no. 1 (Spring 1975): 3-14.

1976

"The Challenge of Liberation Theology — a Lutheran Perspective." In *Consultation on Theological Presuppositions Implicit in the Current Theories of Education,* a Study by the USA National Committee of the Lutheran World Federation, pp. 63-82. 1976.

"The Christian Mission and American Imperialism." In *Religion and the Dilemmas of Nationhood,* Bicentennial Years of the Knubel-Miller-Greever Lectures, edited by Sydney E. Ahlstrom, pp. 64-72. Lutheran Church in America, 1976.

"The Christian Mission and American Imperialism." *dialog: A Journal of Theology* 15, no. 1 (Winter 1976): 70-78.

"American Imperialism and the Christian Mission" (abridged version). *World Encounter* (June 1976): 1-5.

"A Trinitarian Theology of the Cross." *Journal of Religion* 56, no. 1 (January 1976): 113-21.

"Taking Our Bodies Seriously." *Faith at Work* 89, no. 4 (June 1976): 6-7.

"Lutherans on Liberty and Liberation." *dialog: A Journal of Theology* 15, no. 3 (Summer 1976): 166-68.

"The Gospel of Justification *Sola Fide*." *dialog: A Journal of Theology* 15, no. 3 (Summer 1976): 207-13.

1977

"A Personal Odyssey." *Kirche og Folk* 26, no. 19 (November 1977): 43-44.

1978

"Theology and the Body." In *Physical Activity and Human Well-Being*, edited by Fernand Landry and William A. R. Orban. Symposia Specialists, 1978. A collection of the papers presented at the International Congress of Physical Activity Sciences held in Quebec City, July 11-16, 1976.

1979

"The One Universal Church." *Schola: A Pastoral Review of Sacred Heart School of Theology* 2 (1979): 19-32.

"Sex, Marriage, and the Clergy." *dialog: A Journal of Theology* 18, no. 3 (Summer 1979): 169-74.

1980

"Who Do We Say That He Is? On the Uniqueness and Universality of Jesus Christ." *Occasional Bulletin* 4, no. 1 (January 1980): 2-9.

"The Universal Meaning of Jesus Christ." *LCA Partners* 2, no. 6 (December 1980): 13-16.

1981

"The Ordination of Deacons." *dialog: A Journal of Theology* 20, no. 2 (Spring 1981): 101-5.

"Open Letter to David Preus." *dialog: A Journal of Theology* 20, no. 2 (Spring 1981): 136-37.

"The Christian Doctrine of Salvation." *Interpretation* 35, no. 2 (April 1981): 117-31.

"Braaten Responds" (to the critique of Braaten's position regarding universalism). *Partners* 3, no. 3 (June 1981): 20-21.

"Can We Still Hold to the Principle of *'Sola Scriptura'*?" *dialog: A Journal of Theology* 21, no. 3 (Summer 1981): 189-94.

"The Lutheran Confessional Heritage and Key Issues in Theology Today." *Currents in Theology and Mission* 8, no. 5 (October 1981): 260-68.

"Toward an Ecumenical Theology of Human Rights." In *How Christian Are Human Rights?* edited by Eckehart Lorenz, pp. 36-54. Lutheran World Federation, 1981.

"Auf dem weg zu einer Okumenische Theologie der Menschenrechte." In *Zur Sache* 22, pp. 52-79. Lutherisches Verlagshaus, 1981.

"The Uniqueness and Universality of Jesus Christ." In *Mission Trends, No. 5,* edited by Gerald H. Anderson and Thomas F. Stransky, C.S.P., pp. 69-89. Eerdmans, 1981.

"Carl Braaten Responds to Critiques of His December 1980 LCA Partners Article on the Uniqueness of Christ." *LCA Partners* 3, no. 3 (June 1981): 20-21.

1982

"The Contextual Factor in Theological Education." *dialog: A Journal of Theology* 21, no. 3 (Summer 1982): 169-74.

"The Future of the Ecumenical Movement." *Theology Digest* 30, no. 4 (Winter 1982): 303-12.

1983

"Reflections on the St. Louis Forum: Authority and Power in the Church." *ATS Theological Education* 19, no. 2 (Spring 1983): 101-5.

"Ecclesiological Perspectives." *Covenant Quarterly* 41, no. 3 (August 1983): 53-58.

"Evangelization in the Modern World." In *Consulting on Evangelism.* A Document of the Division for World Mission and Ecumenism for the Lutheran Church in America, pp. 33-50. 1983.

"Jesus among the Jews and Gentiles." *Currents in Theology and Mission* 10, no. 4 (August 1983): 197-209.

"Shadows of the Cross: On the Contemporary Significance of Luther's Theology." Chancellor's Address, delivered at Regis College, Toronto, November 21, 1983.

1984

"Praxis: The Trojan Horse of Liberation Theology." *dialog: A Journal of Theology* 23, no. 3 (Summer 1984): 276-80.

"Romans 12:14-21." *Interpretation* 38, no. 3 (July 1984): 291-95.

"Evangelization in the Modern World." In *The Continuing Frontier: Evangelism.* A Document of the Division for World Mission for the Lutheran Church in America (September 1984): 30-45.

"Prolegomena to Christian Dogmatics." In *Christian Dogmatics,* First Locus, vol. 1, edited by Carl E. Braaten and Robert W. Jenson, pp. 5-78. Fortress, 1984.

"The Person of Jesus Christ." In *Christian Dogmatics,* Sixth Locus, vol. 1, edited by Carl E. Braaten and Robert W. Jenson, pp. 465-569. Fortress, 1984.

1985

"The Question of God and the Trinity." In *Festschrift: A Tribute to Dr. William Hordern,* edited by Walter Freitag, pp. 6-16. University of Saskatchewan, 1985.

1986

"Whole Person and Whole Earth." *Lutheran Women* (May 1986): 6-9.

"The Problem of the Absoluteness of Christianity." *Interpretation* 40, no. 4 (October 1986): 341-53.

"Theological Perspectives in the Christian Mission among Muslims." In *God and Jesus: Theological Reflections for Christian-Muslim Dialog,* Division for World Mission and Interchurch Co-operation of the American Lutheran Church, pp. 8-19. 1986.

1987

"Whatever Happened to Law and Gospel?" *Currents in Theology and Mission* 14, no. 2 (Spring 1987): 111-18.

"Let's Talk about the Death of God." *dialog: A Journal of Theology* 26, no. 3 (Summer 1987): 209-14.

"Men, Women, and the Trinity." *Cresset* 51, no. 1 (November 1987): 23-25.

"Christocentric Trinitarianism v. Unitarian Theocentrism: A Response to S. Mark Heim." *Journal of Ecumenical Studies* 24, no. 1 (Winter 1987): 17-21.

"The Problem of the Absoluteness of Christianity: An Apologetic Reflection." In *Worldviews and Warrants,* edited by William Schweiker and Per M. Anderson, pp. 51-70. University Press of America, 1987.

"A Look at CPE from a Lutheran Theological Perspective." *SPC Journal* 10 (1987): 30-33.

1988

"The Doctrine of the Two Kingdoms Re-examined." *Currents in Theology and Mission* 15, no. 6 (December 1988): 497-505.

"The Meaning of Evangelism in the Context of God's Universal Grace." *Journal of the Academy for Evangelism in Theological Education* 3 (1987-1988): 9-19.

"Preaching Both Law and Gospel." *International Christian Digest* 2, no. 4 (May 1988): 37-41.

"Salvation through Christ Alone." *Lutheran Forum* 22, no. 4 (November 1988): 8-12.

"Lutheran Theology and Religious Pluralism." *LWF [Lutheran World Federation] Report* 23/24 (January 1988): 105-28.

1989

"Preaching Christ in an Age of Religious Pluralism." *Word and World* 9, no. 3 (Summer 1989): 244-50.

"Jesus and World Religions." *World Encounter,* no. 3 (1989): 4-7.

"The Mind and Heart of the Lutheran Pastor." *dialog: A Journal of Theology* 28 (Spring 1989): 117-19.

"Introduction: Naming the Name" and "The Problem of God-Language

Today." In *Our Naming of God: Problems and Prospects of God-Talk Today,* edited by Carl E. Braaten, pp. 1-34. Fortress, 1989.

1990

"Whole Person and Whole Earth." In *The Parish Nurse,* edited by Granger Westberg, pp. 77-81. Augsburg, 1990.

"The Triune God: The Source of Unity and Mission." *Missiology: An International Review* 18, no. 4 (October 1990): 417-27.

"God in Public Life — a Rehabilitation of the Lutheran Idea of the 'Orders of Creation.'" *Lutheran Theological Seminary Bulletin* 70, no. 1 (Winter 1990): 34-52.

"God in Public Life: Rehabilitating the 'Orders of Creation.'" *First Things,* no. 8 (December 1990): 32-38.

"Paul Tillich's Message for Our Time." *Anglican Theological Review* 72, no. 1 (Winter 1990): 16-25.

"Gott und das Evangelium: Pluralismus und Apostasie in der amerikanischen Theologie." *Kerygma und Dogma* 36, no. 1 (January/March 1990): 56-71.

"The Identity and Meaning of Jesus Christ." In *Lutherans and the Challenge of Religious Pluralism,* edited by Frank Klos, C. Lynn Nakamura, and Daniel F. Martensen, pp. 103-38. Augsburg, 1990.

1991

"God and the Gospel: Pluralism and Apostasy in American Theology." *Lutheran Theological Journal* 25, no. 1 (May 1991): 38-50.

"The Mission of the Gospel." *F.O.C.L. Point* 2, no. 2 (Fall 1991): 1-2.

1992

"Christian Theology and the History of Religions." *Currents in Theology and Mission* 19, no. 1 (February 1992): 5-13.

"No Other God." *Evangelical Catholic* (Theological and Opinion Journal of the Episcopal Synod of America) 15, no. 2 (November/December 1992): 1-3.

"Response to Paul F. Knitter" ("Religious Pluralism in Theological Education"). *Anglican Theological Review* 74, no. 4 (Fall 1992): 438-42.

1994

"Jesus and the Church." *Ex Auditu: An International Journal of Theological Interpretation of Scripture* 10 (1994): 59-72.

"The Il/Legitimacy of Lutheranism in America?" *Lutheran Forum* 28, no. 1 (February 1994): 38-44.

"Response to Manfred K. Bahmann." *Lutheran Forum* 28, no. 3 (August 1994): 11-12.

"Ecumenical Orthodox Dogmatics?" *Touchstone* 7, no. 1 (Winter 1994): 10-11.

1995

"The Gospel for a Neopagan Culture." In *Either/Or: The Gospel or Neopaganism,* edited by Carl E. Braaten and Robert W. Jenson, pp. 7-22. Eerdmans, 1995.

"No Other Gospel." *Lutheran* 8, no. 10 (October 1995): 20-23.

"Introduction: Gospel, Church, and Scripture." In *Reclaiming the Bible for the Church,* edited by Carl E. Braaten and Robert W. Jenson. Eerdmans, 1995.

1996

"Scripture, Church, and Dogma, An Essay on Theological Method." *Interpretation* 50, no. 2 (April 1996): 142-55.

"Katolicita a reformacia." *Cirkevne Listy* (October 1996): 152-54.

"Die Katholizität der Reformation." *Kerygma und Dogma* 42 (July/September 1996): 186-201.

"The Problem of Authority in the Church." In *The Catholicity of the Reformation,* edited by Carl E. Braaten and Robert W. Jenson, pp. 53-66. Eerdmans, 1996.

"Confessional Integrity in Ecumenical Dialogue." *Lutheran Forum* 30, no. 3 (1996): 24-30.

"A Harvest of Evangelical Theology." *First Things,* no. 63 (May 1996): 45-48.

1997

"Creation, Eschatology, Ecology." In *Caritas Dei, Beiträge zum Verständnis Luthers und der gegenwärtigen Ökumene,* Festschrift for

Tuomo Mannermaa on His Sixtieth Birthday, edited by Oswald Bayer, Robert W. Jenson, and Simo Knuuttila, pp. 128-38. Luther-Agricola Gesellschaft. Helsinki, 1997.

"The Cultural Captivity of Theology: An Evangelical Catholic Perspective." The Inaugural Margaret McKinnon Memorial Lecture on Christianity and Culture, published by the Nepean Presbytery of the Uniting Church in Australia, pp. 1-19. Melbourne, 1997.

"Hearing the Other: The Promise and Problem of Pluralism." *Currents in Theology and Mission* 24, no. 5 (October 1997): 393-400.

"The Role of Dogma in Church and Theology." In *The Task of Theology Today*, edited by Victor Pfitzner and Hilary Regan, pp. 25-57. Australian Theological Forum, 1998.

"Natural Law in Theology and Ethics." In *The Two Cities of God: The Church's Responsibility for the Earthly City*, edited by Carl E. Braaten and Robert W. Jenson, pp. 42-58. Eerdmans, 1977.

"A Response" (to Russell Hittinger on "Natural Law and Catholic Moral Theology"). In *A Preserving Grace: Protestants, Catholics, and Natural Law*, edited by Michael Cromartie, pp. 31-40. Eerdmans, 1997.

"Epilogue: Theology *Pro Ecclesia* — Evangelical, Catholic and Orthodox." In *Reclaiming the Great Tradition*, edited by James S. Cutsinger, pp. 185-98. InterVarsity, 1997.

1998

"The Finnish Breakthrough in Luther Research." In *Union with Christ*, edited by Carl E. Braaten and Robert W. Jenson, pp. vii-ix. Eerdmans, 1988.

1999

"Foreword." In *Christ and Culture in Dialogue*, edited by Angus J. L. Menuge, pp. 7-13. Concordia Academic Press, 1999.

"The Special Ministry of the Ordained." In *Marks of the Body of Christ*, edited by Carl E. Braaten and Robert W. Jenson. Eerdmans, 1999.

"The Significance of New Testament Christology for Systematic Theology." In *Essays on Christology: Who Do You Say That I Am?* edited by Mark Allan Powell and David R. Bauer, in honor of Jack Dean Kingsbury, pp. 216-27. Westminster John Knox, 1999.

"The Last Things." *Christian Century* 116, no. 33 (December 1, 1999): 1174-75.

"The Gospel Proviso: Lessons from 20th-Century Theology for the Next Millennium." *dialog: A Journal of Theology* 38, no. 4 (Fall 1999): 245-52.

"The Resurrection Debate Revisited." *Pro Ecclesia* 8, no. 1 (Spring 1999).

2000

"Powers in Conflict: Christ and the Devil." In *Sin, Death, and the Devil*, edited by Carl E. Braaten and Robert W. Jenson, pp. 94-107. Eerdmans, 2000.

"Robert William Jenson — a Personal Memoir" and "Eschatology and Mission in the Theology of Robert Jenson." In *Trinity, Time, and Church: A Response to the Theology of Robert W. Jenson*, edited by Colin E. Gunton, pp. 1-9 and 298-311. Eerdmans, 2000.

"The Evangelical and Catholic Theology of Paul Tillich: A Lutheran Appreciation." *North American Paul Tillich Society Newsletter* 26, no. 1 (Winter 2000): 2-7.

"*Nullus Diabolus — Nullus Redemptor:* Apocalyptic Perspectives on the Struggle for Life against Death." In *Thinking Theologically about Abortion,* edited by Paul T. Stallsworth, pp. 51-72. Bristol House, 2000.

"Augsburg Confession, Article VII: Its Implications for Church Fellowship and Structure." *Certus Sermo* (an Independent Monthly Review of the Northwest Washington Synod of the Evangelical Lutheran Church in America), no. 119 (March 2000): 1-4. Continued in no. 120 (April 2000): 1-3.

2001

"Introduction." Coauthored with Robert W. Jenson. In *Church Unity and the Papal Office*, pp. 1-9. Eerdmans, 2001.

"The Reality of the Resurrection." In *Nicene Christianity: The Future for a New Ecumenism,* edited by Christopher R. Seitz, pp. 107-18. Brazos, 2001.

"A Shared Dilemma: Catholics and Lutherans on the Authority and Interpretation of Scripture." *Pro Ecclesia* 10, no. 1 (Winter 2001): 63-75.

2002

"The Future of the Apostolic Imperative: At the Crossroads of World Evangelization." In *The Strange New Word of the Gospel: Reevangelizing in the Postmodern World,* edited by Carl E. Braaten and Robert W. Jenson, pp. 159-74. Eerdmans, 2002.

"Christology and the Missionary Crisis of the Church." In *Story Lines: Chapters on Thought, Word, and Deed* (for Gabriel Fackre), edited by Skye Fackre Gibson, pp. 106-12. Eerdmans, 2002.

2003

"Apocalyptic Imagination in Theology." In *The Last Things: Biblical and Theological Perspectives on Eschatology,* edited by Carl E. Braaten and Robert W. Jenson, pp. 14-32. Eerdmans, 2003.

2004

"The Christian Faith in an Inter-Faith Context." *dialog: A Journal of Theology* 43, no. 3 (Fall 2004): 233-37.

2005

"Sins of the Tongue." In *I Am the Lord Your God: Christian Reflections on the Ten Commandments,* edited by Carl E. Braaten and Christopher R. Seitz, pp. 206-17. Eerdmans, 2005.

"The Reality of the Resurrection." *Good News* (the Magazine for United Methodist Renewal) (September/October 2005): 28-30.

2006

"A Response to My Lutheran *Dialog* Responders." *dialog: A Journal of Theology* 45, no. 3 (Summer 2006): 192-96.

2007

"Sexuality and Marriage." In *The Ten Commandments for Jews, Chris-*

tians, and Others, edited by Roger E. Van Harn, pp. 135-47. Eerdmans, 2007.

"Reclaiming the Natural Law for Theological Ethics." *Journal of Lutheran Ethics* 7, no. 10 (October 2007).

2008

"A Critique of the 'Draft Social Statement on Human Sexuality' Prepared by the Task Force for ELCA Studies on Sexuality, Church in Society" (Evangelical Lutheran Church in America). *Journal of Lutheran Ethics* 8, no. 7 (July 2008).

2009

"On Flunking the Theological Test in the ELCA." *dialog: A Journal of Theology* 47, no. 1 (Winter 2009).

Editorials

"Commmunion before Confirmation?" *dialog: A Journal of Theology* 1, no. 3 (Summer 1962): 61-62.

"Against the Becker Amendment." *dialog: A Journal of Theology* 3, no. 4 (Autumn 1964): 295-97.

"The Second Vatican Council's Constitution on the Church." *dialog: A Journal of Theology* 4, no. 2 (Spring 1965): 136-39.

"The Theological Mandate of the Church College." *dialog: A Journal of Theology* 4, no. 3 (Summer 1965): 218-21.

"Dialog — the Fifth Year." *dialog: A Journal of Theology* 5, no. 1 (Winter 1966): 4-6.

"Paul Tillich: Lutheran and Catholic." *dialog: A Journal of Theology* 5, no. 1 (Winter 1966): 6-7.

"The New Social Gospel Movement." *dialog: A Journal of Theology* 5, no. 2 (Spring 1966): 133-35.

"The Next 450 Years." *dialog: A Journal of Theology* 6, no. 4 (Autumn 1967): 244-45.

"Intercommunion." *dialog: A Journal of Theology* 8, no. 2 (Spring 1969): 88.

"Theology and Student Politics." *dialog: A Journal of Theology* 9, no. 1 (Winter 1970): 5-6.

"On Polarization." *dialog: A Journal of Theology* 9, no. 3 (Summer 1970): 167-68.

"Luther at Worms — Some Kind of Revolutionary." *dialog: A Journal of Theology* 10, no. 1 (Winter 1971): 4-5.

"The Grand Inquisitor of Missouri." *dialog: A Journal of Theology* 10, no. 2 (Spring 1971): 84-86.

"Hanoi Ploy." *dialog: A Journal of Theology* 10, no. 2 (Spring 1971): 89.

"Dialog after Ten Years." *dialog: A Journal of Theology* 11, no. 1 (Winter 1972): 4-5.

"The Future Is Not What It Used to Be." *dialog: A Journal of Theology* 11, no. 1 (Winter 1972): 5-8.

"Churches of the Reformation, Unite!" *dialog: A Journal of Theology* 11, no. 1 (Winter 1972): 11-12.

"The Colliding of Eschatology and Establishment." *dialog: A Journal of Theology* 11, no. 1 (Winter 1972): 18-22.

"How Christian Is the New Ethnicity?" *dialog: A Journal of Theology* 11, no. 3 (Summer 1972): 166-67.

"On Leaving America." *dialog: A Journal of Theology* 11, no. 4 (Autumn 1972): 245-46.

"On Getting Keyed Up for Key 73." *dialog: A Journal of Theology* 11, no. 4 (Autumn 1972): 248-49.

"Garbage In, Garbage Out! The Press Report on the St. Louis Faculty." *dialog: A Journal of Theology* 11, no. 4 (Autumn 1972): 250-51.

"Which Key?" *dialog: A Journal of Theology* 12, no. 1 (Winter 1973): 4.

"The Lutheran Church in America's Affirmation of Faith." *dialog: A Journal of Theology* 12, no. 2 (Spring 1973): 92-93.

"The Retreat to Conservatism." *dialog: A Journal of Theology* 12, no. 3 (Summer 1973): 12-15.

"Providence and Watergate." *dialog: A Journal of Theology* 12, no. 4 (Autumn 1973): 249-50.

"The Charismatic Phenomenon." *dialog: A Journal of Theology* 13, no. 1 (Winter 1974): 6-7.

"The Current Controversy in the Missouri Synod." *dialog: A Journal of Theology* 13, no. 2 (Spring 1974): 84-85.

"An Evangelical Papacy?" *dialog: A Journal of Theology* 13, no. 2 (Spring 1974): 90.

"Dialog in Transition." *dialog: A Journal of Theology* 13, no. 4 (Autumn 1974): 244-45.

"The Enemy of My Enemy Is My Friend: On the Hartford Theses." *dialog: A Journal of Theology* 14, no. 2 (Spring 1975): 84-85.

"Goodbye, Lutheran Unity." *dialog: A Journal of Theology* 14, no. 4 (Autumn 1975): 244-46.

"Lutherans Split in Chile." *dialog: A Journal of Theology* 14, no. 4 (Autumn 1975): 250-51.

"Sixty Millions for Missions." *dialog: A Journal of Theology* 16, no. 3 (Summer 1977): 164-65.

"What's Going On in Theology?" *Lutheran School of Theology Epistle* 13, no. 1 (Fall 1977): 2, 4.

"The Myth of the Chicago School." *dialog: A Journal of Theology* 17, no. 2 (Spring 1978): 85-87.

"On Mixing Religion and Politics." *dialog: A Journal of Theology* 19, no. 4 (Autumn 1980): 244-45.

"Beyond Ecumenism, What?" *dialog: A Journal of Theology* 19, no. 1 (Winter 1981): 7-10.

"Where Is the Magisterium?" *dialog: A Journal of Theology* 22, no. 1 (Winter 1983): 4-5.

"What's in a Name?" *dialog: A Journal of Theology* 22, no. 1 (Winter 1983): 7.

"The Future of *dialog*." *dialog: A Journal of Theology* 23, no. 4 (Autumn 1984): 244-45.

"No Breakthrough Whatever" (on the Lutheran-Catholic Dialogue on "Justification by Faith"). *dialog: A Journal of Theology* 23, no. 4 (Autumn 1984): 245-46.

"The Crisis of Authority." *dialog: A Journal of Theology* 23, no. 4 (Autumn 1984): 247-48.

"The New Inquisition." *dialog: A Journal of Theology* 24, no. 1 (Winter 1985): 4-5.

"Is Liberation Theology a Heresy?" *dialog: A Journal of Theology* 24, no. 1 (Winter 1985): 5-6.

"How to Save the Lutheran Church." *dialog: A Journal of Theology* 24, no. 2 (Spring 1985): 84-85.

"Lutheran School of Theology and the Pittsburgh Crisis." *dialog: A Journal of Theology* 24, no. 3 (Summer 1985): 164-65.

"Merger Watch: Theological Education in the New Lutheran Church." *dialog: A Journal of Theology* 24, no. 3 (Summer 1985): 206-7.

"The Bishops Commission and the Pittsburgh Confession." *dialog: A Journal of Theology* 24, no. 4 (Autumn 1985): 243-47.

"Reunion in Our Lifetime?" *dialog: A Journal of Theology* 24, no. 4 (Autumn 1985): 242-43.

"Lutheran Schizophrenia." *dialog: A Journal of Theology* 24, no. 4 (Autumn 1985): 247.

"The Melanchthonian Blight." *dialog: A Journal of Theology* 25, no. 2 (Spring 1986): 82-83.

"Who's the Phony? Tutu, Falwell, and Apartheid." *dialog: A Journal of Theology* 25, no. 2 (Spring 1986): 83.

"Lutherans Concerned Issue Call for Dialogue." *dialog: A Journal of Theology* 25, no. 2 (Spring 1986): 83-84.

"The Name Will Change but the Game Will Remain the Same." *dialog: A Journal of Theology* 25, no. 2 (Spring 1986): 84-85.

"Tourists and Terrorists." *dialog: A Journal of Theology* 25, no. 3 (Summer 1986): 162.

"The Centenaries of Karl Barth and Paul Tillich." *dialog: A Journal of Theology* 25, no. 3 (1986): 164.

"Those Lutheran Church in America Bishops." *dialog: A Journal of Theology* 25, no. 3 (Summer 1986): 214-15.

"True and False Thinking on Repristination." *dialog: A Journal of Theology* 25, no. 4 (Summer 1986): 247-48.

"Does God Cause Aids?" *dialog: A Journal of Theology* 25, no. 4 (Autumn 1986): 246-47.

"Quotas: The New Legalism." *dialog: A Journal of Theology* 25, no. 1 (Winter 1986): 3-4.

"Berger Speaks Out on Apostasy." *dialog: A Journal of Theology* 26, no. 2 (Spring 1987): 82.

"The Ecumenical Impasse and Beyond." *dialog: A Journal of Theology* 26, no. 2 (Spring 1987): 83-87.

"We Have a Bishop." *dialog: A Journal of Theology* 26, no. 3 (Summer 1987): 162.

"God and/or Christ." *dialog: A Journal of Theology* 26, no. 4 (Autumn 1987): 242-43.

"Ecclesiogenesis: On Giving Birth to a New Church." *dialog: A Journal of Theology* 26, no. 4 (Autumn 1987): 243-44.

"The Six Year Study of Ministry." *dialog: A Journal of Theology* 26, no. 1 (Winter 1987): 5-6.

"Theological Issues Facing the Evangelical Lutheran Church in America." *dialog: A Journal of Theology* 27, no. 2 (Spring 1988): 87-89.

"Can the Church Be Saved?" *dialog: A Journal of Theology* 27, no. 3 (Summer 1988): 162.

"Liberation Theology Coming of Age." *dialog: A Journal of Theology* 27, no. 4 (Autumn 1988): 241.

"Neuhaus and the Bishops on Contra Aid." *dialog: A Journal of Theology* 27, no. 4 (Autumn 1988): 242.

"Let's Reorganize the ELCA." *dialog: A Journal of Theology* 28 (Spring 1989): 164-65.

"Should the ELCA Join the WCC and the NCC?" *dialog: A Journal of Theology* 28 (Spring 1989): 166-67.

"The Making of an American Protestant Church." *dialog: A Journal of Theology* 28 (Autumn 1989): 243-44.

"A Call to Faithfulness." *dialog: A Journal of Theology* 28 (Autumn 1989): 246.

"Inappropriate." *dialog: A Journal of Theology* 28, no. 1 (Winter 1989): 3.

"Ecumenical Bottom Lines." *dialog: A Journal of Theology* 29 (Spring 1990): 82.

"On Higgins Bashing." *dialog: A Journal of Theology* 29 (Spring 1990): 84-85.

"The Outrage of the Season." *dialog: A Journal of Theology* 29 (Summer 1990): 164.

"Uncivil War on Ecumenism." *dialog: A Journal of Theology* 29 (Summer 1990): 165-66.

"Can You Top This One?" *dialog: A Journal of Theology* 29 (Autumn 1990): 246-47.

"Richard John Neuhaus: A Tribute to a Friend and Colleague." *dialog: A Journal of Theology* 29 (Autumn 1990): 248-49.

"We Believe in the One Church." *Taking the Lead* (a Publication of the Rocky Mountain Continuing Education Center — ELCA) 2, no. 2 (1994): 8-11.

"What Price Unity?" *Pro Ecclesia: A Journal of Catholic and Evangelical Theology* 3, no. 4 (Fall 1994): 407-10.

"The Historical Jesus and the Church." *Pro Ecclesia: A Journal of Catholic and Evangelical Theology* 4, no. 1 (Winter 1995): 11-12.

"The House of God." *Lutheran Forum* 39, no. 2 (Summer 2005): 8-11.

Index

Index